the Ministry of the HOLY SPIRIT

the Ministry of the HOLY SPIRIT

William Fitch

ZONDERVAN PUBLISHING HOUSE OF THE ZONDERVAN CORPORATION
GRAND RAPIDS, MICHIGAN 49506

THE MINISTRY OF THE HOLY SPIRIT
Copyright © 1974 by The Zondervan Corporation
Grand Rapids, Michigan

Library of Congress Catalog Card Number: 74-11854

Third printing 1978
ISBN 0-310-24380-7

Grateful acknowledgment is made for permission to quote from the following copyrighted material:

The New Testament in Modern English. © 1958 by J. B. Phillips, published by Wm. Collins Sons & Co., Ltd., London, and the Macmillan Company.

The New English Bible: New Testament. © 1961 by The Delegates of the Oxford University Press and The Syndics of the Cambridge University Press.

The Revised Standard Version of the Bible, © 1946, 1952, and © 1971 by the Division of Christian Education, National Council of the Churches of Christ in the United States of America.

Climbing by Rosalind Goforth. © 1940 Evangelical Publishers, Toronto.

The King James version of the Bible has been quoted with only occasional and minor changes; e.g., "Holy Spirit" replaces "Holy Ghost" and "ye" has been changed to "you."

Printed in the United States of America

Contents

Preface

When first I began to write this book, I intended that it should be called "God, the Holy Spirit." As the pages unravelled themselves, however, I found that I was more and more writing, and being forced to write, about "The Ministry of the Holy Spirit" — the manifold ways in which the eternal Spirit of God reveals Himself and works in and through the Church and every true believer in Jesus Christ.

There has therefore been a subtle change in emphasis. But the main thrust of the book is very much as I had originally wanted it to be. Everywhere I find people eager to know more and more about the Person and work of the Holy Spirit. Wherever I go, I find the same kind of questions being asked by Christians. Is there something that I should know of the Holy Spirit that would revolutionize my whole Christian life? Am I less than my best for God by missing out on some authentic personal experience of the Holy Spirit? How can I be sure that I am truly filled with the Spirit and thereby am a true means of grace to others?

These are questions that are being asked by earnest Christians everywhere. In many cases, there has been an experience of true conversion. The believer knows that the Holy Spirit has entered his life and things are different. But he finds it hard to delineate this experience in terms that agree with the New Testament; and his own experience comes short, he feels, of the kind of Christian walk and testimony that he sees there. This book is one attempt among many others to open up the holy Scriptures and note in simple terms what the Holy Spirit can do in the life of every true disciple. Hopefully, it will also help us to test ourselves as to the measure of our reality, security, and success in achieving what God really means us to achieve.

In the writing of this book I have made much use of the thoughts of A. W. Tozer. Here and there the reader may find phrases that are remarkably similar to his, simply because I have virtually memorized them and made them my own. Where I have unwittingly not acknowledged a source, I offer my apologies as well as my grateful thanks.

I have naturally found it necessary to study the elements of Neo-Pentecostalism. I cannot in any way call myself a Pentecostal as that term is currently used. I come from the great Reformed tradition and am deeply indebted for all that I have gained through this branch of the Church. It is, of course, very easy to be obscurantist and to dismiss this whole movement as one of the many things that will shortly pass away. I hope I create no impression like that. At the same time, the more I have studied the material this book comprehends, the more I have become convinced that the classic positions of Neo-Pentecostalism are nonbiblical. I praise God for the many who have found Christ through this branch of the Christian Church. At the same time I must plead for a purer understanding of what the Scriptures say concerning the ministries of the Holy Spirit.

The doctrine of the Person and work of the Holy Spirit is absolutely indispensable to every disciple of Christ. It is my definite conviction, after studying in depth as much relevant material as I have been able to secure, that Neo-Pentecostalism does not accurately represent the teaching of the New Testament on the Holy Spirit. I do not find any commandment in the New Testament to "be baptized with the Spirit." I find there no emphasis in the need for a second work of grace comparable to, but going beyond, conversion. A call to sanctification? Yes! A call to grow in grace and in the knowledge of our Lord and Savior Jesus Christ? Yes! But an experience mandatory to all Christian disciples to be "baptized with the Spirit" and begin "to speak in tongues" is not the teaching of the prophets or the apostles. We are summoned to "be filled with the Spirit" and to "walk in the Spirit." But that is very different from what Neo-Pentecostalism demands.

Yet I also am persuaded that all the gifts of the Holy Spirit as outlined in the New Testament are operative in the Church today. When Paul says, "Forbid not to speak in tongues," I hold that he speaks under the authority of the Spirit of God. This therefore implies that I assume there are certain Christians to whom the Holy Spirit has given this gift of tongues — "dividing to every man as He in His sovereignty wills." Everything flows from sovereign grace through the eternal Spirit. Every Christian receives at the moment of his conversion some gift of the Holy Spirit. This may be a development of a natural talent already possessed. It may be something quite unique and new.

There were "glossolalia" in Acts and "glossolalia" in Corinth. They are different manifestations of the Spirit. It is my earnest prayer that, though at times I may appear to speak forcibly, the real burden of my heart, which is to see every believer filled with the Spirit, will be fulfilled. This filling is free for all to receive. We fail our Lord if we refuse to be thus filled. But we equally fail Him if we add to His words and demand a post-conversion experience for which New Testament warranty is lacking.

The Scriptures — which I hold to be absolutely authoritative, fully inspired by the Holy Spirit, written with the finger of God and inerrant — must be our supreme guide in these matters. In addition, love must be sovereign. Far too much divisiveness has been created already by false emphases. A return to the simplicity of the biblical teaching on the doctrine of the Holy Spirit is among our greatest needs. When that happens, the ministries of the Spirit will be fulfilled, the Spirit will glorify the Son, and the triune God, Father, Son, and Holy Spirit will be our only end and our joy for ever.

WILLIAM FITCH

June 1974

the Ministry of the HOLY SPIRIT

1

The Forgotten One

I will pray the Father, and he shall give you another Comforter, that he may abide with you for ever (John 14:16).

BEFORE LEAVING HIS DISCIPLES, our Lord gave them most explicit teaching about the Holy Spirit.

"The time has come for Me to return to the one who sent Me; and I am telling you the simple truth when I assure you that it is a good thing for you that I go away" (John 16:5, 7, translation mine). He told them then that by His returning to the Father He would be able to send them "another Comforter" — one who would never leave them, one who would be like Himself, and one by whose power they would glorify their Lord.

Great sections of chapters 14 and 16 of John's gospel are devoted to our Savior's teaching about the coming of the Holy Spirit. The Holy Spirit would be the ultimate fact of divine revelation and the most vital force in man's redemption. A new dispensation was before them — the dispensation of the Holy Spirit. The Spirit of God would be from first to last the divine instrument of grace leading men to full salvation. In, through, by, and from Him would come enlightenment and conviction, repentance and regeneration. Wisdom and power would flow from Him. "When He comes, He will force men to see the true significance of sin; He will expose their sin because they don't believe in Me; He will demonstrate truth and goodness, for these will have been won for all by My going to the Father; and He will demonstrate also the meaning of judgment, for the spirit now ruling the world will have been judged" (John 16:8-11 paraphrased).

13

The message was identical after Calvary and the Resurrection. Before leaving them finally, He said: "You will receive power when the Holy Spirit comes on you; and you will be my witnesses in Jerusalem, and in all Judaea and Samaria, and to the ends of the earth" (Acts 1:8 NIV). And everything happened as He had said when on the great day of the Feast of Pentecost the Spirit of God fell upon a praying church. Then they were "all filled with the Holy Spirit" (Acts 2:4). The day and dispensation of the Holy Spirit had come.

Do we believe in the Holy Spirit?

Clearly we should believe in the Holy Spirit. But any stranger entering a church today might never hear that there is a Holy Spirit. We may make many allowances for historical circumstances, but it is a simple fact that the Apostles' Creed contains ten articles on the Person and work of Christ, but only one on the Holy Spirit. A. W. Tozer wonders at this and makes this comment:

> The idea of the Spirit held by the average church member is so vague as to be nearly non-existent. When he thinks of the matter at all he is likely to try to imagine a nebulous substance like a wisp of invisible smoke which is said to be present in churches and to hover over good people when they are dying. Frankly he does not believe in any such thing, but he wants to believe something, and not feeling up to the task of examining the whole truth in the light of scripture, he compromises by holding belief in the Spirit as far out from the centre of his life as possible, letting it make no difference in anything that touches him practically. This describes a surprisingly large number of earnest persons who are sincerely trying to be Christians. [1]

Every time the Church repeats the creed, it reaffirms its faith in the Holy Spirit. But does the Church really know what is being affirmed? There are many who think that the term "the Holy Spirit" is a mere figure of speech for spiritual atmosphere. Evidently they hold that the ascribing of personality to the Holy Spirit is a massive blunder. But how can the Bible be accepted as credible if the Holy Spirit is disregarded as a Person? Our Lord spoke of the Holy Spirit as "the Spirit of truth." He emphasized

---

[1] A. W. Tozer, *The Divine Conquest* (Harrisburg: Fleming H. Revell, 1950), p. 66.

that only through the direct guidance of the Holy Spirit would the Church be led into all truth. The self-testimony of Scripture to its own inspiration is: "Holy men of God spoke as they were moved by the Holy Spirit" (2 Peter 1:21). This means that the Holy Spirit spoke through the prophets. They were many; but the Spirit is the great Author and Inspirer of them all. He holds the key to Scripture; indeed, He is Himself the key; and it is through Him who is the Revealer that revealed truth can be known.

Similarly, the apostle insists that "no one can say Jesus is Lord except by the Holy Spirit" (1 Cor. 12:3 RSV)! It is not through intelligence, reason, or argument that we come to the point of confessing Jesus Christ as Lord. No! It is through the illumination of God the Holy Spirit. Our Lord told Nicodemus: "Except a man be born of . . . the Spirit, he cannot enter into the kingdom of God" (John 3:5). This means that the Church of Jesus Christ is that company of men and women who have been enlightened, begotten, unified, and indwelt by God the Holy Spirit. Do we really believe this? It is vital that we do so. To be ignorant of the wonderful Person of the Holy Spirit is to be ignorant of true salvation. Our prayer, surely, must be:

> Spirit of God that moved of old
> Upon the waters' darkened face,
> Come when our faithless hearts are cold,
> And stir them with an inward grace.
>
> Come, give us still Thy powerful aid,
> And urge us on, and make us Thine;
> Nor leave the hearts that once were made
> Fit temples for Thy grace divine.

> (Cecil Frances Alexander, 1818 - 1895)

*The Christian life is supernatural
and needs supernatural resources*

In the epistle to the Hebrews we read that believers who have been "made partakers of the Holy Spirit, and have tasted the good Word of God," have tasted also "the powers of the world to come" (6:4, 5). This means that when the Holy Spirit indwells a believer, he gives him a foretaste of an absolutely new kind of power — a totally new experience, a power that really belongs to the ages to come. What is going to be known in fullness in the ages of eternity we may here and now experience when we are "sealed with the holy Spirit of promise," who is God's pledge and guarantee that we belong to Him (Eph. 1:13). This describes the operation of the Holy Spirit within the life of a disciple of Christ. Here and now he has a little share of the inheritance of power and glory that await him in the world to come with Christ. Nothing less than this can make the Christian life possible. We must know God's life within us. We do so as we are "indwelt by His Spirit."

Human resources fail. It may be true that never before have the human resources of the Church been so great. But to meet the onslaught of evil that is around us today we need help other than that which man can provide. Samuel Chadwick meditates on this and writes:

> The Church that is man-managed instead of God-governed is doomed to failure. A ministry that is College-trained but not Spirit-filled works no miracles. The Church that multiplies committees and neglects prayer may be fussy, noisy, entertaining and enterprising, but it labours in vain and spends its strength for nought. It is possible to excel in mechanics and fail in dynamic. There is a superabundance of machinery; what is wanting is power. To run an organization needs no God. Man can supply the energy, enterprise and enthusiasm for things human. The real work of a Church depends upon the power of the Spirit. [2]

In order to reach such a position, a church must be emptied of self, even as each individual Christian desiring the fullness of the Holy Spirit must be emptied of self. The way to Pentecost is always by the way of the Cross. Yet the Church too often seems to exist for its own glory: the exaltation of its preaching, the lauding of its program, the comfort of its people. This spells a dead church. There may be crowds; but there is no conviction of sin. There may be philanthropy; but the miracle of regeneration is unknown. The membership may be wealthy, distinguished, and elite in the eyes of men; but there is no corresponding fruit of the Spirit. All is barren unless the Holy Spirit indwells the temple of our bodies as well as the sanctuary we have built for the worship of God. Worship is idolatry until He inspires.

---

[2] Samuel Chadwick, *The Way to Pentecost* (London: Hodder and Stoughton, 1932), p. 15.

The Holy Spirit gives life

In 2 Corinthians 3:6 Paul says: "The letter kills but the Spirit gives life." None but the Holy Spirit can give life to the truth of the New Testament. He alone can make our Lord's teaching a living, supernatural, and powerful way of life for each believer. If you are prepared to read the New Testament with an open mind, you will see that the normal experience of the early Christian was supernatural. Remove the supernatural from the book of Acts, and you are left with something that has no coherence, no significance. The disciples were "filled with the Holy Spirit" and became participants in a life wholly supernatural. Their guidance was supernatural. Their living was supernatural. Their preaching was supernatural. They were supernaturally taught, protected, uplifted, and led. We read in Acts 19:11 that "God wrought special miracles by the hands of Paul." This was when Paul was in Ephesus; and, as has been frequently pointed out, the Greek phrase "special miracles" can best be understood as "miracles of a kind that do happen every day." The Holy Spirit did unusual things when Paul ministered in Ephesus — the kind of things that even Paul was not accustomed to seeing all the time; and Luke, who is so accurate in his reading and writing of history, sees this as something worthy of special record.

It is absolutely essential that we who confess that Jesus Christ is Lord in these latter decades of the twentieth century should ask ourselves why it is that we are not seeing this kind of miracle now. The same Holy Spirit who inspired the New Testament church is with *us*. There is no diminution of His power. But have we forgotten Him? Is He the great forgotten One in all the work we do within the Church? Surely the time has come for us to seek Him with all our heart. Surely in our day when evil stalks the land, when satanism, witchcraft, pornography, sorcery, and cruelty abound everywhere, we should be asking urgently the reason for our impotence. When our Lord came down from the Mount of Transfiguration, He found a demented father with a demon-possessed son surrounded by arguing scribes and a band of helpless disciples. Christ wrought the miracle. The boy was healed. Later, when the disciples came to Him and asked, "Why could not we cast him out?" they received this answer: "This kind can come forth by nothing but by prayer and fasting" (Mark 9:28, 29). Do we hear this answer, too, if we are truly honest with ourselves and with God?

We must rediscover the Holy Spirit. He indwells every believer. But is He permitted to do what needs to be done? Have we quenched the Spirit (1 Thess. 5:19)? Or have we grieved the Spirit (Eph. 4:30)? In the Athanasian Creed, born out of the controversies of the fourth-century Church, there is a reference to the deity and sovereignty of the Holy Spirit that we should all know; it is a beautiful, precise, and comprehensive statement.

> There is one Person of the Father, another of the Son, and another of the Holy Spirit. But the Godhead of the Father, of the Son, and of the Holy Spirit, is all one, the glory equal, the majesty co-eternal. . . . And in this Trinity none is afore, or after other; none is greater, or less than another. But the whole three persons are co-eternal together, and co-equal. So that in all things, as aforesaid, the Unity in Trinity, and the Trinity in Unity is to be worshipped.

It is high time for us to repent of our aggravated transgressions against the blessed Holy Spirit, the third Person of the triune God. But how shall we repent? Surely, by reversing ourselves, our acts, and attitudes towards Him. If we have forgotten Him till now, we must forget Him no more. If we have neglected His direction and directives, we must neglect them no more. "Let the wicked forsake his way, and the unrighteous man his thoughts; and let him return unto the Lord, and he will have mercy upon him; and to our God, for he will abundantly pardon" (Isa. 55:7). The time has come for us to realize that He is One to be worshiped and obeyed. There is urgency in the matter, for further neglect will only cause us further loss. The need of all of us is to open up every avenue of our redeemed personalities in order that He, the Holy One, might possess them wholly as Lord and God. When He comes, and when we offer Him the hospitality of our whole heart, then He will reveal Christ to us as we have never known Him before; He will bless us with a great tenderness of heart, such tenderness of heart as will make us tremble at the approach of sin; He will bring His own credentials, witnessing with our spirit that we are truly the children of God and called with a holy calling to the service of our generation.

Is this possible? John Wesley, preaching on "Scriptural Christianity" (Sermon 4 from his classical work *Forty-Four Sermons*), says:

> Where is the country in which all the inhabitants thereof are filled with the Holy Spirit? — are all of one heart and soul; cannot suffer anyone among them to lack anything, but continually do give to every man as he hath need; who, one and all, have the love of God filling their hearts, and constraining them to love their neighbours as themselves — who offend not in any point, either by word or deed, against justice, mercy, or truth; but in every way do unto all men, as they would these should do unto them?

It was a rhetorical question; but when he preached it on August 24, 1744, at St. Mary's, Oxford, before the entire body of faculty and students, he pled with all his hearers to be "filled with the Holy Spirit." By such "filling" there would be hope of "special miracles."

Let us give heed to this call. Let us no longer forget but reverence and obey the Holy Spirit of God.

> Breathe on me, Breath of God,
> Fill me with life anew,
> That I may love what Thou dost love,
> And do what Thou wouldst do.

> (Edwin Hatch, 1835 - 1889)

2

Glorifying the Son

He shall glorify me; for he shall receive of mine, and shall shew it unto you (John 16:14).

WHEN OUR LORD ASCENDED into heaven, He did so as the glorified One. In this capacity He gave the Holy Spirit, the Spirit of glory; and the work of the Holy Spirit is to glorify Jesus. "He shall glorify Me" (John 16:14). This was His teaching in the upper room; and the disciples never forgot it. When on the day of Pentecost the Holy Spirit was poured upon them, they knew the fulfillment of Joel's prophecy and immediately they began to proclaim that Jesus Christ was a Prince and a Savior. They never ceased to do so.

Now this is the duty and joy of every Christian — to glorify Jesus. But this can be done only in the power of the Spirit. What is this glory? And how can we be instruments of bringing glory to the One whom the Father has already glorified? It is vital that we learn the real meaning of our terms.

The Holy Spirit glorifies Christ in the life of every true Christian. That is, the Holy Spirit recreates in the follower of Christ the image of Christ Himself. The glory of God is the perfection and power of the divine will, the divineness of the mode of His being and working. When our Lord ascended on high, God "highly exalted him, and gave to him a name above every other name" (Phil. 2:9). Now, instead of being limited by flesh, by time and space, He passed as man into the very life of God and was glorified. As the glorified One, He gives the Spirit of glory to the Church; and the Spirit of glory immediately begins to recreate in our lives the image of the glorified Savior. He continually reminds us of the fact that Christ is glorified and in that sense He glorifies the Son. But in addition to that wonderful ministry, He communicates and shares with us the presence and power of the enthroned Christ so that Christ is manifested in us as indeed the Lord of glory.

This means that when our Lord says, "He shall glorify Me," He means that the Holy Spirit will make Christ apparent and glorious *in us*. He will glorify the Son of God in the weakness of the flesh of those who have truly believed and been saved with an ever-lasting salvation. It is in the Church that the glory of Christ is going to be known supremely; and that means that in every true member of the Body of Christ His glory should be seen.

Through suffering His glory appears

This should cause us both to rejoice and to tremble. It is surely a tremendous cause for praise that we shall become channels for the revealing of the glory of the Son of God, our Savior. But when we recall that it was necessary for Christ to suffer and to enter into His glory (Luke 24:26), we should realize that as is the Master, so will the servant be. He was made "perfect through suffering." Likewise, Paul speaks for us all when he prays, "That I may know him, and the power of his resurrection, and the fellowship of his sufferings, being made conformable unto his death" (Phil. 3:10). Glory is born in suffering. When the Holy Spirit begins to glorify Christ in us, He does so in the weakness of our frail human nature; and often He uses the engraving tool of pain. Yet surely, and without interruption, if the Spirit is allowed to work in ungrieved sovereignty within us, the glory of Jesus Christ will be seen in us as year succeeds year. Often, it is only as we suffer with and for Christ that the glory of our Lord is perfectly manifested in us. Even as "it became him, for whom are all things, and by whom are all things, in bringing many sons to glory, to make the captain of their salvation perfect through sufferings" (Heb. 2:10), so does the glory of Christ become manifest in them who suffer for His sake.

Have we not seen this in our day? All around the world men and women are being persecuted for righteousness' sake. I think of Dr. Wurmbrand, prisoner of Jesus Christ for so many years behind the iron curtain; for three of these years, suffering in solitary confinement in a dungeon below the surface of the earth; yet he has emerged from his suffering with a light of glory shining on him that we can only call the glory of the Son of God. Through much suffering we enter into the Kingdom of our God.

And was it not so with the apostle Paul? "Yea, doubtless," he says, "I count all things but loss for the excellency of the knowledge of Christ Jesus my Lord; for whom I have suffered the loss of all things, and do count them but dung, that I may win Christ, and be found in him, not having my own righteousness . . . but the righteousness which is of God by faith" (Phil 3:8, 9). Paul knew himself to have been singled out by the Holy Spirit for a very special ministry — that of being a pattern of "suffering for Christ" for all who would subsequently believe. When Ananias was sent to him, God said, "He is a chosen vessel unto me . . . for I will shew him how great things he must suffer for my names's sake" (Acts 9:15, 16). In this way, Paul was made an instrument to glorify his Lord and Savior, Jesus Christ. Suffering became the badge of service and the means of glorifying the Son of God.

One sole objective

This, then, is clear. There is one sole objective in the Holy Spirit's activities: He is present to glorify Jesus. This means that whatever begins with the Holy Spirit always ends in Jesus Christ. This is the glorious communion of the blessed Trinity: the Father glorifies the Son even as the Son glorifies the Father, and it is the peculiar and exalted ministry of the Holy Spirit to exalt and glorify the Son.

From this we can make some very definite deductions. For one thing, all order and structure derive from the glorifying of the Son. In heaven the highest place is ascribed to Jesus by God the Holy Spirit. Test every place by His preeminence there: Is Christ Jesus exalted in that place to which you go so often? We can likewise test any system of belief by the place given in it to Jesus Christ. Take Jehovah's Witnesses, the Christadelphians, the Christian Scientists, the Mormons, and similar cults. Do they give to Jesus Christ the place that the New Testament gives to Him? The answer is very simple. They do not. At some point there is a diluting of the glory ascribed to Him. His glory is shared with some other or others. But God will not share His glory with any. Nor will the Son. "He shall glorify Me."

The highest place that heaven affords,
Is His, is His by right,
The King of kings and Lord of lords,
And heaven's eternal light. [1]

This is His only rightful place. It is the hallowed work of the Holy Spirit thus to exalt Him and to crown Him with many crowns.

Furthermore, we can test any pursuit or activity in the same way. What about the books we read, the pleasures we enjoy, the friendships we cultivate, the homes we visit, the vacations we take, the hobbies we pursue, the things we love, all the ways we spend our time? As we bring these under the control of the Holy Spirit, He speaks to us. He tells us plainly if by them we are glorifying Jesus. And He reproves us if by any of them we are tarnishing the glory, or blotting out the image of the Son of God as His perfect will wants to form it in us. He will make it very clear to us if what we think and say and do are in fact to the glory of the Son of God, our Prince and Savior.

Drawing on the truth of Christ

We are told by our Lord: "He shall receive of mine, and shall shew it unto you" (John 16:14). In Phillips' translation this reads: "He will draw on my truth, and reveal it to you." We have already been told: "He will show you things to come" (John 16:13). That becomes very clear in many passages in the epistles but most of all in the book of Revelation, which is "the Revelation of Jesus Christ." This revelation is given to show the disciples "things which must shortly come to pass" (Rev. 1:1). The entire book is a revelation of the glory of Jesus Christ. In the Apocalypse the Holy Spirit glorifies Jesus Christ, as epitomized in the song of the angels: "Worthy is the Lamb that was slain to receive power and wealth and wisdom and strength and honor and glory and blessing" (Rev. 5:12 RSV). This is the Holy Spirit's joy. He exalts the Son of God as He reveals Him in His fullness.

He receives the fullness of Christ and imparts it to the children of God. Thus He glorifies the Son. When our Lord says, "He shall receive of mine," we are reminded of very similar words from John

---

[1] From the hymn "The Head That Once Was Crowned With Thorns" by Thomas Kelly (1769 - 1854).

17:10: "And all mine are thine, and thine are mine." This is a glimpse of the wonderful bond that exists between the Father and the Son. All that the Son has, the Father has. All that the Father has, the Son has. God the Father is glorified in the Son and the Son is glorified by the Father. And all this is *through the Holy Spirit,* who with equal rights in this divine unity receives the absolute fullness of God and shares this with God's child. He draws on the truth of Christ and imparts it to us who believe.

We therefore ask ourselves: Is my life glorifying my Savior? It is for this purpose that we came into the world. "Man's chief end is to glorify God and to enjoy Him for ever." So runs the Shorter Catechism. Are we glorifying God through Jesus Christ? Is it Jesus Christ who is being seen in us when men look on us? This is the question we must face. We are not being honest with God or with ourselves or with the fellowship of the saints if we cannot say we have faced this issue squarely. There is a prayer that is expressed in the simple but beautiful words of a little chorus:

> Let the beauty of Jesus be seen in me,
> All His wonderful passion and purity;
> O, Thou Spirit divine,
> All my nature refine,
> Till the beauty of Jesus is seen in me.

(Albert Orsbon)

This is no trite prayer. It touches the depths of our personal sanctification.

The Westminster Confession of Faith sums all this up very succinctly. In chapter 13 the subject of sanctification is dealt with:

> They who are effectually called and regenerated, having a new heart and a new spirit created in them, are further sanctified really and personally, through the virtue of Christ's death and resurrection, by His word and Spirit dwelling in them; the dominion of the whole body of sin is destroyed, and the several lusts thereof are more and more weakened and mortified, and they more and more quickened and strengthened in all saving graces, to the practice of true holiness without which no man shall see the Lord.

There follows a second paragraph that treats of the civil war thus occasioned where the flesh lusts against the Spirit and the Spirit against the flesh. The third paragraph, however, triumphantly declares the victory that the sons of God shall know as they walk in the Spirit:

> In which war, although the remaining corruption for a time may much prevail, yet, through the continual supply of strength from the sanctifying Spirit of Christ, the regenerate part doth overcome: and so the saints grow in grace, perfecting holiness in the fear of God.

May we know the joy of such sanctification. When we do, we will be experiencing the wonder of the Holy Spirit's work as He glorifies Christ within us.

3

The Fruit of the Spirit

The fruit of the Spirit is love, joy, peace, longsuffering, gentleness, goodness, faith, meekness, self-control (Galatians 5:22).

"IT IS, ALAS, sadly too true, and a matter of tragically common experience in Christians, that instead of 'trees of righteousness, the planting of the Lord,' there are everywhere to be seen across the Church dwarfed and scrubby bushes with scarcely enough life to keep up a little show of green."[1] When Alexander Maclaren spoke these words, he spoke for the total Church. For it is still a cause for much heart searching that in so many lives where the fruit of the Holy Spirit should abound, we are in actual fact almost destitute of His graces and show almost nothing of His fruit. Our Lord was concerned that His disciples should "bring forth fruit." He said, "Abide in me, and I in you; as the branch cannot bear fruit by itself, unless it abides in the vine; neither can you, unless you abide in me" (John 15:4 RSV). Almost in the same breath, He had said, "Every branch . . . that beareth fruit, he [the Father] purgeth it, that it may bring forth more fruit" (John 15:2). Further on in the same discussion He added these words: "Herein is my Father glorified, that you bear much fruit; so shall you be my disciples" (John 15:8). Here is our Lord's concern. His disciples must bear fruit: "fruit . . . more fruit . . . much fruit." There is progression in His thinking and expectation. The husbandman, who is the Lord God, the Father Almighty, the God and

---

[1] Quoted by J. Oswald Sanders, *The Holy Spirit of Promise* (Fort Washington, Pennsylvania: Christian Literature Crusade, 1940), p. 88.

Father of our Lord and Savior Jesus Christ, waits to see if we are going to bring forth fruit to His glory.

Chosen to bring forth fruit

St. John obviously thought much about this message our Lord delivered to the disciples. He has recorded it for us with an exactitude and care that are most noteworthy. Indeed, when he speaks of the Lord having chosen them as disciples, he recalls that the Master linked this, too, with fruit bearing. "You have not chosen me, but I have chosen you . . . that you should go and bring forth fruit, and that your fruit should remain" (John 15:16). It was for this that He had called them. They were to be His ambassadors ultimately. Yes! But first they were to be "fruit-bearers."

What is this fruit? It is the likeness of Jesus Christ Himself in His followers. This is why we speak of "fruit" and not "fruits." It is *one* fruit. Christ cannot be subdivided. Nor can the likeness of Christ. But just as He appears in a myriad different forms when we look at Him from all different angles, so also does the likeness of Christ appear different and may be summarized in a host of ways, but the essence of all is *love*. All the other manifestations of the fruit of the Spirit are just evidences or outlets of love. Joy is love smiling. Peace is love resting. Longsuffering is love waiting. Gentleness is love yielding. Goodness is love working. Faith is love trusting. Meekness is love accepting. Self-control is love overcoming. In every case, you find that any virtue is a manifestation of love. In every case, love is the answer and the key to perplexities and problems, especially those that arise on a personal level. Christ has chosen us in order that we should "show forth His love to all men." Has He not said, "By this all men will know that you are my disciples if you have love one for another" (John 13:35 RSV)? Love has manifold manifestations. But love is the true fruit of the Holy Spirit. When Christ's love is shed abroad in our hearts by the Holy Spirit, then all these other gifts and graces will be found as well. This is our destiny — to love as God loves.

The cultivation of fruit

Cultivation is essential if fruit is to be obtained. Our Lord expressly says, "My Father is the husbandman" (John 15:1). Think of that for a moment.

A true gardener is ruthless in his concern for his plants. He knows that the weeds must be rooted out; the branches must be pruned; the soil must be enriched. Yet at the same time he knows full well that he is only an instrument. He cannot create a flower out of the seed. This is a miracle whenever it happens. The seed must go down into the darkness of the soil if it is to germinate, thrust up the green blade, and grow to fruition. So it is with God and His children. God sees to it that we are planted aright. He supplies us with all needed life-producing elements. Gently and firmly He watches over us. As we grow, He permits essential pruning. He holds the knife. He is determined that we should bring forth fruit to His glory.

Pruning may be a hard and chastening process. It is often painful. But there is purpose in it. It is always intended to bring forth more fruit. Let a bush grow wild and you will never get from it its greatest potential. Pruning is an art which only a great master can really employ; and God is such an artist. He knows the branches in each bush that are not bearing fruit. He cuts them down. We should be grateful for such wonderful care. He never gives up. He is determined that His children should "grow in grace" and that thereby they should manifest the fruit of Christian grace in all its purity and glory. So the heavenly husbandman works with us, cleanses us, prunes where necessary, and plans a crop. Do we flinch? Perhaps, but we do not lose courage when we know that there is a purpose in our pain.

Many have found this in the chastening fires of suffering. "My dear friends, do not be bewildered by the fiery ordeal that is upon you, as though it were something extraordinary. It gives you a share in Christ's sufferings, and that is cause for joy; and when His glory is revealed, your joy will be triumphant" (1 Peter 4:12, 13 NEB). I sat long into the night a few days ago with a man to whom great trial has come. He said to me, "I am going over every part, every single square inch of my life, in order to discover, if I may, in the light of the Scriptures where I have gone wrong." God is pruning his life. The searchlight of God is probing the darkened areas of his life which he thought he could hide from God. But God refuses to be left out of any part of our life if we are determined to be holy. He will refine and purify. He will sit, as Malachi saw Him, like a refiner waiting to see His own image in the molten metal (Mal. 3:3).

All the fruit of the Spirit is likeness to Christ

As you go through the various evidences of fruit in the life of the Christian, you soon see that the fruit of the Spirit is another name for likeness to Jesus Christ. As we have said, this is why we speak of "fruit" and not "fruits." The fruit of the Holy Spirit is *one* even as Christ is *one* and His name and character are *one*. It is fruit — singular! We dare not speak of the fruits of the Spirit. We can, of course, speak of the works of the flesh. Paul does. In Ephesians 5 he elaborates on these works and shows how manifold and varied they are. Only after he has written about these sinful works of man does he write about the wonderful fruit of the believer. The fruit of the Holy Spirit is thus placed in direct contrast to the works of the flesh. This is the right order. Idolatry, discord, drunkenness, fornication, indecency of any kind, ruthless greed, shallowness, darkness of understanding, ignorance, falsehood, vice, and evil desire; these are the marks of sin. But the fruit of the Holy Spirit is absolutely different. The fruit of the Holy Spirit begins with the character of the Christian mind; it then passes on to reveal itself in many forms in personal conduct. What a natural contrast! Works belong to the factory. They are part of the whole sequence of dead things. The sinner becomes deluded by Satan and produces works of devilish ingenuity and unholy cunning. The fruit of the Spirit, however, is like the flowers that grow in gardens. Man cannot make flowers. They require his diligence and care, of course, but they are neither his invention nor his creation. No mortal skill can produce unaided the golden fields of corn or the lovely fruit on luscious trees. Fruit needs God. Without God's gracious Spirit we cannot produce the fruit of the Spirit. It is the Lord's doing.

Reduced to very simple and basic English, what Paul says is that the fruit of the Spirit is a loving, affectionate spirit, radiant with peculiar joy, and full of tranquillity; it is very patient in disposition even when provoked; it possesses unusual insights into the needs and wants of others, is generous in judgment and is utterly loyal; it is by nature very humble, forgets itself in the happiness of others, never allows itself to get out of control, and is always reliable because of its unusual adaptability and self-mastery.

What a catalog of virtues! It is a very wonderful catalog. But would you expect anything else when you are speaking of the "fruit of the Holy Spirit"?

His ninefold graces

Seventeen works of the flesh are detailed. But nine specific graces are mentioned as being part of the fruit of the Holy Spirit (Gal. 5:22). Together they form a triad of experience, a triad of conduct, and a triad of character. This is how J. Oswald Sanders in his very explicit book on *The Holy Spirit of Promise* depicts them.[2] It is a natural and fitting division of this ninefold manifestation of the life of God. Experience, conduct, and character mold themselves together to form the perfect evidence of a life that is born of God.

The Scriptures never confuse the gifts of the Spirit with the fruit of the Spirit. It is granted to all God's children to know the fruit of the Spirit. To every child of His, God comes seeking fruit. But the gifts of the Spirit are a different order of things. Fruit should be found in all. Gifts are given by sovereign dispensation. We have gifts that differ according to the grace that is given to us. Some have only one gift. Some may have a number. It is even possible that some may have many. All differing gifts are suited to the kind of service we are called to fulfill, whether of prophecy, ministry, teaching, exhortation, beneficence, administration, speaking in tongues, the interpretation of tongues, or some other service. There are three passages that treat of the subject of spiritual gifts and the lists are all different. We shall note this when we come to study spiritual gifts. What we must emphasize now is that our Lord said:

> I am the true vine, and my Father is the husbandman.
> Every branch in me that beareth not fruit he taketh away;
> and every branch that beareth fruit, he purgeth it,
> that it may bring forth more fruit (John 15:1, 2).

God expects His children to bear much fruit. In this way we show we are disciples indeed. May we all truly bear much fruit.

---

[2] Ibid., p. 90.

4

The Gifts of the Spirit

When he ascended up on high, he led captivity captive, and gave gifts unto men. . . . And he gave some, apostles; and some, prophets; and some, evangelists; and some, pastors and teachers; for the perfecting of the saints, for the work of the ministry, for the edifying of the body of Christ (Ephesians 4:8-12).

THE GREATEST GIFT of our Lord to His Church is the gift of the Holy Spirit. He told His disciples in the upper room: "I will pray the Father and he shall give you another Comforter, that he may abide with you for ever" (John 14:16). This happened on the day of Pentecost. God works according to a calendar. Long centuries earlier God had told His people about the feast of Pentecost; and it was on this very day that the Spirit came. With the Spirit, there came also gifts of the Spirit. "Now there are diversities of gifts, but the same Spirit. And there are differences of administrations, but . . . it is the same God which worketh all in all. But the manifestation of the Spirit is given to every man to profit withal" (1 Cor. 12:4-7). This last verse means that any gift of the Holy Spirit is intended to be used for the profit and advantage of all within the circle of believers. [1]

---

[1] What about gifts to unregenerate people and the place of these in God's plan of redemption? Are the abilities of non-Christian inventors, dentists, and psychiatrists, for example, also gifts of the Holy Spirit?

All natural gifts are God's gifts. He makes us as we are. Without Him we would not be capable of anything. Natural abilities are therefore gifts of God. Of that there can be no question.

But the issue before us is that of spiritual gifts given by the Holy Spirit after regeneration. Are these gifts special addenda to our natural quantum of natural

An unusual diversity of gifts

We should note very carefully that the Holy Spirit knows no restriction in the gifts He bestows. Of course, He will never bestow any gift that is evil — He is the Holy Spirit. What comes from Him is pure and good. But there is an almost infinite mixture of gifts with which He blesses the Church. There are three passages of Scripture that deal with these gifts — in addition to the ministries that our Lord elaborated when He spoke to the disciples on the night He was betrayed. The three passages are in Romans 12, 1 Corinthians 12 and 14, and Ephesians 4. Even the most cursory reading of these passages will immediately demonstrate one thing: the gifts vary in each list. They are diverse, suited to differing individual qualifications, and adaptable to every situation that the Church might face.

The Giver is One. But the gifts are many. And not all persons have the same gifts. "God has appointed in the church first apostles, second prophets, third teachers, then workers of miracles, then healers, helpers, administrators, speakers in various kinds of tongues. Are all apostles? Are all prophets? Are all teachers? Do all work miracles? Do all speak with tongues? Do all interpret?" (1 Cor. 12:28-30 RSV). The answer to these questions is in each case an emphatic negative. No one has all these gifts. As in the parable of the talents in which one is given five talents, another two, another one, so is it with the gifts of the Spirit. All have at least one gift; that is clear from Romans 12:6: we have

---

endowment by God? Surely, the answer is that the Spirit gives a special gift to all believers in addition to natural gifts and qualities. "For by the grace given to me I bid every one among you not to think of himself more highly than he ought to think, but to think with sober judgment, each *according to the measure of faith which God has assigned him"* (Rom. 12:3 RSV). This "measure of faith" is surely a special "charisma" of God to His adopted child. It is a particular gift. So we read in verse 6 of the same chapter: "Having then gifts that differ according to the grace that is given to us. . . ." There is here in the Greek a play on the words "charis" and "charismata," which is difficult to pick up in English.

The plain fact appears to be that while the Holy Spirit dwells within our mortal bodies He quickens them. He awakens dormant faculties and develops the latent. Every part of a person's being is revitalized by the Spirit's presence. The Holy Spirit gives to all who believe "life more abundant." Yet at the same time He gives some special gift that is distinctive and unique over and above all our natural qualifications. That appears to be the clear meaning of Paul in all the passages dealing with spiritual gifts.

gifts that differ "according to the grace that is given to us." But no one has all the gifts. Even apostles are singled out, and prophets too. They do not possess all the gifts. To them has been given a gift of God the Holy Spirit for the edifying of the Church and for the building up of the Body of Christ.

Defense against abuse

It is made clear that counterfeits of these gifts may manifest themselves. This has happened: church history has many a telling illustration of how the gifts of the Holy Spirit have been misused and misapplied. The New Testament shows us men prepared to offer money if only they might obtain the specific gifts seen in the apostles. "Thy money perish with thee" — that was the stern rebuke of God's servant to one who would prostitute a holy gift of God for ignoble and selfish ends. In the church at Corinth, the gifts of the Holy Spirit were commercialized and became a source of rivalry, disorder, envy, and acrimony. There were those who possessed only one gift but claimed precedence over others with more gifts than themselves — they desired priority in importance. What had happened there was that carnal men had come into possession of these gifts and were using them for carnal ends. Now this is very revealing. It is doubtful if these men knew what they were doing. Satan is such a master at bombarding the subconscious that it is quite feasible they did not realize how wrong their acts were. No suggestion is made by Paul that the gifts in the Corinthian church were not genuine; but the gifts were perverted to wrong goals and subverted to unworthy ends. It is indeed strange that in a church of which the apostle Paul could say that "they came behind in no gift, waiting for the coming of the Lord," there were nonetheless carnalities that would have disgraced a properly ordered pagan assembly.

Safeguards must be sought. Otherwise disaster looms. The right kind of safeguard is to cling to the verities and loyalties of the faith. The preeminent loyalty is recognition of the lordship of Christ. Let this point be stressed, this safeguard. Our Lord said of the Holy Spirit that "He shall not speak of himself. . . . He shall glorify me" (John 16:13, 14). In any assembly truly ordered by the Holy Spirit there will be much talk about the Lord whom the Spirit loves to exalt. It is impossible to know Jesus Christ save by the Holy Spirit. Only the Spirit can make Christ real. And only when Jesus Christ is truly Lord does the Holy Spirit come to have His rightful place in the company of the people of God. Overmuch talk or stress on the Holy Spirit with a corresponding diminishing of glory to the Christ of God is a sign that the true way has been missed.

Seek, then, to glorify *Christ*. Whatever gift comes from the Holy Spirit is granted in order that the Christ might be the better seen. "He shall glorify me."

And another safeguard against possible abuse of the gifts of the Spirit is a rightful defense of the Word of God. "All scripture is given by inspiration of God" (2 Tim. 3:16). His gifts will therefore never be at variance with His Word. The Spirit of Christ who is the Spirit of truth will verify, corroborate, affirm, interpret, and attest the Word of God. There is no wisdom given of God that is not in accordance with the holy Scriptures. In the Body of Christ, order will rule, for God is not the author of confusion; edification will be known, for "the meek will he guide in judgment; and the meek will he teach his way" (Ps. 25:9). If there be gifts of prophecy and speaking in tongues with interpretations, none of these should ever conflict with the revelation already fully given. Over all, love reigns supreme.

The uniqueness of the gifts

These gifts transcend natural talents. Yet they are related to them. When God first planned the epistle to the Romans, He foresaw a man who would have such natural talent and such spiritual gift as would make it possible for him to write this wonderful letter. So is it still. The days of the apostles are not past. They are still with us. The Holy Spirit renews, vitalizes native powers, quickens natural endowments, and emphasizes our basic capabilities. Even as fire quickens, so does the Holy Spirit energize and endow us with new powers to God's glory. What is impossible with man becomes possible when He, the Spirit of glory, has come. He works through our natural talents, yet His gifts transcend them. There are many gifts of the Spirit. Every time I read the New Testament to try to enumerate them I find a different number. But somehow that is the way it ought to be. Gifts such as wisdom, faith, miracles, healings, knowledge, discernment of spirits, tongues

and interpretation of tongues, teaching, leading, helping, renewing
— these are all gifts of the Holy Spirit. Without the Spirit of God
we would never know one of them. True, wisdom and knowledge
are clearly related to the mind, to intelligence and to learning;
nonetheless, they cannot be discovered by the natural powers of
man. No more can faith, though it has been called man's sixth
sense, for we walk by faith, we live by faith, we do everything by
faith. What of healing? When James speaks of healing, he refers
to something transcending the normal gifts of medical science.
These normal gifts were not despised by the early Church — was
not Dr. Luke numbered among Paul's party on the second missionary journey? But the gift of healing was a spiritual ministry fulfilled by the elders of the Church who were themselves filled with
the Spirit.

And tongues? We shall speak more of them presently. But here
we note that they were a recognized factor among the gifts of the
Holy Spirit. Paul wished that all who heard him might "speak in
tongues." How often have I longed that all the elders of my church
might thus "speak in tongues." It would be a clear sign that God
was doing something unusual and great among them. The gift of
tongues, however, comes last on the list — and first in controversy.
There is a gift of tongues that is given for a sign, as there is a gift
of tongues for the edifying of the Body of Christ. Careful study
of the New Testament places the gift of tongues among the gifts
of the Spirit and it must be specially preserved from abuse. That
it has been abused, possibly more than any other gift, may be true.
Possibly also there have been more divisions caused through the
exercise of this gift than through any other. We must beware of
grieving the Spirit of God by whom we are "sealed unto the day of
our redemption." Tongues are a gift to a select band. To say anything else is to deny God's Word.

The object of the gifts

Paul points out that the gifts of the Spirit are intended to equip
us for the service of the Lord. In Romans 12:6-8, he says, "Having
then gifts differing according to the grace that is given to us, whether
prophecy, let us prophesy according to the proportion of faith; or
ministry, let us wait on our ministering; or he that teacheth, on
teaching; or he that exhorteth, on exhortation; he that giveth, let

him do it with simplicity; he that ruleth, with diligence; he that showeth mercy, with cheerfulness."

By these gifts, it is planned that we too should glorify Christ even as the Holy Spirit glorifies Christ. Many have argued that some of these special gifts of the Spirit ended with the apostolic age. But the reasoning is suspect. At many other periods of church history these gifts have been seen and it would not be difficult to mount overwhelming evidence to demonstrate that such gifts are visible in the Church today. There is good reason to state that the present age is one in greater need of divine manifestations of the gifts of the Spirit than any other. We live in a time when occult manifestations are multiplied and in many cases they are counterfeits of the divine. The wisdom of this world is mighty in its ability to show forth the exceeding greatness of the powers of evil. Never was there greater need for the exercise of all true spiritual gifts.

The gifts are given to glorify Christ. In so doing, they make Christ desirable. They show that He is Lord over all, King of kings, and Lord of lords. To Him has been given all power in heaven and earth. It is before Him that every one must bow and every tongue confess that Jesus Christ is Lord to the glory of God the Father. Now it is an utter impossibility for man to do this in his own strength. By ourselves, we taint all we touch; we tarnish all we handle. But when the Holy Spirit indwells us and is working in power within and through us, then Christ can be revealed, then the glory of the Son of God can be perceived again in the likeness of sinful flesh.

We must distinguish carefully between fruit and gifts, as we saw earlier. Fruit and gifts are not identical. Gifts are endowments of power. Fruit is a reflection of character. True fruit is an evidence of true holiness of life, but, sad to say, it is possible to possess spiritual gifts without corresponding evidence of Christlikeness in our lives. Gifts may operate immediately, whereas fruit takes time to develop. Fruit is expected of all, the true fruit of the Spirit, in which love is supreme. Gifts are for those for whom they have been prepared. All true believers must bear fruit. Gifts can never be a substitute for fruit.

It is essential that we understand the real object of spiritual gifts. They are given to glorify Christ, to glorify God the Father almighty through Jesus Christ the Son. But for this end to be accomplished, the gifts we have received must be used. The whole thrust of the passage in 1 Corinthians 14:14 is that the gifts of the Spirit are intended to help the Church and that each man has received from the Spirit whatever gift the Spirit knows is best for him to receive. Now some say that all must speak in tongues. But St. Paul expressly asks, "Do all speak in tongues?" and the answer clearly is no. Fruit is demanded of all — every manifestation of the fruit of the Spirit. It is not the case that one Christian should show the fruit of joy, another the fruit of love, while yet another manifests the fruit of peace or longsuffering or self-control. No! A thousand times no. The fruit should be seen in holiness of character in all true Christians. Not so the gifts of the Spirit. "To one . . . to another . . . to another. . . ." That is the scriptural principle. To read from this that all should speak in tongues is a truth alien to the Bible.

Many, of course, did speak in other tongues "as the Spirit gave them utterance." To argue, however, that this speaking in tongues is identical with what the Corinthian church experienced is quite wrong. In Acts 2, it is said that the multitude heard "in [their] own tongues the wonderful works of God." They needed no interpreter. But in Corinth Paul expressly states that there must be no speaking in tongues "without interpretation." This in itself differentiates the tongues of Corinth from the tongues of Acts. We shall later study the question of speaking in tongues in fuller detail. At this point what needs to be said is that this "gift" of the Spirit is for those whom He has selected, as is true of all the other gifts of the Spirit. You cannot come up to some counter where all the gifts of the Spirit are displayed and choose what you want. No! The Holy Spirit alone is the Giver. See to it that when He gives His gift you exercise it to the full.

I know of Christians who, clearly endowed by the Spirit with some special gift for the edification of the Church, have gone through life desiring some other gift than the one they have received. This is very sad. True spiritual discernment, which is one of the gifts of the Spirit that I believe He is prepared to grant to all who truly seek it, should make clear to every Christian what special gift he possesses. It is of this that Paul is thinking when he writes that no man should "think of himself more highly than he ought to think; but to think soberly, according as God has dealt to every man the measure of faith" (Rom. 12:3). When we are prepared for that, asking God for wisdom to know what our special gift is, then God is indeed glorified; Christ is glorified; the Holy Spirit is glorified. We manifest the tokens of divine life and power ordained from all eternity for us to enjoy and use.

God grant to each of us the wisdom to see and use the gift His Spirit has given.

5

The Spirit of Life

The law of the Spirit of life in Christ Jesus has made me free from the law of sin and death (Romans 8:2).

THE APOSTLE PAUL calls the Holy Spirit "the Spirit of life." The same emphasis is given in the Nicene Creed:

> I believe in the Holy Spirit, the Lord and the Giver of life; who proceedeth from the Father and the Son, who with the Father and Son together is worshipped and glorified; who spake by the prophets.

The Westminster Confession of Faith (chapter 2, paragraph 3) discusses "God and the Holy Trinity" in terms particularly fitted to our study now:

> In the unity of the Godhead there be three persons, of one substance, power, and eternity: God the Father, God the Son, and God the Holy Ghost. The Father is of none, neither begotten nor proceeding; the Son is eternally begotten of the Father; the Holy Ghost eternally proceeding from the Father and the Son.

He is the Spirit of life. This can mean nothing less than that He is the Spirit from whom all life flows. He is the life-giving Spirit. That is why He is rightly called the Spirit of regeneration. It is through the eternal Spirit that we are born into the family of God. None can call Jesus Christ Lord except by the Holy Spirit (1 Cor. 12:3). Yet it is the ability to name Jesus Christ as Lord and Savior that brings us into the redeemed family of God. Life comes through the Spirit of life.

He is at the center of the secret of all energy, truth, power, and grace. He gives life. It is for this purpose that He came — that

He might give life to the dead. Life has been defined as a capacity to respond to environment. A corpse is incapable of making sound or movement, or of paying any attention whatever. But life responds. And He who is the Spirit of life gives to the sinner the ability to respond to God. He gives the gift of birth. By the Holy Spirit we are born into God's family. "Except a man be born of water and of the Spirit, he cannot enter into the kingdom of God" (John 3:5). These are the words our Lord used when He talked with Nicodemus in the dead of night. The same Spirit that brooded over the waters of primeval chaos broods over the spirit of man and makes him see the light of truth, thereby enabling him to receive the Spirit of life. The Holy Spirit is the indweller of all sanctified men and women, directing, controlling, sanctifying the whole man. By this He becomes the Spirit of their spirit, the Mind of their mind, the Strength of their strength, the Heart of their heart, and the Life of their life.

The renewal of the image of God

The marks of the new life given by the Holy Spirit are very clear. They are nothing less than the complete renewal in the heart of man of the image of God which was lost at the fall. It is of this that Paul writes to the Galatians: "You are all the children of God by faith in Christ Jesus" (Gal. 3:26). Similarly the apostle John writes, "as many as received him, to them gave he power to become the sons of God, even to them that believe on his name; which were born [when they believed] not of blood, . . . nor of the will of man [like those children adopted by earthly parents in whom no inward change is wrought], but of God" (John 1:12,13).

By this amazing work of the Holy Spirit, we are "renewed in the spirit of [our] mind" (Eph. 4:23). The work of grace is completed. The ruin that the fall left is cast aside and once more the *imago Dei* shines forth within and through us. Of all the doctrines of Christianity that can be called fundamental, two stand forth as unique — the doctrine of justification and the doctrine of the new birth. The former relates to what God does *for* us; the latter relates to what God does *in* us. In *temporal* order, neither of these is before the other. They are exactly contemporaneous. In *logical* order, however, justification may be considered to precede the new birth. We first conceive of God's wrath being turned away, and then we think of the wonderful things that His Spirit does within our hearts.

When God made man in His own image, He made him so with particular reference to His moral image. This, according to the apostle, is "righteousness and true holiness" (Eph. 4:24). God is love; therefore man was originally filled with the love of God. God is spotless purity; therefore in the beginning man was pure from every sinful blot; otherwise God could not have pronounced him, as well as all the other work of His hands, "very good" (Gen. 1:31). He was not, however, made immutable. He was able to stand, but liable to fall. Man fell from his high estate. This is the terrible story of Genesis 3. Man openly declared that he would not have God to rule over him. And in that very day he chose to separate himself from God, he died. He fell under the power of a servile fear. He fled from the presence of God. He became unholy as well as unhappy.

We need not linger over the sad details. All of human lineage has agreed with Adam. "All have sinned and come short of the glory of God" (Rom. 3:23). We are one with our illustrious lineal father. We have chosen our own way. Pride has ruled our wills and we by nature are under the wrath of God. And if we are to be changed so radically that once again the image of God will be stamped upon our personalities, then we must meet the conditions that God has laid down in His great plan of redemption. Gospel holiness is no less than the image of God stamped upon the heart; it is nothing less than the mind which is in Christ Jesus; it consists of all heavenly affection and tempers mingled together in one. This is the image of God. It is this image that is renewed in us when we receive Jesus Christ into our lives and worship Him as Savior and God. No more radical change can be imagined. It makes it natural for us to love every man, for we know ourselves to be loved with an everlasting love. We are brought from darkness into God's own marvelous light and love Him with all our heart.

Thus the image of God is restored. Christ becomes to us the Lord of all. The Holy Spirit within us helps us to make our lives a daily offering and sacrifice to God, acceptable through Jesus Christ. Could any greater work be imagined than that?

The Holy Spirit — the essence of life

All this mighty work is accomplished by the Holy Spirit. He is able to do it, because He is the very essence of life.

As we study biblical references to the work of the Holy Spirit, we see that He was active among men from the beginning of time. It is true that the precise words "Holy Spirit" occur only three times in the Old Testament. But the creative concept of the Spirit is there in the book of Genesis.

He is never thought of as an inanimate force. The word for spirit in Hebrew is "ruah" and this word has two distinct meanings. One is breath. The other is wind. The idea of "wind" is impersonal; but the concept of "breath" is very much more intimate, obviously implying consciousness and understanding, for it is hardly possible to have breath without having one who breathes. At the root of both meanings, however, is the idea of movement. "Ruah" was always in action, always affecting whatever it breathed upon. Another thought basic to the word "ruah" is that of creativity. When the Spirit of God moved across the face of the waters in the beginning, it was with creative movement. And when God made man and he became a living soul, it was because God "breathed into him the breath of life" (Gen. 2:7).

All through the Old Testament we see this same movement, force, power. The men and women of faith who are extolled for their faith in Hebrews 11 were all empowered by the Holy Spirit. He led armies into battle. But He operated in more intimate ways also. In the great penitential Psalm 51, we hear David praying,

> Create in me a clean heart, O God, and put a new and right spirit within me. Cast me not away from thy presence, and take not thy holy Spirit from me (Ps. 51:10, 11 RSV).

In the 139th Psalm we read:

> O Lord, thou hast searched me and known me! . . . Thou dost beset me behind and before, and layest thy hand upon me. . . . Whither shall I go from thy Spirit? Or whither shall I flee from thy presence? (Ps. 139:1, 5, 7 RSV).

The immediacy of God is known through the presence of the Spirit of God. And it was always thus with our Lord. He was "conceived by the Holy Spirit." Simeon was promised by the Spirit that he would see the Messiah before he died. John the Baptist was filled with the Holy Spirit from his mother's womb. It was this same John who said, "I baptize you with water . . . but he who is coming after me . . . will baptize you with the Holy Spirit . . ." (Matt. 3:11 RSV). Not until our Lord was anointed with the Spirit did He begin His ministry. It was through the eternal Spirit that He wrought miracles, taught the multitudes, called His disciples, and sent them forth to preach and heal. As Calvary drew near, He told the disciples more and more about the Holy Spirit and promised that He would be another Comforter who would be with them forever to guide them, teach them, and strengthen them.

After His resurrection, Jesus commanded the disciples to "tarry in Jerusalem" till the fulfillment of His promise was realized. They waited. And when on the day of Pentecost the Spirit came upon the praying Church, each one of that noble band was transformed. Immediately, they launched on a crusade of life-giving, life-creating acts. They were no longer weak, vacillating, powerless. No! The Spirit of God, the Spirit of all-conquering life and love, equipped them with new dynamisms. Life poured into them and through them in such overwhelming force that no one was able to stand against them. They went to the ends of the world and turned it upside down. They were filled with the Spirit. Being thus filled with life abundant, they could do nothing else but demonstrate that life to all the world. And the world has been different ever since.

Baptism or fullness?

It is stated by John the Baptist: "He shall baptize you with the Holy Spirit, and with fire" (Matt. 3:11). What does this mean?

Over this statement controversy has raged. Unfortunately so. There is really nothing doubtful in what the Bible says. In this, as in all other cases, the words of Martin Luther in *Table Talk* are true: "The Holy Spirit is the plainest teacher of all teachers." When the word "baptism" is used of the Holy Spirit, it clearly refers to the incorporation of the believer into Jesus Christ. "By one Spirit are we all baptized into one body, whether we be Jews or Gentiles, whether we be bond or free; and have been all made to drink into one Spirit" (1 Cor. 12:13). Nothing could be simpler. Jesus Christ baptizes with the Holy Spirit and with fire. By the

Holy Spirit, He baptizes us, incorporates us, joins us into His body. Thus on the day of Pentecost, the mystery which had been hidden from the beginning of time was revealed; and in the house of Cornelius there was a further revelation of the mystery: the Gentiles also should be heirs. They too should be baptized into a wonderful unity with the Jew in Christ as Lord. So the separating walls between Jew and Gentile are done away with forever. All are one in Christ Jesus. The baptism of the Spirit is that sovereign and divine act whereby they who believe in Christ are joined forever to Him. This is a divine and spiritual act. Any lower interpretation diminishes the work of the eternal Spirit of God. The apostle Paul stresses this writing to the Galatians:

> After . . . faith is come, we are no longer under a schoolmaster. For you are all the children of God by faith in Christ Jesus. For as many of you as have been baptized into Christ have put on Christ. There is neither Jew nor Greek, there is neither bond nor free, there is neither male nor female: for you are all one in Christ Jesus. And if you be Christ's, then are you Abraham's seed, and heirs according to the promise (Gal. 3:25-29).

The baptism of the Spirit applies to the moment of our acceptance by God and birth into God's family. In this context, baptism is another word for rebirth.

But there is another word used frequently when the work of the Holy Spirit is noted. It is the word "fullness." "They were all *filled* with the Holy Spirit" (Acts 2:4, italics mine). Is this just another word for "baptism"? Surely not! If the Holy Spirit, in His inspiring holy men of God to write as they did and thus to bless the Church with the sacred Scriptures, used distinct words, He surely intended that they should have specific meanings. And they do. "Be not drunk with wine wherein is excess; but be filled with the Spirit" (Eph. 5:18). The tense is present. "Be filling." This is an experience that we should have constantly, and many do. Unfortunately, there are just as many who don't. They belong to Christ. They have been "baptized" by the Holy Spirit into the Body of Christ. But this may be without knowing the blessed fullness of the Holy Spirit. On the day of Pentecost, two events took place in the lives of the disciples. They were "baptized into Christ" and they were "filled with His Spirit." It is our solemn responsibility as believers to so discipline ourselves and to so walk in the steps of our Lord and Master that of us it will be true also — we shall be filled with the Spirit.

This constant infilling by the Holy Spirit is the great watershed between the Old and New Covenants. On the day of Pentecost, the priest of the Jewish economy became the preacher in Christ's Kingdom; the altar became a pulpit; the annual appearance of the high priest in the holy of holies ended, for Christ our High Priest has ascended to make unending intercession for His own; and the Holy Spirit, who in Old Testament times would come and go, is now given to God's children to abide with them forever (John 14: 16). And, most glorious wonder of all wonders, the Jew and the Gentile meet as one at the feet of the living Christ. "He is our peace . . . and hath broken down the middle wall of partition between us (i.e., between Jew and Gentile), having abolished in his flesh the enmity . . . that he might reconcile both unto God in one body by the cross, having slain the enmity thereby" (Eph. 2:14-16).

Both Jew and Gentile may accept Christ as Savior and Lord. Both Jew and Gentile may be "baptized by the Spirit" into the Body of Christ. Both Jew and Gentile may know the joy of being "filled with the Holy Spirit." We acknowledge in this gospel age "one Lord, one faith, one baptism" (Eph. 4:5). *One* baptism. This can happen only once. Our Lord stresses this when He makes a significant change in the use of prepositions. Speaking of the Holy Spirit and His coming to the disciples, He said, "He dwells *with* you, and will be *in* you" (John 14:17 RSV). How right Luther was when he wrote in *Table Talk* that "the heart of the gospel is in the prepositions of the New Testament." The Holy Spirit indwells us. He longs to *fill* us with Himself. This filling we must seek daily. There is one baptism; there should be many fillings. As He infills us, He takes to Himself the oversight of all we are and think and say and do.

It is wonderful to realize that we may be filled with the Spirit of life. This is an experience of friendship, the friendship of God. It is an experience of contact with a Personality, one who deeply cares for us and is able to support us through every experience of life. It is an experience of fellowship with the source and center of all life and this in the most dynamic ways. And it is an experience that all God's children may share. The will of God for us is nothing less than that we should be "filled with all the fulness of God" (Eph. 3:19). God has no favorites. God is no respecter of persons. This gift of the Spirit's fulness is altogether of grace. It is for you. And you will never be able to accomplish all that God means you should accomplish without the actual and real in-filling of the Holy Spirit.

Are there degrees of fullness?

There are degrees of fullness. The mighty ocean holds more water than even the largest fresh-water lake. A cup can hold more than a thimble. So it is with us as we seek the fullness of the Spirit of God. A newborn babe in Christ may have a very limited capacity for fullness. But by dwelling in Christ, by feeding on His Word, by the exercise of disciplined prayer, we grow. Growth means a capacity for greater fullness. And this should be the mark of the Christian's capacity for God. Otherwise we are not growing in grace and in the knowledge of Christ Jesus our Lord.

Growth in grace means that our capacities are constantly being expanded to receive the immeasurable wonders of the love of God. The Spirit of life is the Spirit of love. God is life and God is love. So, as we grow daily, we increase our ability to express the love of God to men wherever we are. This is our Christian duty. It is also our joy. Take a concordance and look up every reference to "growth" in the New Testament. Learn every one of these verses and passages by heart. Let this word dwell in you. As the true spirit of the Scriptures grasps your mind, yield yourself to it and let it bring forth fruit unto life eternal. This is what God wants to do in you and for you. Nothing less will satisfy Him.

Don't forget that you are filled with the Spirit of life when Jesus Christ is Lord of all. Our Lord said, "I am come that they might have life, and that they might have it more abundantly" (or in all its fullness) (John 10:10). To the woman at the well at Sychar He said, "Whosoever drinketh of the water that I shall give him shall never thirst; but the water that I shall give him shall be in him a well of water springing up into everlasting life" (John 4:14). In New Testament times there was a variety of ways in which believers seemed to enter into this experience of the fullness of the Holy Spirit. In Acts 2 we see the Church waiting expectantly for a promised gift. But in Acts 10 the people in the house of Cornelius have no definite expectation of an unusual manifestation of divine life. But it happened in both cases.

And all this is strangely relevant to our own times. Everything we read in the New Testament seems very contemporary. So little has changed today. The same Lord who breathed on His disciples and said, "Receive the Holy Spirit," is the One who meets us in the sanctuary on a Sunday or on any day of the week in the little sanctuary we have prepared for His coming. It is very simple if we take our cue from Scripture alone and follow the Scripture through to the very end. When we do so, the words that I now quote of the late Dr. Graham Scroggie will seem perfect and complete:

> What then about the now currently held doctrine that multitudes of Christians have never received the Baptism of the Spirit, and that all such should seek it until they experience it? All I can say is, that such teaching is not derived from the New Testament, and the spread of it is bringing large numbers into bondage and darkness. This error is due, perhaps, to the confusing of the Fullness of the Spirit with the Baptism; but more especially is it due, I think, to associating the blessing of the Spirit with the gift of tongues. [1]

---

[1] From a message given at the Keswick Convention, 1925, quoted by J. Oswald Sanders, *The Holy Spirit of Promise* (Fort Washington, Pennsylvania: Christian Literature Crusade, n.d.), p. 62.

6

Speaking in Tongues

*Now concerning spiritual gifts, brethren, I would not
have you ignorant* (1 Corinthians 12:1).

NO STUDY OF THE PERSON and work of the Holy Spirit would be
complete without an examination of glossolalia — the phenomenon
of speaking in tongues.

Over the past fifteen years a significant and exciting movement
has stirred the life of the Christian Church. Men and women from
all walks of life, with every pigmentation of skin, some rich, some
poor, school drop-outs and college professors, housewives and
bishops, statesmen and draft-dodgers, have experienced the phenomenon of "speaking in tongues" — or glossolalia, as it is commonly
called. In this ecumenically minded age this experience has been
described as the greatest unifying force that ecumenicity knows; for
the fall-out from this unique visitation in the churches is raining
down on Presbyterians and Lutherans, on Roman Catholics and
high Anglicans, on Congregationalists as well as on Convention
and Independent Baptists. Christians, who twenty years ago would
have crossed the street to avoid one another, are today meeting
in "underground" cell groups and sharing their experiences of "the
second blessing" — i.e., the baptism of the Holy Spirit accompanied
by the gift of speaking in tongues.

There has been much written on this. There will be much more.
I have spoken repeatedly on the subject and have frequently been
asked for a copy of my manuscript. The following pages are a
brief summary of what I have said elsewhere, what I have seen,
what I believe, and what I think the Scriptures teach. I am not
interested in stirring up controversy. I only want the plain teaching
of the Bible to be known.

The Corinthian Christians

Paul writes about spiritual gifts at great length in his first letter to Corinth. Let me first summarize the basic elements that he stresses there.

1. When Paul writes about speaking in tongues, there is no note of surprise in his letter. On the contrary. He deliberately lists this phenomenon as one of the gifts of the Holy Spirit. He is familiar with these gifts. He accepts them as a genuine part of Christian experience. He writes only in order to insure that there should be no misuse of the gift.

2. He obviously considers the Holy Spirit to be the source of tongues. Why else would he include them in the gifts of the Spirit? That the Holy Spirit had given this gift he does not question. What he does question is the maladministration of the gift; from that point he strives to maintain the true balance of a mature Christian.

3. There is clearly no doubt in his mind that because it is a gift of the Spirit, those who possess it are appointed by God. "And God has appointed in the Church . . . speakers in various kinds of tongues" (1 Cor. 12:28 RSV).

4. Having said this, we must add that he regards this gift as only one among many. He lists a number of spiritual gifts — the word of wisdom, the word of knowledge, faith, the gifts of healing, working of miracles, prophecy, discerning of spirits, different kinds of tongues, interpretation of tongues. At no point does he imply that any one believer has all these gifts. On the contrary, his logical mind moves in the opposite direction. "Do all speak in tongues?" (1 Cor. 12:30). It is very clear that as the other gifts were distributed in the sovereign providence of God by the Holy Spirit, so it is with the gift of tongues. It is to a select band that this gift is given. It is to a company of men and women, chosen from the foundation of the world through predestinating grace, that this gift is granted by God the Holy Spirit.

5. Paul stresses that all gifts, including tongues, are given for a very definite reason. "Each man is given his gift by the Spirit that he may use it for the common good" (1 Cor. 12:7 *Phillips*). The New English Bible translates this a little differently: "In each of

us the Spirit is manifested in one particular way, for some useful purpose." The gift, in other words, is intended to bless the Church.

6. In the case of tongues, the object of their use is the strengthening of the believer personally. "He that speaketh in an unknown tongue edifieth himself" (1 Cor. 14:4). It may be a personal act of worship in which he alone is involved and by use of this gift he helps to build himself up in his most holy faith.

7. When however, interpretation is added — and Paul insists that in every public gathering where tongues are employed there should be such interpretation — the whole church may well be edified and strengthened. "When you come together, each one has . . . a tongue, or an interpretation. Let all things be done decently and in order" (1 Cor. 14:26, 40 RSV).

8. The apostle evidently regards such speaking in tongues as a form of prayer. "For if I pray in a tongue . . ." (1 Cor. 14: 14 RSV).

9. He is speaking out of personal experience. "I thank my God, I speak with tongues more than you all" (1 Cor. 14:18). This is a very significant saying; though we would be foolish to underestimate the force of the verse that follows: "Yet in the church I had rather speak five words with my understanding . . . than ten thousand words in an unknown tongue." Paul was a very remarkable man. He had at one time in his experience been lifted up from earth and carried away to the third heaven where he heard things that it is not lawful for man to utter. How natural, then, that this gift of glossolalia should be his. But he states quite categorically that it is better to speak five words with his understanding than ten thousand in an unknown language.

10. He recognizes that there is an essential difference between the tongues of Acts 2 and those practiced in the Corinthian church. "One who speaks in a tongue speaks not to men but to God, for no one understands him" (1 Cor. 14:2 RSV). On the day of Pentecost, the very opposite was the case: "How hear we every man in our own tongue, wherein we were born?" (Acts 2:8).

11. Paul goes so far as to say that he wished they all spoke in tongues, though he immediately qualifies this. "I would that you

all spoke with tongues, but rather that you prophesied: for greater is he that prophesieth than he that speaketh with tongues" (1 Cor. 14:5).

12. One final note. Paul expressly says, "Forbid not to speak with tongues," though he qualifies this again with particular emphasis when he says in the same verse, "Covet to prophesy" (1 Cor. 14:39). Prophecy at this time had both the meaning of "fore-telling" the future and of "forth-telling" the Gospel. The ministry of foretelling continued to be very important in the early Church. We have only to think of Agabus, the prophet, who came down from Jerusalem to Antioch and prophesied concerning the great famine that was about to come and did indeed come in the days of Claudius Caesar. That was important. But when Paul spoke of prophecy, he was thinking of his own ministry — the burning words that came hot from his heart when he proclaimed the Gospel of free grace and undying love. Nothing less than this is true prophecy — the telling forth of the greatness of our God, His everlasting mercy, His abundant redemption.

Order or disorder

Paul closes this classic chapter of 1 Corinthians 14 with the words: "Let all things be done decently and in order."

Disorder had crept into the Corinthian church. There were times when a number of people were speaking together in tongues and the result was plain discord. Paul therefore limited the number of people who should share in this ministry to three and they had to speak one after the other, with interpretation given immediately after the message in tongues (1 Cor. 14:27). God is not the author of confusion but of order. The marvelous order of the universe around us, with all the stars in their courses, is a pattern of the kind of order we should see within the worshiping Christian fellowship. Anything that promotes discord should be abandoned at once. Naturally we must ask the question "Is the Pauline commandment being observed today in every gathering where God's people meet and where the ministry of tongues is being exercised?" Regrettably, the answer can only be no.

In the words of Dr. Kurt Koch, theologian, missionary traveler, preacher, and writer,

The rules that Paul enunciates here, being biblical principles at their best, are ignored almost entirely by today's tongues' movement. Often there is praying without interpretation and with a lack of order and control. Many people pray and they frequently pray at the same time and the women invariably take precedence. [1]

In another passage taken from his book *Occult Bondage and Deliverance* he tells of an incident in the work of Peter Octavian, an evangelist being greatly used by God in the revival in Indonesia. (Octavian came to Stuttgart and Dr. Koch worked with him there.)

On account of the 3,000 people present in the evening, the meeting overflowed into two other halls. At the end of his talk Peter Octavian called upon the people to accept the Lord Jesus Christ as their Saviour. He waited quietly for maybe one or two minutes. Suddenly a man on the rostrum began to speak in tongues. I wondered how Peter Octavian would react to this. "In the name of the Lord Jesus," he began, "I command this man to be quiet." He could not have spoken more plainly. Afterwards I asked, "Why did you stop that man?" He replied, "It was clear to me that the enemy was trying to disturb the meeting." [2]

Paul saw that the act of speaking in tongues was a real problem to the Corinthian church. A great deal of confusion had arisen because of it. Much perplexity and disorder abounded. By this means, Satan had gained a mastery he was never intended to hold. Therefore the apostle warns the people tenderly, as a true shepherd of the flock of God, and shows to them the supreme need that Christ be exalted in all things and that nothing should be permitted that might detract from the glory that was His and His alone. It is obvious that in and among the Corinthian Christians something in the nature of a physical epidemic had occurred. This had to be stopped immediately. It was. And it is surely not without importance that while in every case where the gift of tongues is mentioned in the book of Acts, all the people involved spoke in tongues, yet in the church of Corinth, only twenty years later, no longer did everyone speak in tongues. There was a lessening of impact from this gift of tongues. Why?

---

[1] Kurt Koch, *The Strife of Tongues* (Grand Rapids: Kregel, 1966), p. 39.

[2] Kurt Koch, *Occult Bondage and Deliverance* (Grand Rapids: Kregel, 1970), p. 95.

Pentecostalism and Neo-Pentecostalism

Pentecostals have come to be known as the third great force in Christendom. It is so because of the numbers linked with Pentecostal churches — at least 10,000,000 members — and also because they are to be found in almost every part of the world. Pentecostals look back to New Year's Eve, 1900, as one of the key dates of their history. At 7 o'clock that evening, Charles Parham, who for years had been seeking an anointing of the Holy Spirit like in quality and strength to that which he perceived in the New Testament Christians, gently placed his hands on the head of one of the women in the Bible school they had established. Immediately, from her lips came a flow of words which none of them could understand. Parham is one of the great names of modern church history. He took his message to the streets of the southern states. Later he opened another Bible school in Houston, Texas. To that school came W. J. Seymour, an ordained Negro minister. It was Seymour who carried the Pentecostal message to California, to one of the most famous addresses in Pentecostal history: 312 Azuza Street, Los Angeles.

For three years revival days continued. Beginning in 1906, the spreading flame claimed a great multitude for the Kingdom of God; people came from all over the world to learn of what God was doing. Rich and poor alike came to see what was going on. Without fanfare, without Madison Avenue advertising techniques, the movement which was first born in an old livery stable swept onwards — all day, all night, for over a thousand days.

Thus the Pentecostal church was born. Since that day, many branches of this movement have developed and there are a number of Pentecostal denominations. Growth was their hallmark. Between 1926 and 1936 the historic churches lost nearly two million members — eight percent of their total. In the same period, Pentecostals showed this growth:

Pentecostal Assemblies:	up 264%
Assemblies of God:	up 209%
Church of God:	up 92% [3]

---

[3] John L. Sherrill, *They Speak With Other Tongues* (New York: McGraw-Hill, 1964), p. 50.

Was it possible that some of the eight percent of the loss from the historic churches was to be found among the extraordinary increases of the Pentecostal Christians? Some bitter feelings were displayed. The old-line churches regarded the movement of Pentecostalism as a passing fad which would have its day and then cease. On the Pentecostals' part, there was a dismissal of the older churches as being totally out of touch with the real power of Christianity. Thus, for well-nigh fifty years the situation continued and the developments mentioned above seemed only to accelerate. Behind inviolate walls of defense each lived and moved and had its being in complete isolation from the other.

But then came change.

Neo-Pentecostalism

Only a hint has entered into the account of the previous section of the place that Neo-Pentecostalism was to take. The time has come to take up this enthralling part of the story.

This segment of history is well told by John Sherrill in chapter 6 of his book *They Speak With Other Tongues.*[4] Here I merely summarize the essential detail. David du Plessis was from South Africa and deeply involved in the spread of Pentecostalism worldwide. He grew up at a time when there was much hostility against Pentecostals and when he determined to go into the Pentecostal ministry, he knew that sin, the devil, and liberal churchmen would be his most virulent foes.

For twenty years after ordination he stayed in Africa, working in the latter part of that period as executive secretary of the Pentecostal Fellowship of South Africa. Soon however, larger fields called him and by 1949 he was secretary-general of the World Conference of Pentecostal Fellowships. Then came tragedy. He was injured in an auto accident. This couldn't have happened at a worse time, as he was making preparations for the Second World Conference of Pentecostals to be held in Paris in the summer of 1949. Gradually he was healed, and in his own words, "The only real effect of the accident was to slow down my bull-headed, steamroller approach to the Paris Conference. All of a sudden I had to let some of the arrangements out of my hands. I had to ask

---

[4] Ibid., chapter 6.

God to enable me to ask for help both from Himself and from other people."[5]

Then came the strangest of "commands." After the conference in Paris, which went well, he found himself thinking more and more about a group of men whom he had dismissed from his mind as being totally outside his orbit. For him, it was not difficult to give a name to these men: it would be the World Council of Churches. God was leading him to seek out a meeting with them.

"All right Lord, if You say so, I'll go." He met with many of them and told them very directly of all that God had done in his life through the ministry of the Holy Spirit. The men listened and paid attention.

That was the beginning. Subsequently he found himself being propelled through many doors, meeting continually with the men he had spent a lifetime avoiding. One theological professor would call him and introduce him to another. He was given powers of expression which he knew were not native to him. He spoke as the Spirit urged him to speak. He met with leaders of all the mainline denominations. At last, breakthrough happened. It occurred in a large Episcopal church in Van Nuys, California.

Father Dennis Bennett was a successful man. He had taken over the struggling church in Van Nuys in 1953 and by the time he met with David du Plessis, the church had a membership of 2,300. In a very natural way he was led into an experience of speaking in tongues.

So the term "Neo-Pentecostalism" was created. For he was only the first of many from old-line churches who entered into the same experience as the Pentecostal church had been proclaiming since the year 1900. Every denominational barrier seemed to be broken by the onrushing tide of glossolalia and other associated gifts of the Spirit, such as interpretation and the gift of healing. Bible scholars, ministers, theologians, and concerned laymen began to scrutinize eagerly those biblical passages that dealt with the gifts of the Holy Spirit. The charismatic movement took hold of many segments of church life, penetrating large areas of the historic communions. High Anglicans found a common meeting ground with members of the Assemblies of God. The fall-out from this

---

[5] Ibid., p. 55.

extraordinary wave of spiritual activity descended on Methodists, Lutherans, Presbyterians, and Congregationalists, as well as on many smaller denominations. The Roman Catholic Church found itself in a unique position, for it too felt this potent movement among its own ranks and there have been many who have begun to find a truly Christian fellowship with Christians of other denominations by reason of this gift of speaking in tongues.

Questions that must be faced

One outcome has been a flood of questions. Devout Christians who are wanting to be the best for God ask, "Is there something here that I am missing?" "Is there something in me that is blocking the Holy Spirit?" "Is it possible for me to receive a new endowment of power by my obtaining this gift through the laying on of the hands of one who is empowered in this way?" "Is it likely that God would permit this movement to develop as it has at this point in the history of the Church if He had not some sovereign purpose of grace and love to fulfill?" "Should I begin to ask for this gift? Or would that seem presumptuous in the light of those passages that say that the Holy Spirit gives gifts in accordance with His sovereign will?"

There is no doubt that many sincere Christians have been greatly agitated about this whole issue. But again we must plead for a disciplined reading of the holy Scriptures. Whatever we do must be biblical. The Holy Spirit will never command anything that is contrary to the plain teaching of the Bible. Very well, then, is there really any doubt about what the Bible teaches? We must study the question most carefully.

The Bible says, "Forbid not to speak with tongues" (1 Cor. 14: 39). The gift of tongues, therefore, is one that cannot be denied. There is no real evidence that this gift has been wholly withdrawn from the Church. The Bible, however, also says, "Covet to prophesy" (1 Cor. 14:39); and it instructs us, in 1 Corinthians 12:31, to "covet earnestly the best gifts." Immediately after saying this, Paul moves into his great hymn of love, and then (in the fourteenth chapter) he says, "Follow then the way of love, while you set your heart on the gifts of the Spirit" (1 Cor. 14:1 *Phillips*). At once he goes on to say, "The highest gift you can wish for is to be able to speak the messages of God." This word which we translate "to speak the messages of God" is the simple word "to prophesy,"which at this time, as we have seen, held two meanings — of foretelling the future and also of forth-telling the good news of the Gospel. To be able to fulfill this ministry is the "best gift." It is this "best gift" we are commanded to follow. There is no doubt at all that where the apostle speaks to the Corinthians of the gifts of the Spirit, he is setting in perspective this lesser gift of glossolalia. He reminds them that he speaks in tongues more than any one of them. But he would rather speak five words with his understanding than ten thousand words in an unknown tongue.

The only sure sign?

The Pentecostals say that speaking in tongues is the only sure sign that we are filled with the Holy Spirit. And what heartache this has caused to many a sincere disciple! Countless people have been led to believe that they do not know the blessed infilling of the Holy Spirit if they do not speak in tongues. But where is the scriptural authority for this? Surely everything that we have noted thus far from Paul's writings tends toward the conviction that tongues are in no way to be regarded as the only evidence of the infilling of the Spirit. There is really only one great evidence for the fullness of the Spirit — that is Christlikeness. "He shall glorify me." The Spirit makes us like our Lord "whom having not seen [we] love" (1 Peter 1:8). It is His unique and specialized ministry to make glorious the Son of God and to reveal Him through the lives of true believers.

To say that all Christians who are filled with the Spirit speak in tongues is utterly contrary to the Word of God. I know that Pentecostals, in order to get around the difficulty of Paul's words "Do all speak in tongues?" have developed a theory that all Christians when they first believe do speak in tongues, but this gift may not be maintained in them. This to me is wresting the Scripture from its context and giving it a meaning it was never intended to have. The plain fact is that the fullness of the Spirit is demonstrated when the "fruit of the Spirit" is clearly seen — "love, joy, peace, longsuffering, gentleness, goodness, meekness, faith, self-control." As we have seen already, all these are marks of the walk, the conversation and the character of Jesus Christ, our Lord.

There is another point that should be stressed. Pentecostals are accustomed when quoting from Romans 8:26 to say that the phrase "with groanings which cannot be uttered" refers to the inward agony of the soul of the believer. But surely everything in this verse is glorifying the Holy Spirit and rejoicing in the mighty words that He is wont to fulfill. Surely, therefore, it is He who makes intercession "with groanings that are inexpressible." Anything other than this would seem to be taking the Scriptures and interpreting them to fit in with some preconceived ideas of our own.

Shortcuts to spiritual power

By nature we are always looking for shortcuts in our spiritual lives. We are prone to do anything other than take up our cross and follow after our Lord (Matt. 16:24). Donald W. Burdick reminds us that

> spiritual accomplishment is not easily come by. It is the result of agonizing growth, of defeat after defeat followed by victory, of wrestling in prayer and searching the Word of God. Christian character is forged by blow after blow on the anvil of daily experience. It never comes quickly, but, like maturity of any kind, it is the product of the slow process of growth. How shallow, then, is the view of many glossolaliacs who assume that spiritual maturity has suddenly arrived in one short hour of ecstatic experience. This is not exaggerating. For such has been the testimony of some, and such is the apparent testimony of others who are not quite as frank. Francis Geddes, director of the Religious Research Foundation, says, "Those who speak in tongues say you get spiritual maturity for nothing." Herein lies its deceptiveness — the promise of easy accomplishment when in reality such is impossible. Tongues are no substitute for holiness of life; ecstasy cannot take the place of uprightness and Christian integrity. [6]

Ours is of course an impatient age. We want instant coffee, instant rice, crash programs, and express highways. But God is not in a hurry. His word is "He that believeth shall not make haste" (Isa. 28:16) and adds, "Be still, and know that I am God" (Ps. 46:10).

No, spiritual maturity is not to be obtained by any instant prescription. This is one of the greatest lessons that the child of God has to learn. He receives the Spirit of adoption and knows God

---

[6] Donald W. Burdick, *Tongues: To Speak or Not to Speak* (Chicago: Moody Press, 1969), p. 86.

as Father; but from that early infant stage he must go on to perfection. One of the facts that the charismatic movement has to face
is its encouragement of this short-cut type of Christian experience.
It is still true that

> There is no expeditious road
> To pack and label men for God
> And save them by the barrow load. [7]

We need to dwell on such wise counsel as this:

> The way to deeper knowledge of God is through the lonely valleys
> of soul poverty and abnegation of things. The blessed ones are
> they who have repudiated every external thing and have rooted
> from their hearts all sense of possessing. These are the "poor in
> spirit." They have reached an inward stage paralleling the outward
> circumstances of the common beggar in the streets of Jerusalem;
> that is what the word "poor" as Christ actually used it means. Free
> from all sense of possessing, they yet possess all things. "Theirs is
> the Kingdom of God." [8]

There is no shortcut to spiritual joy, power, and effectiveness in
the service of our great God and Savior. There is no once-for-all
experience that will, at a single stroke, solve all the problems of the
Christian community or of the individual Christian. Our Lord in-
tends that we should be entirely dependent upon Him. That is why
we walk by faith and not by sight. That is why we learn to trust
in Him moment by moment. Anything different from this is not the
life of faith that the New Testament commands. We are told to
take up our cross daily (Luke 9:23). We are urged to reckon ourselves indeed "dead unto sin, but alive unto God" (Rom. 6:11).
When our Lord was tempted by Satan in the wilderness, there was
no attempt made to have our Lord change His goals, but only that
He should use quicker methods of achieving them. Each of these
temptations, however, our Lord repulsed. We must follow Him in
word and deed.

That there is an endowment of spiritual power that we may know
through a deepening experience and knowledge of the Word of
God and through an ever-expanding life of prayer is beyond question. We should all seek such an endowment in accordance with

---

[7] From "A Judgment in Heaven, Epilogue," by Francis Thompson.

[8] A. W. Tozer, *The Pursuit of God* (Harrisburg, Pennsylvania: Christian Publications, 1948), p. 23.

the teachings of the apostles and prophets as well as by following the example of our Lord. But to expect some unique gift accompanied by speaking in tongues as we have been describing them is to tempt the Lord. He has taught us clearly the way of the cross and of death to self. The Holy Spirit can undertake to fill the vacuum created when we are emptied of self, when we die to all self-praise, self-glory, self-assertion, self-pity, and self-affection. By following the path that our Lord Himself took — the Calvary road — we shall be fitted for His service and filled with the power that is altogether divine. This is the fullness of the Holy Spirit which we should desire and into which we should increasingly grow. He will never deny this to any of His servants.

Illustrations of dangers

Some years ago, while ministering in New Jersey, I met with Raymond W. Frame, a member of the Overseas Missionary Fellowship. In the course of one of his talks he related a very significant experience. Accepting 1 John 4:1-3 as a guide in all matters affecting the lordship of Christ and the reality of the Spirit filling and inspiring a man to particular utterances, he felt led to carry out a test in the case of a Chinese brother who was well known among the Shanghai churches for his fluency, dignity, and graciousness in the exercise of his gift of tongues. On two separate occasions the tongues messages had been tape-recorded together with the interpretation given by another Christian; there were certain inconsistencies in the recordings, and finally Mr. Frame decided to carry out a public test of this man.

While the Chinese brother with the gift of tongues was actually speaking under supernatural power, a clearly articulated message of some kind, the question was put to the spirit who was in control of him at that time: "Thou, spirit, art speaking in an unknown tongue, dost thou confess that Jesus Christ is come in the flesh?"

The reaction was first of all, total disregard of the question. Later, as the question was frequently repeated, a note of irritation came into the voice. Then an angry outburst in a kind of Chinese which was understandable: "Why do you not believe? Do you not know that I have come to do a great work! Ha-ha-ha-ha-ha!" Not once did the spirit that was in the man clearly confess that Christ had come in the flesh.

As a result of this, he was branded as a false prophet and put out of the church and discredited among the other churches of Shanghai.

Mr. Frame gladly gave me the privilege of repeating this illustration and citing him as the authority on which the report was made. It is highly significant; for if it is possible for such types of speaking in tongues to enter the sanctuary of God and purportedly bring messages in the name of Christ, then the danger signals are clear. Every spirit must be tested. "Try the spirits whether they are of God" (1 John 4:1).

I should add another illustration from the same man and with the same privilege of reporting. When Mr. Frame was still a young and inexperienced missionary in China, he nearly fell into the error of believing that all gifts of tongues were clear evidences of the presence and power of the Holy Spirit. He told me how an unusually charming and gifted Chinese preacher came to their area in the province of Honan. He brought with him a small team of like-minded missionaries from Shantung province. The main thrust of their ministry was to underline the importance of the charismata in all Christian life and service. They related the before-and-after of many Christian workers, including their own. "The effect upon the Chinese present was that we became convinced that we were all in that lamentable 'before' condition — irritable, touchy, prayerless, fruitless, joyless, ineffective — and that we were all cold in our love to God and to the souls of men. We longed to attain the 'after' state in which each member of the team seemed to be rejoicing. But how? What was the secret?"

"Pray. Let your mind go blank and let human wisdom cease to control you. Allow the Holy Spirit to make you as plastic clay, and thereby fashion you as a usable vessel in His hands. Pray until the Holy Spirit can declare Himself sovereign of your whole being by taking control of that most unruly member, the tongue, and by making it speak forth the praises of God in an unknown language." That was the counsel.

The meeting was opened for free and vocal prayer — each person voicing his petition aloud. Many voices were heard at once. The sound of praying, crying, and shouting increased mightily. As this developed, Mr. Frame thought, *I have had warnings against this kind of display.* Then he began to have warning lights flashing in his mind telling him to be careful and to keep his feet firm on the Word of God.

One of his missionary associates, however, standing beside him suddenly became very agitated and began shouting in excellent Chinese, leaping and waving his arms, obviously under the control of a power quite beyond himself. As this happened, Mr. Frame began to feel he did not wish to miss any special blessing that might be there; gradually he allowed his mind to go blank, began to yield himself to the external power outside of himself that seemed to be pleading for full control over him. As he did so, a sense of paralysis began to numb his feet. It soon affected his legs. Then it clearly was spreading up into his arms. And at that moment he realized that what was coming upon him was coming from the wrong direction. From beneath! Surely the wrong direction. Without hesitating one moment longer, he cried aloud, "May the blood of Christ protect me from this." The paralysis vanished at once. He was normal again.

One month later he met his co-worker who had been so strangely moved during that meeting. This, in brief, was his comment: "You know, Ray, that thing that happened to me that night at S.K.T. was not of God. It was of the devil."

In the light of experiences such as these, I feel that the statement prepared by the Latin America Mission, giving some guidelines for facing the charismatic movement in Colombia, is extremely wise and should be widely spread abroad. It says among many other things:

> We do not believe that every outward manifestation of a so-called gift is necessarily from the Spirit of God. On the contrary, the Bible teaches that the opposite is true. "And many will say to Me in that day, Lord, Lord, have we not prophesied in thy name? and in thy name have cast out devils? and in thy name done many wonderful works? And then will I profess unto them, I never knew you; depart from me, you that work iniquity" (Matt. 7:22, 23). "For there shall arise false Christs, and false prophets, and shall show great signs and wonders; insomuch that, if it were possible, they shall deceive the very elect" (Matt. 24:24). Thus the devil may counterfeit the gifts of the Spirit, and this requires constant vigilance on our part, warning and instructing our brethren against such errors. [9]

---

[9] San José, Costa Rica: Latin American Mission, 1967.

This clearly stresses an all-important fact. No single gift is the indispensable sign of the fullness of the Holy Spirit. Everyone has some gift of the Spirit. No one has all the gifts of the Spirit. And there is no one gift that may be singled out to mark the owner of this gift as the one who is going to be of greatest service in the vineyard of the Lord. Nowhere does the Bible show that all believers must experience glossolalia. The teaching that tongues must accompany the true fullness of the Holy Spirit is unbiblical, unedifying, unnatural. "Yea," as the apostle says, "let God be true and every man a liar" (Rom. 3:4). Let us refuse to wrest Scripture from its context. Let our appeal be ever and only "to the law and to the testimony" (Isa. 8:20).

Safety is found there alone.

The possibility of deception

The New Testament carries many warnings about the possibility of being misled. Paul saw that very clearly. He reminds his Corinthian friends that they must constantly be on guard against Satanic wiles. "You know," he reminds them, "in the days when you were still pagan, you were swept off your feet and carried away to those dumb heathen gods, being led hither and thither without any true direction" (1 Cor. 12:2, translation mine). He returns to the theme when he writes his second letter. Bluntly he declares that many whom they had known and had regarded as true servants of God, were in reality false and lying people. They were "false apostles, deceitful workmen, disguising themselves as apostles of Christ" (2 Cor. 11:13 RSV). He goes even further, for he wants to explain that such men were not God's messengers. God's messengers? They were counterfeits of the real thing, dishonest practitioners, masqueraders in deceit. John is no less strong. "Don't trust every spirit, dear friends of mine, but test them to discover whether they come from God or not. For the world is full of false prophets. You can test them in this simple way: every spirit that acknowledges the fact that Jesus Christ actually became man, comes from God, but the spirit which denies this fact does not come from God" (1 John 4:1-3 *Phillips*).

It is clearly of importance, then, that we test all spirits whether they be of God. The twentieth century is no stranger to falsehood, the big lie, the facile attempt to beguile the unwary. The stresses of our culture and countercultures have summoned from the vast deep the spirits of darkness that are working their evil spell in areas where they should never have been given admittance. The Church is under attack. War on the saints is an awesome reality. The occult, witchcraft, sorcery, white and black magic, palmistry, and ouija boards have found an entrance into the very citadels of our churches. It is very easy for us to be deceived. "Let him that thinketh he standeth, take heed lest he fall" (1 Cor. 10:12).

Our hope is to allow the Holy Spirit to guide our steps daily. He has covenanted to do so. Our Lord said of Him, "He will guide you into all truth" (John 16:13). This he delights to do.

How does He guide us? By bringing us back again and again to the Word of God written. The Holy Spirit is always associated in the Scriptures with the enlightening of the mind and the illumining of the understanding. And it is the Scriptures He uses, for He is Himself the author of them all. "Wherewithal shall a young man cleanse his way? by taking heed thereto according to thy word" (Ps. 119:9). It is right therefore to stress that the Holy Spirit, through whom our Savior offered Himself without spot unto God, will also keep us and enable us to offer up daily sacrifices of praise and joyful service. "All scripture is given by inspiration of God, and is profitable" (2 Tim. 3:16). What follows from that statement? "That the man of God may be perfect, thoroughly furnished unto all good works" (2 Tim. 3:17).

Against the possibility of lying deceit and demon deception, we must bring ourselves totally under the guidance and sovereignty of the Scriptures of truth and permit the Holy Spirit to make clear what He knows we need to learn. As we do so, He will unmistakably be for us a "refuge and strength, a very present help in trouble" (Ps. 46:1).

As we test the spirits under the direction of the Holy Spirit and in the light of the Scriptures, we shall soon see that some very important things must be noted in any discussion of glossolalia. Let me illustrate.

I want to discuss four principal matters: (1) the fact of glossolalia in other religions or cults, (2) the good effects that should be marked as derivatives of glossolalia, (3) some possible explanations of the phenomenon, (4) a reexamination of the use of tongues as a possible substitute for the truly divine and supernatural.

Glossolalia in other cults

In many parts of the world glossolalia is a well-known fact of life. Buddhist and Shintoist priests speak in alien tongues while in a trance. Speaking in tongues exists as much in South America as it does in India or Australia. Racial and cultural barriers are unknown where the tongues movement holds sway. It breaks through any intellectual strata that we may have erected in society. This by itself would be commendable; however, the fact that it is not limited to Christian fellowships should constitute a warning signal to any Christian eager to express himself in glossolalia. But it seldom does. Even though the most irrefutable evidence of tongues-speaking at the heart of pagan and devilish rites be produced, too many Christians refuse to heed the warning this evidence clearly bespeaks. Yet the need to "try the spirits" is, as we have seen, in no place more essential than in this realm of speaking in tongues.

Considerable research has been done in various cultures. In "A Survey of Glossolalia and Related Phenomena in Non-Christian Religions" L. Carlyle May presents extensive data concerning tongues, particularly as these are employed by medicine men or priests of pagan rites. This article appeared in 1956 in the *American Anthropologist*. Speaking in tongues, May points out, happens often during rituals associated with healings. In Micronesia in the Mortlock Islands the spirits are said to open wide the mouth of the priest and to speak through him in a language of their own. May cites another case from *The Life of a South African Tribe* by Henri A. Junod.[10] It comes from the Thonga people of Africa and describes how when a demon is being exorcized, the person sings a curative song which he himself composes, usually in the Zulu tongue. The conclusion reached by May is most interesting:

> This survey has shown that speaking in tongues is widespread and very ancient. Indeed it is probable that as long as man has had divination, curing, sorcery, and propitiation of spirits he has had glossolalia.[11]

Whatever else we may say about glossolalia, we cannot escape

[10] New York: Universal, 1962.
[11] L. Carlyle May as quoted by Burdick, *Tongues*, p. 67.

the fact that it is not a phenomenon unique to Christianity. There may be a hundred explanations of the facts. It may be necessary to consider things like ecstatic utterances, self-hypnosis, play-acting, and demon-possession. What is certain is that among multitudes of people who have known nothing of Christianity, glossolalic experiences have been known, observed, recorded, and discussed. There is no such thing as "glossolalia for Christians only."

This is neither the time nor the place to follow the trail leading to an explanation of this existential fact. It is in my opinion impossible to listen to a Christian speaking in tongues and conclude that this is the result of self-delusion or of any fake origin. The tongues flow too naturally; they are frequently most beautiful; and in many cases they are spoken by people of proved integrity. I would completely disavow any suggestion that tongues spoken by a Christian are the result of connivance or contrivance. When we set such Christian glossolalia with the others we have been considering, it would be far more reasonable to assume that speaking in tongues originates within the area of the psychological, i.e., within the personality of the one who uses tongues as a medium of expression of something deeply rooted within himself. We shall return to this. It is enough to make mention of this as the area in which fundamental research must continue.

Ecstasy may play a part in producing this particular happening. Indeed, this is one of the oldest and commonest ways of accounting for glossolalia. In all forms of ecstasy there is an experience of elevated emotionalism with a consequent loss of awareness of the external world. This may account for some of the factors that distinguish glossolalia; but it certainly does not explain all, especially the experiences of many of the Neo-Pentecostals whose testimony is that when speaking in tongues they feel no undue or excessive wave of emotional pressure. There may be emotion. It would be strange if there were not something of that. But to represent their experience as anything approaching emotional exaltation would be wrong.

Positive values in Christian glossolalia

We must not forget that we are speaking of the "gifts of the Holy Spirit." Numbered among them is this gift of speaking in tongues. We have already stressed that at no point does the New Testament suggest that this gift was taken away totally from the Church. It is therefore still with us. It is still the possession of what I like to call "a certain elect band."

It has been good to know many of these Christians. In my own ministry I have encountered a goodly number of saintly men and women to whom this gift of speaking in tongues has clearly been given. I have discussed this with them, of course. I asked them if there were any special reason why the gift came and sought from them some assessment on their own part of what the gift had meant to them. I wish to be absolutely objective here. I know a number of Christians for whom this gift of tongues has proved a disaster; but from much of what has been said already there are good reasons why this should and could be so. Nevertheless, there are also the others — men and women through whom the Holy Spirit has spoken in language that is not human and they have found this a source of deep joy and great cause for praise. Let me try to summarize some of the things I have seen in the lives of those who in my judgment have truly received this special gift of the Holy Spirit and who speak in tongues "as the Spirit [gives] them utterance."

I have found *a renewed devotion* to Jesus Christ. Perhaps this is the most vital and important result of their experience. The gift has not come to them merely to exalt their ego. On the contrary. It has awakened in them a new desire to serve Jesus Christ and to know Him only as Lord of all they have. It has been exciting to see some who were merely church-goers, with little enthusiasm for the deep things of God, transformed completely through the action of His almighty Spirit. Tongues have accompanied this experience in a number of cases. With new, cleansed, and sanctified tongues they praise the Lord, their Redeemer and Savior. I have, of course, seen the same experience come to others who have not received the gift of speaking in tongues. This for me is perfectly right and good. It is always wonderful to see any backslider restored or anyone following afar off brought nigh to Jesus. Whether the experience is accompanied by tongues or not, I cannot care. The all-important thing is to see Christians growing in grace and in the knowledge of their Lord and Savior Jesus Christ.

Another feature I have seen in a number of Christians to whom the gift of tongues has been given is *a new steadfastness in the faith and a fuller realization of the joy of walking with God.* In so many cases our worship in church has become sterile and barren. We err and lie to ourselves if we do not confess this freely. But with the gift of tongues there has invariably come a surging thrill of joy and wonder at the marvelous grace of a loving God. With this gift of tongues also there ought to be a fresh sense of stability in the work and worship of God. Even as I write, I think of a young man who for many years has made a profession of faith in Jesus Christ as Savior and Lord. He became the husband of a girl with similar precious faith. But there was little evidence of growth; there was an inconsistency about him that made it impossible for us to trust him with major responsibility. But then the Holy Spirit revealed Christ to him again. With that experience came the gift of tongues; and with the gift, there came a new reality, integrity, certainty, and vitality of personal faith. The result? We are throwing more and more work at him week by week and it is all being done with great gladness of heart.

An expanded prayer life has marked others who have received this gift. A very wonderful young couple come to my mind as I think of this. I have found that they pray prayers that God answers and I have often coveted their special prayers for some special projects. On the night on which she was converted this young woman prayed with her whole soul to the God who had saved her. Suddenly she found herself praying in a language she did not understand, but it was all so beautiful and marvelous. For her, since that day, the ministry of speaking in tongues has been a sacred and private medium of communication between herself and God. She never speaks about this experience except when asked to do so and even then with great diffidence. But the radiance of her life, the constancy of her walk, the beauty of her faith have helped her win many to the Lord. Her husband? He is different. As different as one person could possibly be from another. But together they have been led into a life of ministry for the salvation of souls and the bringing of wanderers back to their Father and home. Prayer is truly their native air. It has been a joy to know them and to see God work through them.

"God moves in a mysterious way His wonders to perform." I always think of that line when thinking of the following case. It was 1953. An Anglican evangelist was conducting meetings in a Canadian city where another very self-assured Anglican clergyman pastored a small congregation. Thinking it right to encourage his people to attend services which his Bishop had commended, he went himself and took a number of his people with him. Something exceptional happened that night. This self-assured Canadian rector was born again. The following night he knelt by his bedside and found himself speaking in tongues. The evangelist does not speak in tongues and had never mentioned such a possibility. But the ever-sovereign Spirit gave His gift. To this day the clergyman has kept the secret except from a very few with whom he has intimate fellowship. Now there is *new power* in his preaching, *a new authority, a new life.*

All these are positive factors. I have seen them myself and rejoiced in them. For the Christian friends God has given me in whom I have seen so much of Christ and whose lives have been given an inner radiance because of the Spirit's gift of tongues I daily thank God. Some of the finest work being done in the Christian groups I know is being done by men and women who have shared in this heavenly gift of glossolalia.

At the same time, I would add that wherever I have learned of this I have noticed that there has been no desire to make any ostentatious show about the gift. In some cases, as I have said, it has never been mentioned except to a privileged few. Many have been hesitant to show that this gift has come to them. They want the glory to belong to God alone. They are content if He and He alone knows about it.

Of course, there are those who feel called by the Spirit to speak in tongues in public. Once again we have Paul to counsel us. "Forbid not to speak with tongues (1 Cor. 14:39). You must not forbid this kind of ecstatic utterance. If it is of God, there will be someone there who will truly interpret what is being said. And even though we may wonder why God permits this roundabout way of sending us His message, we shall be grateful that He has visited us and blessed us with the voice of His love.

A word of caution. Anyone to whom the Holy Spirit has given the gift of discernment will know when the tongues being employed are not from heaven. We have noted some examples and will be commenting on more. But for the moment, as we mark and underline those positive values of glossolalia, let us not be deluded in any way. Not everyone speaking in some strange tongue is of necessity speaking the mind and will of God. The spirits must be tried. It is our Christian responsibility to try them; and we have seen how this can and should be done. Sometimes the length of the interpretation will greatly overreach the length of the speech in a tongue. This should in itself be a warning. But wherever God does visit His Church in this way, let every heart rejoice and sing.

The Word of God and the power of God

Having said this, we must again examine the Scriptures and note their teaching concerning the "gift" and the "gifts" of the Holy Spirit. It has been said that sometimes "in a sect the life is often better than the teaching, while in the Church, the teaching is usually better than the life." I say this only to emphasize how vital it is that we know exactly what the Bible says about the coming of the Holy Spirit and His divine ministry in the Church. It is very possible that some may have entered into a real experience of the Holy Spirit's power while still retaining a distorted or incomplete understanding of the Word of God as it declares the sovereignty of the work of God the Holy Spirit. We cannot study with too great zeal or earnestness what He, the Spirit of truth, has written into the text of the holy Scriptures. Those passages that speak of Him — and they are many — must be our particular concern as we survey these tremendous themes.

When the Holy Spirit fell upon the disciples in the upper room on the day of Pentecost, there were a number of unique events — speaking in tongues, healings, miracles, prophesyings — and these continued strongly through the apostolic age. Why were these signs necessary? Principally to authenticate the apostles as the servants of God and the true messengers of His Gospel. The same is true of the signs that followed the ministry of our Lord — "These are written, that you might believe that Jesus is the Christ, the Son of God, and that believing you might have life through his name" (John 20:31). John has been writing about the "signs" he has narrated and about the multitude of other signs, so numerous that, if recorded, "the world itself could not contain the books that should be written" (John 21:25). The signs proved the deity of Jesus and demonstrated that He was indeed the Messiah. Similarly, the signs on Pentecost manifested that the Kingdom of God had now come in all its fullness and that the new covenant which God had promised His people was fulfilled. The signs surrounded the disciples and made them marked men before the eyes of all the world. They were heralds of the Kingdom of God. The Comforter promised by Jesus had come. The utter fulfillment of the plan of God is manifest before the wondering eyes of the tense and listening multitude.

Peter said so on that sun-filled day of Pentecost. "This Jesus . . . being therefore exalted at the right hand of God, and having received from the Father the promise of the Holy Spirit, he has poured out this which you see and hear" (Acts 2:32, 33 RSV). He went on: "Let all the house of Israel know assuredly, that God hath made that same Jesus, whom you have crucified, both Lord and Christ" (Acts 2:36).

And all the crowds on the streets of Jerusalem heard this in their own language. It is as though the confusion of tongues which God sent among the nations of the world at Babel was overturned and all men heard this divine communication spoken by the disciples of Jesus. No wonder they marveled! "How hear we every man in our own tongue, wherein we were born?" (Acts 2:8). But Peter countered their thoughts and speech. "Ye men of Judaea, and all you that dwell at Jerusalem, be this known to you and hearken to my words: For these are not drunken, as you suppose, seeing it is but the third hour of the day." Then followed the most dramatic and climactic word that Peter was to utter: "This is that which was spoken by the prophet Joel; and it shall come to pass in the last days, saith God, I will pour out my Spirit upon all flesh: and your sons and your daughters shall prophesy, and your young men shall see visions, and your old men shall dream dreams; and on my servants and on my handmaidens I will pour out in those days of my Spirit; and they shall prophesy" (Acts 2:14-18).

One can sense the tremendous hush that began to fall on the crowd. Here was no man trained in the schools. He was a humble man; but as they listened, his hearers knew that there was a power in his words that was more than mortal. "They were pricked in their heart." That was the result of his words; and then "they said to Peter and to the rest of the apostles, Men and brethren, What shall we do?" (Acts 2:37). The reply? Surely the words for which all creation has been waiting since the day that through Adam's sin it was delivered over to suffering and evil! "Then Peter said unto them, Repent, and be baptized every one of you in the name of Jesus Christ for the remission of sins, and *you shall receive the gift of the Holy Spirit"* (Acts 2:38). Could anything be plainer? All who hear and turn from their sins to God in penitence and faith will be forgiven freely through the everlasting mercy and will receive the gift of the Holy Spirit. God, the almighty Spirit, will indwell them according to His promise.

All God's promises fulfilled

This gift of the Holy Spirit to men through the Gospel is the fulfillment of an age-old promise to Abraham that in him and in his seed all the nations of the earth would be blessed. (See Genesis 12:3; 22:18.) Paul stresses this when he says, "Christ redeemed us from the curse of the law . . . that in Christ Jesus the blessing of Abraham might come upon the Gentiles, that we might receive the promise of the Spirit through faith" (Gal. 3:13, 14 RSV).

God is true to His promise. Before He could fulfill all His promises concerning the coming of the Holy Spirit, God had first to send His Son to be the Savior of the world. Christ had to suffer. Atonement had to be made for sin. All this was fulfilled at Calvary. The empty tomb is God's signature that the work of Christ is perfect and finished. When He came to His disciples in the upper room, He said to them, "Behold I send the promise of the Father upon you: but tarry ye in the city of Jerusalem, until you are endued with power from on high" (Luke 24:49). He breathed on them and said: "Receive the Holy Spirit" (John 20:22 RSV). This is part of His preparing the disciples for their baptism in the Holy Spirit. The gift was not immediately given; that had to await the day appointed from all eternity on the calendar of God — the day of Pentecost.

But time sped on. The hour was near when, Christ having been glorified, the Holy Spirit might be given. That was the moment when the work of the Trinity for man's redemption was to be completed. Let Paul summarize the matter:

> But when the time had fully come, God sent forth his Son, born of woman, born under the law, to redeem those who were under the law, so that we might receive adoption as sons. And because you are sons, God has sent the Spirit of his Son into our hearts, crying, "Abba! Father!" (Gal. 4:4-6 RSV).

From this it is clear that the entrance of the Holy Spirit into our hearts is the consummation, climax, and completion of the activity of God the Father, the Son, and the Spirit on our behalf.

This brings us to the nub of the whole matter. What we are now about to say is something that every new Christian should be taught as carefully as he is taught the fundamental truths of Christ's death for sin and His rising for our justification. To err here is to err terribly in a multitude of ways concerning the life of the Holy Spirit with us who believe.

When we believe in Jesus and become Christians, a host of things happen. Though they are all aspects of one great experience, yet they can be separated in our thinking and they are definitely separated in the New Testament teaching. Among the many things that happen are the receiving of the forgiveness of God, cleansing from all unrighteousness, justification before God — made to be as though we had never sinned — adoption, reconciliation to God, regeneration or rebirth, access to God. Is that all? No! The greatest fact has not yet been stated. The greatest fact of all, the fact that makes all those other things possible, is the entrance of the Holy Spirit into the personality and body of the believer. That is what Peter said. "Repent, and be baptized. . . , and you shall receive the gift of the Holy Spirit" (Acts 2:38 RSV). So when I believe in Jesus, He baptizes me in His Spirit and thereby I am incorporated into the Body of Christ. As I have noted before, Paul stresses this in writing to Corinth: "For by one Spirit are we all baptized into one body, whether we be Jews or Gentiles, whether we be bond or free; and have been all made to drink into one Spirit" (1 Cor. 12:13). The Holy Spirit takes up His residence within me. He who is the essence of life makes me to experience the life of God within my soul. This is the only baptism of the Spirit that the Scriptures speak about. God's promise to Abraham is fulfilled. The Holy Spirit enters and I am now a member of the Body of Christ.

The life of God within the soul of man

This subheading was a favorite phrase of John Wesley. It is a fact to which the Scriptures continually recur. Think of some of the Scripture passages for a moment.

In Romans 5 Paul paints in glorious colors the extraordinary consequences of our being "justified by faith." Not the least of these blessings is the fact that "the love of God is shed abroad in our hearts by the Holy Ghost which is given unto us" (Rom. 5:5). He repeats this in Romans 8:9-11 when he is reciting God's many blessings to His children: a new mind, the gift of life and peace, and daily guidance, together with the hope of resurrection in years to come. And all this is possible because of one supreme reality: the Holy Spirit dwells with us. "If any man have not the Spirit of Christ, he is none of his" (Rom. 8:9). It is impossible to be a Christian without having received the Holy Spirit. That is the Pauline argument; and it is both logical and incontrovertible.

We can add to these emphatic statements. Look at 1 Thessalonians 4:7, 8. "God has not called us for uncleanness but in holiness. Therefore whoever disregards this, disregards not man but God, who gives his Holy Spirit to you" (RSV). The argument of the passage is that God has made possible a holy life for all His children because He has given them His Holy Spirit. "It is not for nothing that the Spirit God gives us is called the *Holy* Spirit" (1 Thess. 4:8 *Phillips*). It is no longer necessary for God's child to "wait for" the Holy Spirit. The Holy Spirit has come to him, and God's call is now to "walk in the Spirit, and you shall not fulfil the lust of the flesh" (Gal. 5:16).

This is our high calling. Indwelt by the Holy Spirit, baptized by Christ with the Holy Spirit and with the holy fire of God, incorporated into Christ through faith, we are nothing less than temples of the Holy Spirit, who is given to us from God (1 Cor. 6:19). Elsewhere Paul speaks of the Holy Spirit as "the seal" of our ingrafting into Christ. "You, too, when you had heard the message of the truth, the good news of your salvation, and had believed it, became incorporate in Christ and received the seal of the promised Holy Spirit" (Eph. 1:13 NEB). The Holy Spirit is Himself God's seal that we are His and His forever, even as our Lord said, "He dwelleth with you, and shall be in you" (John 14:17). And John adds his witness when he says, "By this we know that He abides in us, by the Spirit which he has given us" (1 John 3:24 RSV). He is not content with saying this only once. He repeats himself. "Hereby know we that we dwell in him, and he in us, because he hath given us of his Spirit" (1 John 4:13). What was planned in the eternal counsels of the Trinity is now fulfilled. God dwells in and with His people *by the Holy Spirit*.

An unmistakable message

It is hard to believe that such plain teaching could be so terribly misunderstood. A true Christian has received God's gift of His indwelling Spirit. You are not a Christian in any New Testament sense of the term unless you are indwelt by the Holy Spirit. Yet, there are still those who say that the Holy Spirit cannot be received until some time after you become a Christian. Sacerdotalists, ritualists, and others of like persuasion affirm that some laying on of hands by a bishop is necessary before this gift can be known. Many Pentecostalists teach that you may not know the Holy Spirit until there is a repeated act of faith leading to a conscious "baptism" in the Spirit accompanied by the gift of speaking in tongues. Surely the Scriptures we have quoted deny such teaching on every line.

At every point the New Testament affirms that under the new covenant of grace the Holy Spirit indwells all believers from the moment when first in trembling faith they look to Jesus Christ as Savior and call Him Lord. They may not be fully aware of the miracle that has happened — God dwelling within their hearts by the Holy Spirit. Yet it is the ultimate miracle of our redemption and salvation. It was for this cause that the Son of God took our humanity and died in place of sinners — to make possible the indwelling of our hearts by the Spirit of holiness and love. Indwelling us as He does, He summons us to live as children of God in a dark world. Inhabiting the temple of our lives, He leads us into a life of joy, assurance, and hope. With us forever, He witnesses with our spirits that we are born of God, and therefore heirs of God and joint-heirs with Jesus Christ.

Can any greater wonder be told?

You shall know the truth

How vital, then, that every new Christian be fully instructed in these truths! Yet, is it not true that many preachers of the Gospel stress that through the death and resurrection of Christ Jesus we may know our sins forgiven and be set on the way to heaven, but go no further? Certainly, the gifts we discover at Calvary are very great. But if we are to know the full-orbed salvation of God, it is necessary for the Christian teacher to stress that He who died for sinners and is now at the right hand of God has claimed from the Father the gift of the Holy Spirit and baptized all who believe in Him with the Holy Spirit. We simply do not spend enough time with young Christians explaining to them the full extent of their inheritance. This must be done. We must tell them, over and over again, that by the baptism of the Holy Spirit they have been born from above and thereby have been incorporated into the Body of Christ. To repeat again what we have noted already so often: "By one Spirit are we all baptized into one body" (1 Cor. 12:13) — the "Body" is the Church and the baptizer is the King of glory, Jesus Christ our Lord. All the New Testament declares it is the singular prerogative of Jesus Christ, Son of God, Savior of men, to baptize with the Spirit; John the Baptist could baptize only with water. Christ alone can baptize with the Spirit.

To seek another baptism after Christ has already baptized us by the Holy Spirit into His Body is quite contrary to the Scriptures. To say that there is a set difference between regeneration and a baptism in the Holy Spirit is not in accordance with the revelation of the prophets and apostles. That there are endowments of power that we may know as we go deeper and deeper still into the heart of God is unquestionable. But that is quite different from what is so frequently spoken of as "baptism by the Holy Spirit" accompanied with speaking in tongues. The biblical guidelines must never be effaced. We fail our Lord, we fail the Church, we fail those we teach if we add our own interpretation to the simple glories of holy Scripture.

> For when the Lord, my Saviour,
> Made me to "look and live,"
> He gave to me His Spirit
> To help me to receive
> His life of grace and meekness,
> His life of deathless love,
> His graciousness and goodness,
> His faithfulness to prove.

> He sealed me with His Spirit,
> Empowering, passionate, free,
> He claimed me for His temple
> In holy purity;
> And then He told me simply
> His Spirit would abide,
> Within me and beside me,
> To keep me near His side.

Thus God fulfilled the promise
He made so long ago
To Abraham, His faithful friend —
That all the world should know
How God will dwell within us,
Father, Redeemer, Lord,
Deep in our hearts forever,
And ever more adored.

All glory to the Father,
All glory to the Son,
All glory to the Spirit,
Through endless ages One;
Praise Him whose covenant mercies
Are still so freely giv'n,
Praise Him, you ransomed sinners
With all the hosts of heaven. [12]

The real dangers in glossolalia

The time has come to summarize some of the things we have learned and to make certain deductions from them. Let us note each point most carefully.

1. *Every Christian has some "gift" of the Holy Spirit.* This is made very clear in Romans 12:6: "Having then gifts differing according to the grace that is given to us, whether prophecy, let us prophesy according to the proportion of faith."

There is a lovely play on words in the original Greek here. The word for grace is "charis" and the word for gift is "charisma." In our translation we have "gifts" and "grace." But Paul is stressing his point that it is not possible to receive "charis" (grace) without receiving also a "charisma" (gift). There are various lists of the gifts of the Holy Spirit in the New Testament; but in every case it is emphasized that the Holy Spirit, when He enters the life of a believer, imparts some special "charisma" — in some cases He may impart several of these gifts to one person. But there is no Christian without some special gift of the Spirit. It may be that the "charisma" is a natural talent that God takes over and by His Spirit sanctifies, empowers, and uses. That may or may not be. Any survey of church history will show men and women upon whom the Spirit has bestowed gifts that appear almost contrary to the natural bent of their personality. The point for us to emphasize,

---

[12] Written by the author — ed.

meantime, is that every believer possesses some particular gift of the Holy Spirit.

2. *No Christian has all the gifts.*   That should scarcely require mentioning. Paul however deals with it in writing the Corinthian Christians. "Are all apostles? Are all prophets? Are all teachers? Are all workers of miracles?" (1 Cor. 12:29). The inference is, of course, that there is no one who possesses *all* these gifts of the Holy Spirit. No! Grace is given to us individually out of the rich diversity of Christ's giving. His gifts are varied and diverse. All the gifts, however, are bestowed with one end in view. Paul states what this is in Ephesians 4:12: "His gifts were made that Christians might be properly equipped for their service, that the whole body might be built up until the time comes when, in the unity of common knowledge of the Son of God, we arrive at real maturity — that measure of development which is meant by 'the fullness of Christ'" (*Phillips*).

This is very clear. No Christian has all the gifts of the Holy Spirit. Each person's particular gift has to be used for the edification of the Church and the maturing of the individual believer.

3. *There is no one gift of the Holy Spirit that every Christian has received.*   Perhaps we should have expressed this otherwise; saying, instead of "has received," "is intended by God to receive." We must be precise. It is obvious that not all Corinthian Christians spoke in tongues. It is further obvious that many in Corinth were speaking in tongues who should not have been. One activity — and it can rightly be called a gift of the Holy Spirit — in which all Christians should participate is "witnessing" (this is what "prophesying" signified when Paul wrote). "Covet to prophesy" is Paul's emphatic command (1 Cor. 14:39). It appears that this is a gift for which we should pray earnestly. But, as far as speaking in tongues is concerned, the farthest that Paul will go is to say, "Forbid not to speak with tongues" (1 Cor. 14:39). That there was a genuine exercise of this gift by true believers, Paul does not dispute. But he would be the first to clash with anyone who asserted that *all* must speak in tongues.

4. *To seek a so-called "baptism of the Spirit" is to be blind to all that God did for us in the moment of our adoption into the heavenly family.*   It is important that we stress to new believers

all their full inheritance through grace in the Kingdom of God. If we neglect this, there can be very unfortunate consequences.

In the moment of regeneration, God gives His Holy Spirit to His child. This cannot be overstressed. If this truth is not made clear to a young Christian, he may not know that he is indwelt by the Holy Spirit. But as he grows in grace, there will develop in him a hunger to be one hundred percent for God. He reads the New Testament and sees there that only through the empowering of the Holy Spirit can he be what God wants him to be. He is therefore open to the opinions of other Christians that what he needs is a new baptism of the Holy Spirit, a further gift of the Spirit, a new reception of the Holy Spirit. This he seeks as something independent from the salvation he has known thus far. It is very sad; but it happens, often.

At the risk of overemphasis, I must repeat that the New Testament knows nothing of such a "second blessing." There is an interesting note on this which is worth recording. I recall an exposition by a Pentecostal preacher in which he expounded Ephesians 1:13. The Authorized Version reads, "In whom also, after you believed, you were sealed with the Holy Spirit of promise." Great play was made of this word "after." From it, the teacher deduced that here was the clearest evidence that Paul taught a sealing by the Holy Spirit at some point subsequent to the act of hearing and faith. But the simple truth is that there is no "after" in the original text. All that is there is a plural participle governing both "hearing" and "believing" — and the tense of the participle is a past tense signifying "once and for all." In other words, Paul in that verse is stressing that in the very moment of the exercise of faith, the Holy Spirit entered as God's executive, seal, and Comforter. If this is taught in all its wonder and glory from the first days of Christian discipleship, there should be no danger of blasphemy against the Holy Spirit. For blasphemy indeed it is when we affirm that the first work of the Holy Spirit is not enough.

5. *In writing to the church in Corinth, Paul especially stresses that tongues-speaking is to be regarded as a lesser gift.* He does this in various ways. In listing the gifts of the Spirit, he places glossolalia at the end. And in 1 Corinthians 14:5 he goes so far as to say: "I would much rather that you all preached the Word of God. For the preacher of the Word does a greater work than

the speaker with "tongues," unless of course the latter interprets his words for the benefit of the Church" (*Phillips*). Is it conceivable that the apostle Paul would make such an emphatic downgrading of the gift of tongues if tongues were among the most vital of all gifts of the Spirit?

It should be a matter of sincere and earnest concern for all of us to seek out and obtain the best gifts. To what extent we may by specially pleading with God for some particular gift obtain it, I would not venture to say. We certainly are told to "covet earnestly the best gifts" (1 Cor. 12:31). Nowhere are we told to covet the blessing of speaking in tongues. We wrest the Scriptures from their context if we try to make such an appeal.

6. *There is a difference between the "tongues" of Acts and those of Corinth.*   The history of Acts 2 is one of miracle. On that day of Pentecost the Holy Spirit came upon the Church in fulfillment of God's age-old promise. "Suddenly there came a sound from heaven as of a rushing mighty wind . . . and they were all filled with the Holy Spirit" (Acts 2:2, 4). Tongues of flame rested on each head. The tongues are a symbol of the Gospel age: now men shall hear everywhere the good news of God in Christ and shall hear through tongues of fire. At Pentecost, the "tongues" were understandable and clear. Not so in Corinth. Here is a different kind of speech which only an interpreter can understand and therefore must declare. Pentecost was a divine miracle in which the entire Gospel age was symbolically manifested and the confusion of Babel overcome. Too frequently, tongues in Corinth were Babel resurrected.

7. *Glossolalia and the subconscious.*   It would be quite impossible to establish any meaningful evaluation of glossolalia if we did not realize that this exercise can very easily be a psychological substitute for the supernatural.

We are fearfully and wonderfully made. We don't need to go to Freud to learn that the subconscious plays a very decisive part in all our lives. Indeed, our conscious lives are really only like the tip of the iceberg showing above water, while nearly nine-tenths of the total ice surface is submerged. It is wholly possible that nothing we have ever spoken or heard is really forgotten — that it is tape-recorded in some miraculous way and stored in the recesses of our subconscious being. If that is so, how easy it would be in certain moments of transport for the subconscious to break through and to demand utterance that has otherwise been denied.

There is another school of thought that holds that there is a collective subconscious, in which is vested the real substratum of the collective imagination of a total people; and, under the right circumstances, this will come to expression in a foreign way.

Over against this view, we must set again the positive revelation of the Bible. In the time of Isaiah, when some claimed that they spoke through mediums or other spirits the messages of God, a test was given: "To the law and to the testimony: if they speak not according to this word, it is because there is no light in them" (Isa. 8:20). In the same connection Paul spoke when he reminded the Corinthian Christians: "Therefore I want you to understand that no one speaking by the Spirit of God ever says, 'Jesus be cursed!' and no one can say 'Jesus is Lord' except by the Holy Spirit" (1 Cor. 12:3 RSV).

God never meant the seat of rationality to become occupied by irrationality. There is always this danger when glossolalia abound.

8. *Glossolalia and Church renewal.* There has been much talk in the Church about revival when special manifestations of tongues-speaking have appeared. But one must walk warily here. It is very significant that in the revival which Indonesia has known over the past five years, there has been a remarkable absence of speaking in tongues. Yet it can scarcely be doubted that this is the greatest revival of Christianity that the twentieth century has seen. On the other hand, it is equally evident that the Corinthian Church, where this gift was so much in evidence, presented some of the biggest problems that Paul faced in his care of all the churches. It would not be exaggerating to say that the Christians in Corinth, in spite of their preoccupation with diverse gifts of the Holy Spirit, were nevertheless among the most immoral, flighty, mismanaged and immature Christians that Paul ever met.

The New Testament certainly does not say that in any movement of spiritual quickening we must expect to see such gifts in operation. Love will be found in overflowing fullness when revival is known. Paul underwrites that very carefully in 1 Corinthians 13. Where there are gifts without love there is nothing real or divine. We should add that nowhere does the New Testament encourage Christians to seek the gift of speaking in tongues, nor suggest that any

Christian should regard himself superior to others if he possesses this gift or spiritually inferior or below God's perfect standard if he does not possess such a gift. I would further add that I cannot discover any place in the Scriptures that supports the position that this kind of spiritual manifestation is a harbinger of new days of blessing.

On the contrary, we are warned against the danger of spiritual pride. How essential it is to heed such a warning. Pride will enter at every level and Satan is a past master at evoking such a spirit. Too frequently we hear those who emphasize tongues-speaking saying, "If you do not have the gift of speaking in tongues, you do not know the Holy Spirit." This is not only foolish, it is vain. As we have demonstrated, this kind of language is contrary to the teaching of the Word of God.

Side by side with this danger, we should set another, namely, that of so overstressing the Holy Spirit that the scriptural order of the Godhead is altered. The scriptural order is Father, Son, and Holy Spirit. Not only so, our Lord when teaching His disciples about the coming of the Holy Spirit said, "He shall not speak of himself" (John 16:13). In the following verse our Lord says "He shall glorify me." That means that the one great objective of the Holy Spirit's ministry is to glorify the Son of God and thereby God, the Father almighty, will be equally glorified. The Holy Spirit is the Spirit of Christ. He proceeds from the Father and the Son. This means that we cannot know Jesus Christ apart from the Holy Spirit; nor can we know the Holy Spirit apart from the Son of God; nor can we know the Father aright except within the glorious unity of the Son and the Spirit. This must be stressed when we are considering the Person and work of the Holy Spirit and in particular the exercise of the gifts He brings. Any tendency to overstress in an unscriptural way the ministry of the Spirit — by speaking, for example, about full Gospel, the latter rain, the second blessing, the necessity of glossolalia — must be most carefully watched and guarded against. Otherwise, once again pride will enter; superciliousness will take over, vanity and self-esteem will be in control. The spirit of Diotrephes, who loved "to have the preeminence" (3 John 9) will become very evident. Such a spirit must be dealt with in the way John indicates.

All of this is really far removed from the spirit of true revival.

In the day when God visits His people in revival blessing, He will share His glory with none other. God in Christ by the Holy Spirit will alone be extolled. Let us watch our way most carefully. Let us pray constantly that God will grant us the quickening we need and that His Holy Spirit will clearly show the way.

9. *The limitation of glossolalia.* I use this phrase to point out that while the disciples to whom the Holy Spirit was given on the day of Pentecost spoke in tongues, there is no record that the three thousand, who that day heard and believed the Gospel, also spoke in tongues. They were promised the same "baptism" and they were undoubtedly baptized by the Holy Spirit into the Body of Christ; but there is not the slightest mention made of them sharing in the gift of glossolalia.

Now this must be significant. Luke is a careful historian. If this had happened to the three thousand, is it conceivable that he would not have made mention of it? Any argument from silence is a doubtful one; but in this day of divine manifestation when God is consummating the plan of redemption planned from all eternity, surely such a detail would require careful documentation. Nothing is said, however. Why not?

Surely the reason is that this gift was not given the three thousand. That the disciples to whom the Lord had promised His Spirit and whom He had commanded to wait until they were endued with power from on high were singled out for particular endowment is perfectly obvious. The inspired Scriptures emphasize their speaking "as the Spirit gave them utterance" and they do so in such a way that men from all over the world hear in their own tongue the wonderful works of God. But the gift was limited to them.

Still further limitation may be noted when we see that while all the disciples in the upper room apparently were given this holy endowment of supernatural oratory and ability, when we reach the church in Corinth, twenty years later, not all the members there speak in tongues. This means that within less than a generation from the initial outpouring of the Holy Spirit at Pentecost, there is a marked decline in speaking in tongues. We do not know how large the church in Corinth was; what we do know is that not all the members spoke in tongues.

Around this question there has been much debate. Many affirm that the gift of tongues has been increasing mightily. We have noted this; and we have asked, "What kind of tongues?" On the other hand, there are those who contend that speaking in tongues becomes less and less prominent in the New Testament and that by the time the New Testament canon was closed the necessity for such a gift of the Holy Spirit had passed, for He was now able fully and constantly to refer His people to the inspired Scriptures of truth. What shall we say of this?

The discussion could be endless. In an age in which the Bible has been so terribly disavowed by so many preachers and at a time when the Church as a whole refuses to accept the Bible as "the written and infallible Word of God," can we not recognize the possibility of God breaking through in a new way to our generation and speaking again through Spirit-inspired tongues? Our Lord once said, "I tell you that, if these should hold their peace, the stones would immediately cry out" (Luke 19:40). Is it beyond imagination that God would choose this hour once again "to put down the mighty from their seats, and exalted them of low degree"? (Luke 1:52). Surely not!

It may well be true that with the closing of the New Testament canon all special and classical revelation came to an end. But this does not mean that God need limit Himself and that in His divine sovereignty He may not see fit from time to time to renew the gift of speaking in tongues throughout His Church.

Yet, we must constantly urge that the greatest watchfulness be exercised by believers against the possibility of deception, strife, and division. We have already noted so many ways in which the enemy of souls can launch some of his fiercest attacks against the disciple of Christ and have had cause to question much of what passes as being revelation of God in the person and tongue of one speaking in tongues, that we would be foolish indeed if we did not continually set ourselves to "watch and pray."

The tongues movement — a modern heresy?

Modern theology is not interested in heresy. Modern churchmen are more prone to demand freedom of viewpoint for everyone who may want to take the name Christian. Some weak attempts have been made in the past twenty years to charge leading theologians with heresy; but the result has been debacle and derision.

Yet for anyone who is prepared to accept the Bible as the Word of God written and infallible in all its parts, there clearly must be such a thing as heresy. Heresy is departure from the truth as revealed in the holy Scriptures. Heresy is any teaching contrary to that of the prophets and apostles as well as that of our Lord Himself. We must "stand fast in the faith" if we would defend it. This is therefore a legitimate question in our present discussion: Are there points at which the tongues-movement can be shown to be heretical in its emphases? Are there stresses made by ardent devotees of this movement that are clearly contrary to the plain teaching of God's Word?

We must very directly answer this question in the affirmative and for the following reasons:

1. *To say that the only certain sign of the presence of the Holy Spirit is glossolalia is contrary to the Word of God.* We note this again to designate this claim of heresy. Paul returns to this issue repeatedly. His words are clear. His teaching is unmistakable. When he says, "By one Spirit are we all baptized into one body . . . and have been all made to drink into one Spirit" (1 Cor. 12:13), he is refuting this so common saying of glossolalists. In verses 29 and 30 of the same chapter he expressly rules that not all have the gift of tongues.

How then can we defend a position that states the very opposite of what Paul is saying here? To do so is to act contrary "to the word and to the testimony." We fail our Lord and we act completely contrary to the express teaching of the oracles of God if we spread abroad such untruths. The plain fact is that it is the "fruit of the Spirit" that is the only sure sign of the Spirit's indwelling. For that fruit we should pray daily. By that fruit we shall be known as His disciples, for we shall by our love for Him be found keeping His commandments.

2. *To say that after regeneration we need a further baptism of the Holy Spirit is heresy.* We have already noted this at some length. I mention it again at this stage in our discussion because we are underlining those specific aspects of tongues speaking that we consider heretical.

When God calls us to Himself, He imparts His Holy Spirit. "He shall be *with* you and *in* you" — so our Lord promised. To receive Jesus Christ as Savior and Lord is to receive the Lord of all life who immediately gives to us the Holy Spirit without measure. It is of course essential that we allow the Spirit to work as He wills within us. We can hinder the Spirit. If we do such things, then the work of the Spirit in our lives will be stultified and the image of Christ will not emerge as it should. From such a condition we must return in penitence and tears to the God of all mercy and, if we do so, He will abundantly pardon and will again remind us of the amazing grace that has granted us the gift of the Spirit. We may then begin to grow in grace and in the knowledge of our Lord. We shall walk in the light as He is in the light. Then will the blood of Jesus cleanse us, and keep on cleansing us, from all sin. This is the wonderful promise of 1 John 1:9. But the action we take must not be confused. We are not receiving a new baptism of the Spirit; we are simply claiming the inheritance that is ours through Jesus Christ. We are possessing our possessions. We are becoming what we already are. We are fulfilling God's holy plan for us when He gave to us His Spirit and adopted us into His redeemed family by grace divine.

3. *To say that tongues speaking is essential to a full Christian life denies the teaching of our Lord and the history of the early church.* Our Lord did not teach this. The passage near the end of Mark's gospel where reference is made to speaking in tongues is not found in the major manuscripts of this gospel. In Jesus' great message before He went out to die He told the disciples much about the Person and work of the Holy Spirit, but no mention whatsoever is made about "speaking in tongues." The fullness of life which He promises His own is going to be experienced through the indwelling power of another like Himself, the Comforter as He called Him, and in that power they would remember, be led, speak with authority, pray, and be Christ's representatives on earth for as long as He left them there.

And when we look into the other writings of the New Testament, surely it is most significant that none of the other writers refer to this gift. When John writes under the guidance of his ascended Lord to the seven churches in Asia Minor, there is no reference made to this particular gift. None! Where we would expect constant reiteration if this gift were indeed so vital, we have nothing but silence. The witness of the larger body of the early church is therefore against this being essential to a full Christian experience and a victorious life of discipleship.

4. *One thing more must be added. Anything that diverts our focus of vision from Jesus Christ is clearly heretical.* We have noted how this happens. The very order of the Godhead goes into reverse in much teaching from glossolalists. Could anything be more dangerous?

Church history is full of sad tales of heretical movements within the Church and invariably these have come to pass because of a loss of scriptural bearings and a consequent failure to focus constantly on Jesus Christ. The New Testament is wholly Christocentric. So is the Old Testament, rightly understood. Christ alone is "the author and finisher of our faith" (Heb. 12:2), and we must look to Him continually as such. Anything that tends to minimize the office of Christ Jesus our Savior must be instantly suspect and corrected. Anything that tends to exclude the Person of Christ is a false and errant interpretation of the holy Scriptures.

When we turn our attention away from Christ, we may concentrate too much on the Holy Spirit; and at the other end of the spectrum we may find ourselves concentrating too much on the work of the devil. When this happens we all too often blame the devil for many evil things that have their origin within our own sinful hearts. The "works of the flesh" (Gal. 5:19-21) are primarily the works of hearts over which Christ has no sway. When He secures control, there is a speedy return to works of love and mercy.

The earliest Christian creed was "Jesus Christ is Lord." For the Christian in the twentieth century this is still the only true way to live the Christian life. It is to such a confession that the Holy Spirit will lead us. It is into such a glorious experience that He will bring us if we are resolved that God will be all in all. To that blessed and glorious life in God we are summoned by the Spirit. In that life Christ is our only Lord.

Let us turn, therefore, from all that would draw us away from Him. We must learn increasingly to love one another. All too frequently those who claim the gift of tongues have been instruments of division rather than of Christian unity. This in itself is an outcrop of heretical teaching. Let it be put away from us forever. Let us learn to "walk in the Spirit" so that we will "not fulfil the lust of the flesh" (Gal. 5:16). Let us seek to be filled with the Spirit and in the name of our Lord Jesus Christ give thanks every day for everything to our God and Father (Eph. 5:18, 20).

7

The Spirit of Power

*You will receive power when the Holy Spirit comes upon
you; and you will bear witness for me in Jerusalem, and
all over Judaea and Samaria, and away to the ends of the
earth* (Acts 1:8, translation mine).

TWO WORDS FOR POWER recur in the New Testament. One means
authority and the other signifies dynamic force. It is the word with
the second of these meanings that we find in Acts 1:8. Our Lord
promised the disciples an ability, a capacity, a potency, and a dynamism by means of which they would become altogether different
from what they had been before. They would of course exercise
that power under authority — the "exousia" granted them by their
Lord, true authority and right, the authority of which He spoke
when He said, "All power is given unto me in heaven and in earth"
(Matt. 28:18). Under such authority they would know a liberation
into a new dimension of power. This would be nothing less than
the dynamism of the Holy Spirit of God.

It is for this that God created man. God made man "to have
dominion." And in our fallen state we still lust after power. Of all
the attributes of God that we covet, power surely must come first.
The history of man is the struggle for power. The eagerness to
possess things and to hold others under our control is native to us
all. Babylon stands in the Bible as symbol of all the crude lust of
humanity for power. Babel was intended to reach to heaven and
thereby its builders would hold power that would forever endure.
Satan's temptation of our first parents in the Garden was to their
hunger for power: "You will be like gods" (Gen. 3:5).

Power, however, was lost when man sinned. Made by God for the heights, man became a groveller in the mire and mists of a stricken earth. That is the entail of sin. "The wages of sin is death" (Rom. 6:23). If we are to recover Paradise, if we are to know again the power for which God in the beginning made us, we must come under the authority of Him to whom belong the Kingdom, the power, and the glory. If this is to be, we must part company with the devil and all his works. His doctrine is that might is right, that nothing must stand between man and his desire, that assertion of self is the only way of self-realization, and that the passion to get and hold is our spring of action. But that is not God's way. The cross is God's way. The way to sovereignty is by the way of Calvary. The cross leads to the crown. The power that in our deepest hearts we know we need can be ours if we will obey the voice of the Lord our God, turn from the sin that has emasculated and weakened us so radically, and yield ourselves up as a living sacrifice for the fulfillment of God's will. This is the pathway to power.

It is also the pathway to Pentecost. No man can do what he ought to do according to his ability without the power to accomplish it. And this Christ promises by His Holy Spirit. "You shall receive power when the Holy Spirit has come upon you" (Acts 1: 8 RSV). Our Lord told the apostles plainly that the indwelling Spirit would be in them an all-prevailing source of power. In Him their greatest need would be fully met. The Holy Spirit would come upon them and thereby new vitality, energy, and spiritual power would be theirs. God's Spirit is always associated in the Scriptures with elemental force. He brooded over the darkness of the deep in the first of times and there emerged an ordered creation. In a similar way He came upon men chosen by God in Old Testament times and they were endowed with the kind of power they needed to do God's bidding. As the prophets looked down the corridors of time, they saw a day when the divine breath would come upon God's children and mighty things would be done. It is this that happened at Pentecost.

A liberating power

We must first emphasize that the Holy Spirit is the Spirit of freedom. "The law of the Spirit of life in Christ Jesus hath made me free from the law of sin and death" (Rom. 8:2). Law cannot liberate. God's law condemns and binds those that transgress the law. But the Holy Spirit comes in newness of power to the believer and sets him free. The new spiritual principle of life in Christ to which the Holy Spirit introduces us lifts and liberates us from the old vicious circle of sin and death.

This is a tremendous theme. Freedom is God's gift — by the Holy Spirit. "Where the Spirit of the Lord is, there is liberty" (2 Cor. 3:17). The Spirit we receive when we receive Christ as Savior is not one who will lead us back into bondage. Never! "The Spirit you have received is not a spirit of slavery leading you back into a life of fear, but a Spirit that makes us sons, enabling us to cry 'Abba! Father!'" (Rom. 8:15 NEB). All creation will one day know this freedom. "The universe itself is to be freed from the shackles of mortality and enter upon the liberty and splendour of the children of God" (Rom. 8:21 NEB).

We are set free from guilt, fear, judgment, and the power of indwelling sin. The Holy Spirit shows us a Savior dying for our sins upon a cross and leads us to trust in Him completely. The Holy Spirit applies to us the "blood of the cross" and cleanses us from sin. He teaches us that "if we walk in the light as God Himself is in the light, then we share a common life with God, and the blood of Jesus Christ keeps on cleansing us from all sin" (1 John 1:7, translation mine). In this living process, the old knots, snarls of carnality, and distortions of evil begin to be removed and we find ourselves wanting to seek after, to know, to serve, and to love God alone. This is the start of Christian liberty. We are by the divine power of the eternal Spirit set free to serve God as we ought, to love Him with all our hearts, and to pray that He may see nothing but His image in us.

There is a paradox here. But the Christian has to learn to live with paradox. The simple paradox is that the freedom he finds is in utter surrender to the rule of Christ. The Christian is a "bond-slave" of Jesus Christ. Christ's freemen are also His bond-servants. We surrender ourselves willingly as servants to righteousness (Rom. 6:18), to Christ Jesus our Lord (1 Cor. 7:22), to our fellowmen and the Gospel (2 Cor. 4:5; 1 Cor. 9:19-23). What this means is that Christian liberty is not license. We are delivered from the curse of the law, yet we bring ourselves immediately under the new commandment He gives. Love to Jesus Christ is shown by the freedom

with which we set ourselves to "fulfil the law of Christ" (Gal. 6:2).
No truer freedom can man know.

How necessary it is that we realize the freedom that is ours! We
dare not go back to the bondage of trying to save ourselves or to a
license that denies the will of Christ. It is very easy to fall a prey
to legalism and traditionalism, to the bondage of other people's
opinions and the fear of man. A true Christian knows discipline.
He knows the perils of licentiousness. He therefore shuns "the lust
of the flesh, and the lust of the eyes, and the pride of life" (1 John 2:
16). He realizes, for the Holy Spirit has taught him, that the whole
world system, based as it is on men's primitive desires, their greedy
ambitions, and the glamour of all that they think splendid, is not derived from the Father at all, but from the world itself. The warning
of Jude about men who "pervert the grace of God into licentiousness" (Jude 4 RSV) is eagerly heeded. God's children have learned
that they have not been freed by the Holy Spirit in order that they
should allow their members to be weapons of evil for the devil's
purpose. They are set free to do the will of God. Sin must therefore
have no dominion over them. They are living under grace.

Is this freedom something that we can enjoy continually? Yes,
if we will. "Walk in the Spirit, and you shall not fulfil the lust cf the
flesh" (Gal. 5:16). Walking means a deliberate moving forward towards a goal. There is an old Chinese proverb that says, "If you are
going to walk ten miles, you must first take the initial step." That is
what we must do if we want to retain the blessedness we knew when
first we saw the Lord. We must move forward with Him. As we do,
the Holy Spirit will daily give us more and still more power — power
to be free. The cause of freedom is the cause of God.

Power to speak

We have already written much about the gift of tongues. There
is one further angle, however, of utmost importance. When the
Holy Spirit came upon the waiting disciples in the upper room,
then, among other things, this happened: "They began to speak."
Their tongues were unlocked and they began to tell forth the wonders of God's mighty salvation. They had seen the Son of God after
His resurrection. This was verified to them by many infallible
proofs. But until that moment they had been tongue-tied. They

had not witnessed to their faith. The world had not yet heard of all that God had done. They began to tell it all.

The gift of prophecy was given the disciples on the day of Pentecost. "They *all* began to speak." Prophecy must not be restricted to a limited sense of foretelling. Prophecy is witnessing. In prophecy, what is vital becomes vocal. "Greater is he that prophesieth than he that speaketh with tongues" (1 Cor. 14:5). Peter soon emerged as the chosen representative of the Holy Spirit for the manifestation of this gift. Yet Peter was no man of the schools. He had never been known as one skilled in the art of oratory. However, he spoke the Word of God "with boldness" and in doing so commanded the attention of a great multitude. The result? A great number of men and women came to the valley of decision. William Arthur graphically portrays the scene and the effects of this preaching:

> Peter's sermon is no more than quoting passages from the Word of God, and reasoning from them; yet, as in this strain he proceeds, the tongue of fire by degrees burns its way into the feelings of the multitude. The murmur gradually subsides; the mob becomes a congregation; the voice of the fisherman sweeps from end to end of that multitude unbroken by a single sound; and, as the words rush on, they act like a stream of fire. . . . At length, shame and tears and sobs overspread that whole assembly. The voice of the preacher is crossed by a cry . . . and at this cry, the whole multitude is carried away and exclaim, "Men and brethren, what must we do?" [1]

This power abides with the Church. Paul recognized that only the Holy Spirit could give the power necessary to make words glow with divine fire. He begged his friends to pray that "utterance" might be given him. "Preaching" is God's gift. "It pleased God by the foolishness of preaching to save them that believe" (1 Cor. 1: 21).

And it is this power we need still. Our words fall like dead leaves on frozen ground unless the Holy Spirit quickens them. It is the joy of the Holy Spirit, however, to give power to those who will open their mouths to declare the mighty acts of God. The power given by Jesus to His disciples in the gift of His Spirit was the power to speak, power to be witnesses to Him. The power of the Holy

---

[1] William Arthur, *The Tongue of Fire*, first publ. 1901 (Winona Lake, Indiana: Light and Life Press, n.d.), p. 60.

Spirit is the power to think God's thoughts after Him, to speak His words to all men.

Power to pray

Prayer is one of the great signs of power in the Spirit-filled disciples. Jesus' followers gained a new power in prayer.

It was from a ten-day prayer retreat that they burst out onto the streets of Jerusalem. In the upper room as well as in the temple where they went frequently during that time, they learned to pray. They were drawn closer to one another in bonds of unity and love. They sought forgiveness from one another for wrongs they had done. The result was that when they reached the fiftieth day, "they were all with one accord in one place" (Acts 2:1).

Their prayer life deepened. In Acts 2:42 we are told, "They met constantly to hear the apostles teach, and to share the common life, to break bread, and to pray" (NEB). When persecution arose over the healing of the lame man at the beautiful gate of the temple, Peter and John were commanded to teach and preach no more. However, as soon as they were discharged they returned to their friends to tell them all that the chief priests and elders had said. What then? More prayer! Here is one of the greatest prayers recorded in all the Bible. They pled the sovereignty of God. They recalled the fulfillment of the divine promises in days gone by. They asked that they themselves might be strengthened, that as His servants they might speak God's Word with boldness (Acts 4: 29). Can we wonder that after such prayer "the building where they were assembled rocked, all were filled with the Holy Spirit, and spoke the word of God with boldness" (Acts 4:31 NEB)?

When prayer languishes in us, when we find ourselves unwilling to spend time alone with God, when we feel little hunger or thirst for the things of God, we must heed the countless warnings that are strewn across the pages of the Scriptures. David's prayer, "Renew a right spirit within me" (Ps. 51:10), must become ours. Prayer is the Christian's vital breath, his native air. Any loss of spiritual appetite is serious. It reveals an anemic condition of spiritual life which looks ripe for Satanic attack and overthrow. In times like these, what we need is a return to the place where we can receive a fresh infilling of the Holy Spirit and be empowered anew to pray. If this is your need as you read this page, let not an hour pass without seeking afresh the renewal of the Spirit. He waits to bless all who seek after God in humility and with a contrite heart.

> I hunger and I thirst,
> Jesus my manna be;
> O living waters, burst
> Out of the rock for me.
>
> Thou bruised and broken Bread,
> My lifelong wants supply;
> As living souls are fed
> O feed me, or I die.
>
> Thou true life-giving Vine,
> Let me Thy sweetness prove;
> Renew my life with Thine,
> Refresh my soul with love.
>
> For still the desert lies
> My thirsting soul before;
> O living waters, rise
> Within me evermore.

(John Monsell, 1811 - 1875)

"Men ought always to pray, and not to faint" (Luke 18:1). It is the teaching of our Lord as it was His constant activity. Though He was the strongest, He was constantly to be found at the feet of God. So may we. The Holy Spirit will always lead us there.

Power to obey

Obedience became the badge of the disciples of Christ. This means they brought themselves under the controlling power of Jesus Christ their Lord, learned His commandments as the Holy Spirit brought them to their remembrance, and followed in Christ's footsteps eagerly, continually, wholly.

This was made possible because through the Holy Spirit they received a new mind. "They that are after the flesh do mind the things of the flesh; but they that are after the Spirit, the things of the Spirit. For to be carnally minded is death; but to be spiritually minded is life and peace" (Rom. 8:5, 6). A carnal mind is inevitably opposed to the purposes of God. It neither can nor will follow His ways of living. To please God is therefore impossible.

But the Holy Spirit gives power to obey. What does this really mean? For the first disciples it involved total obedience to all the moral law of God as expressed by the prophets and revealed fully in Jesus Christ their Lord. For us today it involves even more, for we have now the full record of divine revelation in all the sixty-six books of the Bible. The Holy Spirit is the Author of these Scriptures. To have the mind of the Spirit, then, means that we accept the record, the histories, the commandments and judgments of the Scriptures. The Bible becomes for us not an object of worship but a source of knowledge, the knowledge of the will of God; and having learned what the Lord God requires of us, we go and do it in the power of the Holy Spirit. The Scriptures are our basic textbook for living the Christian life. The Holy Spirit is our teacher and guide. The Scriptures are given to us "for teaching, for reproof, for correction, and for training in righteousness, that the man of God may be complete, equipped for every good work" (2 Tim. 3:16, 17 RSV).

Disciplined, regular, and systematic reading and study of the Bible becomes part of our daily life. This is indispensable if we are to know the power of the Holy Spirit as well as the spiritual laws of the Kingdom of God. Obviously, we bring ourselves under suzerainty of the Scriptures when we accept Jesus Christ as Savior and Lord. He Himself was nurtured and taught by them. He Himself taught us to "search the scriptures" (John 5:39). We must do so. We must study them not merely to get a head knowledge of all that is in the Bible but in order that we might walk according to the pattern of life we see there. Bible study must be practical. We must search eagerly for the full knowledge of the will of God. Then we obey. By faith we accept what we find there as being indeed the word and will of God for us. We trust and obey.

Christian maturity comes through this kind of obedience. All the commandments and plans of God for our lives are detailed here with a fullness and clarity that leaves us without excuse. Moreover, the Holy Spirit is within us and by His power we now can do what previously was impossible. "The righteousness of the law [will] be fulfilled in us [as we] walk not after the flesh, but after the Spirit" (Rom. 8:4). We receive power to obey. What the labors of our hands could not fulfill, the Holy Spirit with our active co-operation will perfect in us. This is His promise. Ours is the joy of sharing in the work of sanctification.

We must therefore be ready at all times to yield to the sovereign overruling of the Spirit of God. He does not come to take life's joys from us. On the contrary, He indwells us in order to conform us to the fullness of the riches of Christ Jesus, the wellspring of all abundant joy. Holiness is not easily acquired. It is a stern and hard-fought fight that we shall know if we are to receive the crown of righteousness. To change us from our carnal image into the likeness of Christ will take time, much time. We are all prone to wander, prone to leave the God of love. Daily we need the cleansing that comes with daily forgiveness. Hour by hour we must give ourselves to every kind of training in righteousness. Constantly we must accept as from the hand of God those experiences by which He "disciplines us for our good, that we may share his holiness" (Heb. 12:10 RSV).

"To obey is better than sacrifice" (1 Sam. 15:22). Praise God, the Holy Spirit gives us the ability, the grace, the power to obey.

Power to discern

The atmosphere of the New Testament church is charged with power. Power of speech, power of miracle, power to pray, power to live victoriously, power to quench the fiery darts of the evil one, power for battle, power to die. Signs and wonders accompanied the disciples' testimony. Disease fled at their touch. Rulers trembled in their presence. They asked and received, for they prayed in the Spirit. The church was inspired, empowered, and triumphant because of the fullness of the Holy Spirit.

There was something else that must be stressed. These believers had a unique quality of spiritual discernment. They were able to see what God was planning. They possessed the power, and it was Spirit-given power, to discern the will of God, to discern the spirits whether they were of God or not, to discern the pathway God meant them to take for His glory.

When I think of the gifts of the Holy Spirit, I often find myself thinking that among the greatest of these is the gift of spiritual discernment. Yet how rarely do we find this gift! I have known many Christians who have had every opportunity of growing in grace. They sit under godly preaching. They are faithful in their attendance at Bible school. They accept the Scriptures as the Word of God. Yet, I would not dare, in a multitude of cases, entrust the welfare of a single soul to them. What is lacking? This holy gift of seeing with the eyes of the Spirit. We should certainly pray for this. We should covet earnestly the best gifts, and this surely is one of them. To be able to know what God is doing at a given time and to be in tune with God — this is something devoutly to be desired.

Whence comes this gift? From no other source than the Holy Spirit. Look again at the disciples after Pentecost. They were able to see the inner heart of a lame man outside the temple. They were able to tell the Sanhedrin that they must obey God rather than man. They could pierce through the camouflage of an Ananias and Sapphira and condemn their secret hypocrisy. And Stephen, outstandingly, was filled with the Holy Spirit and spoke in power and radiant discernment as He recounted God's mighty acts in the history of the chosen people.

Yes, discernment is among the greatest of the Spirit's gifts. Therefore we must seek it with all our hearts.

Discrimination is another word for this gift. It signifies a capacity for moral decision. It means prudence and wisdom conjoined. It is the fulfillment of Paul's prayer for the Philippian Christians: "My prayer for you is that you may have still more love — a love that is full of knowledge and wise insight. I want you to be able always to recognize the highest and the best, and to live sincere and blameless lives until the day of Christ. I want to see your lives full of true goodness, produced by the power that Jesus Christ gives you to the praise and glory of God" (Phil. 1:9-11 *Phillips*).

Idealistic? Of course. Too idealistic? Never! The standard that God sets us is a standard of perfection. If He set any lower standard, He would not Himself be perfect. It is a standard that can be met as we "walk in the Spirit." This kind of discernment or spiritual discrimination does not mean that we compile a list of things that we do and another list of things we don't do. The Bible is no kind of Baedecker guide to which we may turn under a given set of circumstances. No! God's Word reveals to us Him who is the life, the truth, and the way. Under His mastery, we learn what it is to own a complete series of Christian principles and standards, and how we may apply these best and to the greatest glory of God.

We may well lament the absence of this power in the Church

today. For it is indeed very thinly sown. "Where is the God of Elijah?" someone has asked — but the real question goes deeper. "Where is Elijah?" The power that rested on Elijah came because he was a man who stood in the presence of God. Therefore he could stand in the presence of kings. The Spirit waits to anoint with power all those who truly seek it. God grant us grace to strive, to seek, to pray, and not to yield until all that we are and have are possessed utterly by the mighty Spirit of the living God. Then shall God's power be known throughout the land.

8

The Spirit of Truth

But when the Comforter is come, whom I will send unto you from the Father, even the Spirit of Truth, which proceedeth from the Father, he shall testify of me (John 15:26).

When he, the Spirit of truth, is come, he will guide you into all truth: for he shall not speak of himself; but whatsoever he shall hear, that shall he speak (John 16:13).

OUR LORD REFERRED to Himself as the truth and He called the Holy Spirit the Spirit of truth. Truth is the opposite of error even as light is the opposite of darkness. What is truth? Chaucer speaks of truth in *The Franklin's Tale* and says:

Trouthe is the hyeste thyng that men may keep.

There is really no need, however, to define truth, for men know what truth is. We may believe what is false; but we can *know* only what is true. Love rejoices in the truth. Truth is honesty, sincerity, uprightness, light, and life. Every man willing to be honest with himself understands this statement by J. Robert Oppenheimer:

In some sort of crude sense which no vulgarity, no humour, no overstatement can quite extinguish, the physicists have known sin; and this is a knowledge which they cannot lose. [1]

---

[1] From a lecture, "Physics in the Contemporary World," delivered at M.I.T., Nov. 25, 1947.

What does it mean when the Holy Spirit is called "the Spirit of truth"? We must naturally ask what are the implications of this fact, and what we must do about it.

Jesus said: "I am the Truth" (John 14:6). His word is true. He speaks to man the truth of God and we are deaf at our peril.

> Nothing I do or know or speak or feel
> or ever shall
> but this One puts into my hands
> and fully comprehends,
>
> Entering wholly in,
> heard to the end, and known,
> it brings me on to silence,
> and into listening presence.
>
> Words become the Word, the choice
> offered one, a voice. [2]

This is what happens when the Holy Spirit enters. As He is the Spirit of Christ who is the truth, so is He the Spirit of truth. And, since it is His joy to "glorify the Son" so is it His joy to exalt the truth. Through Him we know the truth and the truth makes us free.

The Bible is full of urgent pleas that men should follow the truth. "Fear the Lord, and serve him in sincerity and in truth" (John. 24:14) is among the last of the counsels Joshua gave Israel. When David muses on the man who will stand in the presence of God, he describes him as one walking uprightly, working righteousness, and speaking the truth in his heart (Ps. 15:2). The Psalter returns frequently to this theme. "Thou desirest truth in the inward parts" (Ps. 51:6); "I have chosen the way of truth" (Ps. 119:30); "The Lord is nigh unto all them that call upon him, to all that call upon him in truth" (Ps. 145:18); "Take not the word of truth utterly out of my mouth" (Ps. 119:43). When Malachi describes the true priests of God he writes: "The law of truth was in his mouth, and iniquity was not found in his lips: he walked with me in peace and equity, and did turn many away from iniquity" (Mal. 2:6).

A like emphasis pervades the New Testament, not least in the teaching of our Lord. "You shall know the truth, and the truth shall make you free" (John 8:32); and again when He says, "I am

---

[2] Specially written for this book by Margaret Avison, Toronto.

the way, the truth and the life: no man cometh unto the Father but by me" (John 14:6). Paul urges his followers to speak the truth in love (Eph. 4:15); and, when warring against principalities and powers of darkness, to stand, having their "loins girt about with truth" (Eph. 6:14). Writing to Timothy, he describes the Church as "the pillar and ground of the truth" (1 Tim. 3:15). Similarly, John says, "I have no greater joy than to hear that my children walk in truth" (3 John 4). Truth is the canon of a righteous life. Truth and love are inseparables. To "walk in the truth" is a description of eternal life. To follow Him who is the truth is to live the life of the sanctified.

A special revelation

Truth can be known only if God reveals it. That is obvious; but it is also the heart of Christianity. God speaks. It is His nature to communicate. "In the beginning was the Word" (John 1:1). That means that in the beginningless beginning there was at the heart of God a principle of communication. God longs to share Himself with others. Can a man "by searching find out God?" (Job 11:7). The answer is no; so God must take the initiative, and He does. He is able to do so. No one can stay the power of God. God is able to speak because He is omnipotent and He does speak because He is love. A study of the nature of man reveals the necessity for such a communication from God, for man's nature is both finite and sinful. And the heart of Christianity is that this divine communication, this special revelation, is given in Jesus Christ. This we accept by faith. We further accept by faith that the revelation from God is accurately retained and revealed in the Bible, for the holy Scriptures are God-breathed, given by inspiration of the Spirit of God, the Spirit of truth.

Without such special revelation, we would know absolutely nothing about God. Man needs a guide in things that transcend him. Being sinful, he is dependent on a holy God to give him the illumination he requires. Through all the changing scenes of life he needs one to direct him, to chart his course, to show the way. In the midst of sin and sorrow, surrounded by trials, problems, fears, and difficulties, he cannot move forward or upward without an authoritative guide concerning salvation, holiness, and eternal life with God. Where can this be found? Only in Jesus Christ with the aid of the Holy Spirit. The Holy Spirit of truth reveals the truth about God, man, forgiveness, and all that pertains to life and godliness. This is special revelation. Without such special revelation, we are hopeless and helpless. Because of such special revelation, there are "given unto us exceeding great and precious promises," by means of which we become "partakers of the divine nature, having escaped the corruption that is in the world through lust" (2 Peter 1:4); and all this is because God in divine power "has bestowed on us everything that makes for life and true religion, enabling us to know the One who called us by his own splendour and might" (2 Peter 1:3 NEB).

Truth about God

This is the supreme ministry of the Holy Spirit. He is the Agent of the Godhead. This means that while all things come to us from the Father, and come through the Son, they are actually bestowed on us, worked out in us, revealed in us, by the Holy Spirit. Our greatest need is to know God in all His glory. The Holy Spirit reveals to us that God is a Spirit, infinite, eternal, and unchangeable in His being, wisdom, power, holiness, justice, goodness, and truth. He reveals to us that there is but one only living and true God; but within the mystery of the Godhead there are three persons — the Father, the Son, and the Holy Spirit — the same in substance, equal in power and glory.

The Spirit shows us that it is in Jesus Christ that God the Father is seen and known. "No man hath seen God at any time; the only begotten Son, who is in the bosom of the Father, he hath declared him" (John 1:18). Everything that Jesus did while with His disciples was to help them know the Father. We detect a note of wonder, almost a note of incredulity, in the words of our Lord to Philip at a point when the cross was very near. Philip asked: "Lord, show us the Father and we ask no more." To this Jesus answered: "Have I been all this time with you, Philip, and you still do not know me? Anyone who has seen me has seen the Father. Then how can you say, 'Show us the Father'?" (John 14: 8, 9 NEB). Men looked at Jesus and what they saw, if their understanding was opened by the Holy Spirit, was God, the Father almighty. So, when the Holy Spirit glorifies the Son, He is doing so in order that we may know what God is like and that we may hear the everlasting love of God through the lips of the only-begotten Son.

It is said of Samuel Rutherford that "his whole life was like one vast window through which he constantly looked to one surpassing face beyond."[3] The face to which he looked was that of Jesus, his Lord and Savior. And this is the abiding ministry of the Holy Spirit: to show us the Father in the Son.

Truth about man

Jesus Christ is the answer to the riddle of life itself. He is so because He makes us see the vision of truth and gives us power to overcome all hindrances in our quest for it. He answers the riddle by forcing us to see ourselves as we really are, for it is His will that we should not walk in the darkness of error, but may know the truth and be made free.

He promised His disciples the gift of another Comforter. He said, "When he comes, he will confute the world, and show where wrong and right and judgment lie. He will convict them of wrong, by their refusal to believe in me; he will convince them that right is on my side, by showing that I go to the Father when I pass from your sight; and he will convince them of divine judgment, by showing that the Prince of this world stands condemned" (John 16:8-11 NEB). What did our Lord mean? The Spirit would reveal the sin of man. He would show that the essence of sin is rejection of Jesus Christ. Sins are symptoms. Sin is a malady. Sin is rejection of the Son of God. Further, the Spirit would show that Jesus Christ was right. Righteousness was His throne. By going to the Father via the cross He would demonstrate that God is righteous and just, giving His own Son to die for the sin of the world. Still more, the Spirit would show that judgment is upon the world, for the prince of this world, Satan the adversary, was about to be judged at Calvary and revealed as an imposter, a liar, and a deceiver from the beginning.

But what has this to say about man? Briefly, that man is a sinner for whom the only hope is salvation through the Savior God has sent. Sin? It takes every form. Supremely, the form of "knowing

---

[3] R. S. Stevenson, *Commentary on Pilgrim's Progress* (Edinburgh: A. & C. Black, 1907), p. 73.

Him not." Unbelief is aversion of heart. From unbelief flows wickedness, rottenness, greed, and malice; envy, murder, deceitfulness, quarrelsomeness, and spite; insolence, pride, and boastfulness; sexual immorality, impurity, and sensuality; witchcraft, sorcery, and worship of false gods; jealousy, bad temper, and rivalries; drunkenness, orgies, and false witnessing. The list goes on and on. It is a terrible list indeed. Yet, among the more remarkable facts of biblical inspiration is this: we are incapable of devising a new sin. All the sins that men are sinning tonight are found in the Bible and condemned there. "The heart is deceitful above all things, and desperately wicked" (Jer. 17:9). This is what man is like in his heart of hearts; and it is the Holy Spirit who shows us this truth about ourselves. None other can do it.

The reason for this is that when the Holy Spirit convicts us of sin, He sets us against the standard of the holy law of God. If we were to measure ourselves by the standards of our fellowmen, we might fare not too badly. But God will not have us do that. The Holy Spirit shows us ourselves, shows us as we really are "in the dark," as God Himself sees us. "Man looketh on the outward appearance, but the Lord looketh on the heart" (1 Sam. 16:7). God did this for John Bunyan. He showed him what he was really like in the sight of God. And then, Bunyan tells us:

> I read: "He that shall blaspheme against the Holy Ghost hath never forgiveness, but is in danger of eternal damnation" (Mark 3:29). . . . And now was I both a burden and a terror to myself, nor did I ever so know, as now, what it was to be weary of life, and yet afraid to die. Oh, how gladly now would I have been anybody but myself! For there was nothing did pass more frequently over my mind, than that it was impossible for me to be forgiven my transgression, and to be saved from the wrath to come. [4]

The Spirit of truth will tell us nothing but the truth. Apart from Christ we are sinners in the sight of God and "God is angry with the wicked every day" (Ps. 7:11). What we need to know about ourselves is the truth, the whole truth, and nothing but the truth. The great trouble with man is that he has built up walls of self-deception and self-righteousness about himself and as a result he

---

[4] John Bunyan, *Grace Abounding: Life and Death of Mr. Badman* (New York: Dutton, n.d.), p. 46.

cannot see himself. Humanism, intellectualism, mysticism, spiritism, ecclesiasticism, idealism, satanism — all have clouded the mind and made man think himself just a little lower than God. Only the Spirit of truth can save. Cry to Him while yet there is time.

Truth about the Scriptures

"All scripture is given by inspiration of God" (2 Tim. 3:16). That is the Bible's witness to its own authorship. Peter affirms this in his own colorful way when, while recalling the Mount of Transfiguration, he says that "no prophecy came because a man wanted it to come: holy men of God spoke because they were inspired by the Holy Spirit" (2 Peter 1:21, translation mine). Thus do the Scriptures authenticate themselves.

It is a tremendous claim. No other book makes a claim like it. But the Bible is emphatic. The Holy Spirit is both inspiration and ultimate author. This is why the Nicene Creed expresses the truth that the Holy Spirit was associated with the writing of the Old Testament: "who spake by the prophets." The Spirit of God moved the writers of three continents, from every conceivable walk of life and covering possibly a span of two thousand years to write a work that is consonant in all its parts with the whole, uniform in its judgment concerning evil and righteousness, and united in pointing forward to a coming King who would be the Messiah of God.

The Bible is a unique book. In all the literature of the world it stands alone, by reason of divine inspiration. That is a Christian claim, a dogma of belief, an absolute truth for all who accept the authority of Jesus Christ. He Himself stated that the Scriptures testified of Him (John 5:39). For Him, the Scriptures were the last court of appeal: "It is written." Beyond that He refused to go. He was no victim of delusion. He was no dupe of the prejudices and ignorance of His day. He was "the Truth." Truth cannot lie.

This must be tested by experience. How do I know that the Bible is true? By putting it to the test. This is how I myself became a Christian. I noted that the Bible made a certain promise, provided conditions were met by me. I met them by the grace of God, and the Word of God came through triumphantly. I discovered that Jesus Christ is quite unlike the caricatures that modern man holds concerning Him. He was like a volcano. He forced me to think about everything in a way I had not intended. Money, laziness, anger, petulance, pride, lust, all the libidos of my hidden personality, all my fears and especially my fear of God — He dragged all these out into the open and made me look at them — made me look at them in the light of God, which is the light of the Bible inspired by the Holy Spirit. I realized then that He wanted one thing supremely in me — truth working by love. I realized also that I couldn't fool Him in any way, for all my petty efforts at cover-up were foolish and futile. This drew me more and more to the Word of God written. I saw soon that revelation culminates in Jesus Christ and this again meant that He and the Scriptures were inseparable. Without Him the Bible would be a meaningless book, a tale told by an idiot, full of sound and fury. It was He that gave meaning to the whole — the histories, prophecies, symbols, and ceremonials. He fulfilled all that the prophets had long before promised. "To him give all the prophets witness" (Acts 10: 43). So said the apostles. So He claimed Himself.

The first Christians accepted this without reserve. They taught the Church that the Scriptures were *theopneustai* — God breathed. And He showed them further that there would be an inspired record also of the New Testament. He taught them that the Holy Spirit would take control and that as He had inspired the writers of the Old Covenant, so would He inspire new writers for the New. In this way the whole Bible was written and given to the Church. The Spirit of truth governed its creation by His divine inspiration. He saw to it that the revelation would be fully recorded by the creative inspiration He would give. Thus it came to pass that we hold in our hands today the miracle of a Book, God's Book, the only Book that can make us wise unto salvation. By inspiration of the Holy Spirit of truth the record rolled forth. Multitudes in every generation have listened and believed. It is a living Book. Multitudes have come to know that God lives and Christ is Lord because the Holy Spirit "breathed the breath of God" into this Book and made it to be the Book of truth.

Not all accept this. The past hundred years has seen the Bible assaulted in every conceivable way. The Bible of higher criticism and classic liberalism is very different from the Bible the early Church received. The so-called traditional view has been ignorantly or willfully misinterpreted, or else flippantly caricatured. I have listened to countless men stating that the Bible of their Sunday school days they could no longer accept. But I must confess to seeing in many of these men mere place-seekers masquerading under the claims of modernity and scientific criticism. I find it hard to be patient with men who enter the ministry and spend most of their time discrediting the Bible. Their specious shallowness and colossal vanity are anathema. But there is still a remnant by grace to whom God has revealed the truth by His Holy Spirit. Revelation, inspiration, illumination, and interpretation all come from Him. He is the Holy Spirit of truth. He cannot lie.

Still, wonders happen when men believe what God has said. No more telling illustration of this have I read than the words of C. S. Lewis when he describes the night of his conversion:

> You must picture me alone in that room in Magdalen College, night after night, feeling, whenever my mind lifted even for a second from my work, the steady, relentless approach of Him whom I so earnestly desired not to meet. That which I greatly feared had at last come upon me. In the Trinity Term of 1929 I gave in, and admitted that God was God, and knelt and prayed: perhaps, that night, the most dejected and reluctant convert in England. I did not see what is now the most shining and obvious thing: the Divine humility which will accept a convert even on such terms. The Prodigal Son at least walked home on his feet. But who can duly adore that love which will open the high gates to a prodigal who is brought in kicking, struggling, resentful, and darting his eyes in every direction for a chance to escape? The words *compelle intrare*, compel them to come in, have been so abused by wicked men that we shudder at them; but, properly understood, they plumb the depths of the Divine mercy. The hardness of God is kinder than the softness of men, and His compulsion is our liberation. [5]

This is the everlasting mercy. It rises in the mountains of eternity where the holy Triune God planned man's salvation. It is the story of a love that passes knowledge. The grace of Christ is immeasurable. The glory of Christ is unfathomable. Deep calls to deep and glory to glory. And all this the Spirit of truth reveals to every seeker after truth. He prepares our mind to accept the immensities of revelation. He renews our mind and thereby prepares a transformed life and the learning of God's perfect will. He takes of the

---

[5] C. S. Lewis, *Surprised By Joy* (London: Geoffrey Bles, 1955), p. 215.

things of Christ and reveals them to us; and always the textbook is the Bible. Thus Christ becomes to us by the Spirit wisdom and righteousness and sanctification and redemption (1 Cor. 1:30).

Truth about service

It is very interesting to note how God has called men and women into His service by the Holy Spirit. One brief illustration must suffice. It comes from an organization for which I have had a life-long love — the Salvation Army.

Commissioner Samuel Logan Brengle is a household name in every Salvationist home. He describes how he was led into service for God.

> As I read the scriptures my heart melted like wax before fire. Jesus Christ was revealed to my spiritual consciousness, revealed in me, and my soul was filled with unutterable love. I walked in a heaven of love. Then one day, with amazement, I said to a friend: "This is the perfect love about which the Apostle John wrote: but it is beyond all I dreamed of; it is personality; this love thinks, wills, talks with me, corrects me, instructs me and teaches me." And then I knew the Holy Spirit was in this love and this love was God, for God is love. [6]

Out of this came preaching, witness, and testimony. Soon he found himself pleading with William Booth to take him into the Army and Booth, who felt that this man might prove insubordinate, was hesitant. But God overruled. Brengle was accepted. The Holy Spirit had prepared him for special duty. The life that followed demonstrated daily the sure leading of the Spirit of God.

This is for us all. The Spirit of truth waits to teach. Let us learn from Him.

---

[6] Samuel L. Brengle, *When the Holy Ghost Is Come* (New York: Salvationist Publishing and Supplies, 1896), p. 57.

9

The Spirit of Holiness

He was declared to be the Son of God with power, according to the Spirit of holiness, by the resurrection from the dead (Romans 1:4).

PENTECOST WAS CONSUMMATED when the disciples "were all filled with the Holy Spirit" (Acts 2:4). By whatever other name we call the Spirit of God, He is pre-eminently the *Holy* Spirit. God is holy. Our Lord Jesus Christ was "holy, harmless, undefiled, separate from sinners, and made higher than the heavens" (Heb. 7:26). Likewise the Spirit, being the Spirit of Christ, is the Spirit of holiness. Without holiness, no man shall see God (Heb. 12:14). This means that without the aid of the Holy Spirit, who alone can sanctify us and make us holy, we shall never stand before the burning bliss and purity of the God who made us all. The Church can be made a glorious Church, without spot or wrinkle, only by the Holy Spirit.

The word has fallen into disuse in many quarters. It has become associated with a type of piety that is alien and forbidding. Thus Satan demonstrates again his ingenuity in deceiving even the saints of God. Though they are called unto holiness, they are nonetheless wary of being classified as "holy people." Yet anyone familiar with the New Testament knows that there is only one true objective before the children of God — likeness to Jesus Christ, which is holiness in every sense of the term. The New Testament insists on the necessity of holiness, urges its experience, and enforces its conditions and obligations.

The natural man cannot understand holiness. Nor indeed can

109

the man who knows the life of the Holy Spirit within him, unless he is daily setting himself to seek the life of the Spirit. God's holiness is not simply the best we know made infinitely better. The divine holiness stands apart, solitary, unique, unapproachable, incomprehensible, and unobtainable. God must manifest Himself to us as He is before we catch even the first faint glimmering of what holiness is. Job had heard of God by the hearing of the ear, but when God revealed Himself, something unusual happened: "Now mine eye seeth thee. Wherefore I abhor myself, and repent in dust and ashes" (Job 42:5, 6). So with Isaiah. He entered the temple in the year that King Uzziah died and there he saw God. "I saw also the Lord sitting upon a throne, high and lifted up, and his train filled the temple." He saw the six-winged seraphim and heard them sing, "Holy, holy, holy, is the Lord of hosts: the whole earth is full of his glory." At this, the posts of the door moved and the house was filled with smoke; and Isaiah, overwhelmed with the wonder of everything he saw, cried out, "Woe is me! for I am undone; because I am a man of unclean lips, and I dwell in the midst of a people of unclean lips: for mine eyes have seen the King, the Lord of hosts" (Isa. 6:1-5). All his disguises were torn from him in that moment when God revealed Himself. Before the ineffable glory of the King of heaven he knew himself as sinful and undone.

The life of holiness is the life of God. To know God is to know the meaning of holiness. This life is open to those who seek it. It is not a special deluxe edition of Christianity specially packaged for an elite and privileged few. It ought to be the normal state of every true believer. It is "the mystery which hath been hid from ages and from generations, but now is made manifest to his saints: to whom God would make known what is the riches of the glory of this mystery among the Gentiles: which is Christ in you, the hope of glory" (Col. 1:26, 27). Of this life, it is ever true that they that seek it, find it. Faber has given us words that are fitting and apt as we pray for this gift of holiness from the Spirit of holiness:

> Ocean, wide flowing Ocean, Thou,
> Of uncreated Love;
> I tremble as within my soul
> I feel Thy waters move.

> Thou art a sea without a shore;
> Awful, immense Thou art;
> A sea which can contract itself
> Within my narrow heart. [1]

Let this be our prayer until we see God face to face and love Him with unsinning heart.

What true holiness is

God is holy. To be so, He conforms to no standard, for He is that standard. He is absolutely holy with a fullness of purity that is incapable of being other than it is. All God's attributes are holy. "In him is no darkness at all" (1 John 1:5). Since He is holy, He has made holiness the moral condition essential to the health of all His creation. Holiness is health. Holiness is wholeness. The English word "holy" derives from the Anglo-Saxon *halig, hal,* meaning "well, whole."

Whatever is contrary to the moral health of His universe is of necessity under His displeasure. Sin, being the opposite of holiness, is therefore under judgment. Sin is un-health, dis-ease, mal-function, dis-order. God is described in the Scriptures as angry when He rises against sin; but the very fact that God thus arises is the only hope for this poor, dying world. Sin will make the universe to suffocate in its own pollution; and we are seeing much of that today. God's wrath is a holy act of preservation of His creation. Judgment from the throne of God speeds against everything that degrades, disturbs, and destroys.

Some lines from A. W. Tozer come to mind as I write of this. I shall never forget that wonderful servant of God. I see him still as he expounded the Scriptures he loved so well, and the memory is itself a blessing. He was to my eyes a holy man. He was transparent. There was no trace of insincerity in his speech and his life faithfully mantled all he said. By his writings, multitudes were blest; and I counted myself also within that number. And when he wrote of the holiness of God he said,

> God is holy with an absolute holiness that knows no degrees, and this He cannot impart to His creatures. But there is a relative and contingent holiness which He shares with angels and seraphim

---

[1] Frederick W. Faber, from *Faber's Hymns and Songs.*

in heaven and with redeemed men on earth as their preparation for heaven. This holiness God does impart to His children. He shares it with them by imputation and by impartation, and because He has made it available to them through the blood of the Lamb, He requires it of them. To Israel first and later to His Church God spoke, saying, "Be ye holy; for I am holy." He did not say, "Be ye as holy as I am holy," for that would be to demand of us absolute holiness, something that belongs to God alone. [2]

I know no better statement of the essence of true holiness. To this condition God would lead us. And in the ongoing work of making us holy, it is always the Holy Spirit who is the Agent of the Godhead.

God's will — our sanctification

The biblical idea of holiness is found nowhere else than in the Bible. Even in Israel the idea developed slowly; but infinitely patient as always, God led His people on in progressive revelation of His will for them. He chose Israel to be a special kind of nation. "Now therefore, if you will obey My voice indeed, and keep My covenant, then you will become out of all My possessions a special possession; for the whole earth is mine. You shall be My kingdom of priests, My holy nation" (Exod. 19:5, 6).

God's purpose or plan never changed. The New Testament therefore re-echoes the emphases we find in the Old. "This is the will of God, even your sanctification" (1 Thess. 4:3). "God hath from the beginning chosen you to salvation through sanctification of the Spirit and belief of the truth" (2 Thess. 2:13). Our Lord prayed for His disciples that they might be sanctified and added these amazing words: "For their sakes I sanctify myself that they also might be sanctified through the truth" (John 17:19). In the process of sanctification the Holy Spirit takes the Word of God as revealed in the Bible and applies it to us. Thereby Christ is made to us sanctification and redemption. This is how we glorify God. Every day and in every way we should become more like our Savior. This is sanctification. This is God imputing and imparting to us holiness. In the heart of God there is no greater desire than that we should become holy, become like Himself.

---

2 A. W. Tozer, *Knowledge of the Holy* (New York: Harper & Row, n.d.), p. 113.

There may be many methods of reaching this goal. But the Holy Spirit is central in them all. "The law of the Spirit of life in Christ Jesus hath made me free from the law of sin and death" (Rom. 8:2). No two experiences are identical. As varied as our fingerprints or faces, so are the experiences God's people know in becoming holy. Usually there is an arousing of heart and mind to discern the will of God and then come vision and persuasion. We begin to hunger and thirst after God. In Him we are increasingly satisfied.

Of course, we can expect Satan to hinder us by every means in his power. He does not want to see us grow in grace. He opposes every instrument that God uses in the work of sanctification. He will keep us by every possible means from reading our Bible. He will interrupt us in our praying. The telephone will ring just at the moment when we are trying to be alone with God. Distractions will fill our minds. Wandering thoughts will pursue us. We will find it often difficult to concentrate; and sometimes we will discover within our own hearts a coldness and distaste for spiritual things. The will of Satan is that we remain carnal. He will use every trick in his book to keep us from following hard after God.

What then? What shall we do? What must be our reaction to this kind of persuasion of our adversary, the devil?

We must seek the fullness of the Holy Spirit. And that means seeking Him with our whole heart. It implies that we are in absolute earnest when we say we want the fullness of the Spirit. Remember, we thus declare a willingness on our part to allow the Holy Spirit to have His own way and to claim from us unquestioning obedience in everything. He will not tolerate in us many of the sins that are condoned by other Christians, sins like self-righteousness, self-defense, self-confidence, self-love, self-pity. No! He will demand the right to take from us many things we like and thus He will discipline us. But through it all He will enfold us in a love so great, so all-consuming, so wondrous that our losses will appear more like gains when we balance everything up. Why does the Holy Spirit do this? For one supreme reason — to detach us from the passing interests of life and to throw us back upon eternity. He does so, that is, to insure that we really want God and God alone, that we want to know Jesus Christ and Him crucified, that we want above all other things to be filled with the Holy Spirit of God. When this really happens, we are indeed being sanctified.

Holiness, humility, and simplicity

Part and parcel of true holiness is obedience to the will of God. From obedience, some specific fruits grow. Humility and simplicity are two of the most notable and these are really inseparable from holiness. Let me illustrate what I mean.

Humility is learned when we discover the greatness of God. There is a specious kind of humility that stems from self-discouragement and self-disgust with the kind of shabby lives we live for the greater part of the time. But that is not true humility. The humble man realizes that all his personal, self-originated intentions are works of straw. He therefore clings to something, to *Someone,* infinitely higher than himself.

This is not easily learned. Pride is a hard foe to conquer. But pride is the antithesis of holiness. We are proud of our cleverness in business competition. We are proud of the way we are known far and near. We covet flattery. We are conceited. The elevation of the superiority motive pulls us onward to goals that enhance our egos. We seek powerful friends. We wish to be known as people who are in touch with the great ones of the land. A place in the establishment means much to us. And, one of the devil's oldest tricks, we become proud of our own humility.

But true humility is of God. "Humility rests upon a holy blindness, like the blindness of him who looks steadily at the sun. For wherever he turns his eyes on earth, he sees only the sun."[3] The "God-blinded" man sees only the will of God and longs for that will to be done in and through him on earth. Here humility and holiness meet. God helps us die to the things on which we spend our time, the things that, while enhancing ourselves, waste our years. As we die to these empty trifles, God renews us in His own image by His Spirit and we become lovers of holiness.

Simplicity too is given, the simplicity of a trusting child. This simplicity is the beginning of spiritual maturity and follows that period of our lives in which we have been so busy we have not

---

[3] Thomas Kelly, *A Testament of Devotion* (London: Hodder and Stoughton, 1943), p. 55.

had time to give to others or to think of things eternal. Christian simplicity breaks through the mad rush of crowded calendars and makes us to be still and know that God is God. When this happens poise and peace are rediscovered. We enter on a deeper, an internal simplification of the whole personality. We are learning to walk with God. The taste of new wine is given us. We possess the stilled, tranquil trust of those who, led by the Spirit of God, move joyfully into the dark.

I find very little of this simple life today. The reason? We do not know the meaning of true holiness. We are unwell. We are unwhole — unholy. Life in the twentieth century is too often one mad scramble for things, a fevered strain for possessing, a relentless urge to grab and get. Holiness counteracts this totally. The holy life is lived beside still waters and knows the wonder of the Good Shepherd's presence. Holiness is a life beyond strain, a life of power and joy and love through abandonment to God and forgetfulness of self. We may have left it a little late but it is not yet too late. There is still time for us to seek after Him who is the Lord of all. There is still time to love Him utterly and to be baptized with the power of the apostolic life. There is still time to seek after holiness, humility, simplicity. But we must take time. We must make time, as William D. Longstaff reminds us in his hymn:

> Take time to be holy,
>   Speak oft with thy Lord;
> Abide in Him always,
>   And feed on His Word;
> Make friends of God's children,
>   Help those who are weak,
> Forgetting in nothing
>   His blessing to seek.
>
> Take time to be holy,
>   The world rushes on;
> Spend much time in secret
>   With Jesus alone;
>   .   .   .
>
> Thus led by His Spirit
>   To fountains of love,
> Thou soon shalt be fitted
>   For service above.

As Augustine in *The Confessions* writes: "When I shall with my whole soul cleave to Thee, I shall nowhere have sorrow or labour, and my life shall live as wholly full of Thee."

Holiness through the Spirit

In questing after holiness, we must always remember that holiness is in the spirit of our personality and that it comes from the divine Spirit. No number of forms or ordinances, no multiplicity of will-worship and proud self-humilities, will ever bring us near to holiness. It is not to be found in prohibitions nor in self-denial. Holiness is a spirit of life, a dynamic, a principle that must be born in us by the Holy Spirit even as the Christ-Child was conceived by the Holy Spirit in the Virgin Mary's womb.

God the Holy Spirit dwells within the temple of the believer's body. In a sense, He clothes Himself with a human person, and that person is thereby clothed with the presence and power of the Holy Spirit. Even as the mantle of Elijah fell on Elisha, so does the Spirit of God empower the Christian. The body is the temple of the Holy Spirit. There Christ dwells within men by His Holy Spirit. Christ is not a great example; He is a living Lord. Christian faith does not copy Christ; Christ is reproduced in the heart of a disciple by the Holy Spirit. All life is made holy because the Holy Spirit holds it, transforms it, makes it to glow with the light of God, makes it fragrant with the love of God. The Holy Spirit does not work *on* us; He lives in us. This is the supreme difference between the works of the flesh and the fruit of the Spirit. Works denote sweat and toil; fruit denotes life and growth. Works belong to men; fruit comes from God. Holiness makes our lives fruitful because a holy life abides in the living Word and thereby full and free scope is given to the Spirit of life. The Holy Spirit makes our hearts clean, our minds pure, our faculties to work at their full capacity, and our lives thereby fruitful to the glory of God.

Thus God makes His holiness ours. This is no theoretical layout of a type of Christian life. This is vital Christianity and the world is dying to see this kind of Christianity lived out before it.

What does it see instead? Carnal lives. Lives without the power of the Holy Spirit. Vain and intemperate men and women holding office within the Church and turning the Church into copy-plates of themselves. I have seen too much of this type of Christianity. I want to see it no more. I know of churches where men living openly in sin hold the positions of dominance and do so because of their position in society. I know of a church where there are five elders: two of them are alcoholics, two of them never attend, the fifth is mayor of the town and appears on ceremonial occasions. What kind of Christianity is this? Can we not hear God saying, "I will spew thee out of my mouth"?

The great need of the hour is for holy men and women, holy young people to turn to God and ask for the fullness of the Holy Spirit without measure and to plead that God will cleanse them utterly from all secret faults. When this begins to happen, we can expect God to have mercy upon His Zion. Until it does happen, there is little hope. A holy Church will awaken men to their need of God and will draw them to the cross of Christ. A carnal Church will drive them away and encourage them in their sin. God grant us, then, true hunger after holiness. May the communion of the Holy Spirit be our joy and life.

10

The Spirit of Love

The fruit of the Spirit is love (Galatians 5:22).

THE APOSTLE JOHN, by the Spirit, wrote, "God is love" (1 John 4:8). By this he meant that love is a fundamental attribute of God. All the other attributes of God that are revealed in the Bible teach us what this love is like. Since God is immutable, we know His love cannot change. Since God is self-existent, we understand that His love had no beginning and will never end. Since God is infinite, His love is infinite. Since God is holy, His love is purity in its very essence. Since God is great, omnipotent and almighty, we cannot but believe that His love is an incomprehensibly vast, bottomless, shoreless sea before which we bow in wonder, love, adoration, and praise.

> O love divine, how sweet Thou art!
>   When shall I find my willing heart
>   All taken up in Thee?
> I thirst, I faint, I die to prove
> The greatness of redeeming love,
>   The love of Christ to me.
>
>   (Charles Wesley, 1707-1788)

This is the depth of the love of Christ for His Church. Since the Spirit is the Spirit of Christ, this is also the love with which the Holy Spirit yearns over us, longing to see us conformed to the perfect image of the One He glorifies.

Love defies definition. It cannot, however, deny description; and it has been very wonderfully portrayed in some of the parables of our Lord — the love of the father for his prodigal son, the love that made the Samaritan pick up the wounded Jew and take him to an inn, the love that goes out to seek the wandering sheep in the wilderness. These suggest to us that love is never possessive, is always constructive, and has no joy in the suffering of others. Love keeps no records of ills committed against itself. It is tolerant, patient, and longsuffering. True love is gentle. It never covets the limelight. It has no inflated ideas of its own importance. All this we learn from the illustrations of the love of God that are strewn so lavishly across the pages of the Scriptures. And the Holy Spirit is the Spirit of love. That means that He is Himself love in its quintessence of purity and power. He also is the One through whom this kind of love can be shed abroad in our hearts.

The fruit of the Spirit

"The fruit of the Spirit is love" (Gal. 5:22). There follow eight other expressions of this fruit; but the greatest of all is love. Indeed, as we have noted earlier, each of the other eight aspects of the fruit of the Spirit may well be regarded as aspects of love. In this case, love is the total fruit of the Spirit manifesting itself in many different ways.

Certainly of all the Christian virtues, the greatest is love. Certainly, too, the fruit of the Spirit is singular not plural. Paul does not speak of the "fruits" of the Spirit as he does of the "works of the flesh." The fruit is one. It is an expression of life. We cannot grow the fruit of the Spirit. This would be like attempting to create a part of the Godhead. Fruit comes by our abiding in Christ; and that occurs when the Spirit of love is indwelling us.

In another Pauline passage we see how this love manifests itself. Paul is writing to the Colossians and speaks about Epaphras — a dear fellow-servant — emphasizing that "it was he who brought us the news of your love within the fellowship of the Spirit" (Col. 1:8 NEB margin). Paul was stirred deeply as he learned how greatly the Colossian Christians loved him, and possibly most of all because he saw that there was spiritual growth indicated by this love. Love such as they were showing had grown because of the Holy Spirit. In no way could their love be described as human in origin. It was not mere good nature nor good will that grace had perfected. No! It was a work of the Holy Spirit within them by reason of which they had come to love the servant of God even as God Himself loved His servant.

Love is therefore born of the Holy Spirit. His love is seen in joy, peace, gentleness, goodness, meekness, longsuffering, faith, self-control. Just as He brings assurance and truth and power, so does He shed abroad in us the spirit of love. Where this love is, all other tokens of the fruit of the Spirit will be seen. The "fruit" of the Holy Spirit is vastly different from the "gifts" of the Spirit. Gifts differ in every experience. The Holy Spirit in sovereignty gives gifts as He wills. Not so with the "fruit" of the Spirit. God does not mean one of His children to have "joy," another to have "peace," and yet another to possess "patience." Not at all! Every child of God is intended to possess the full fruit of the Spirit and this many-sided fruit should be seen in the life of every true believer. Pray that it is daily seen in you.

Gifts and fruit

We need not labor the point, but we must be sure that it is understood. Too many Christians simply do not know the difference between the gifts and the fruit of the Spirit. Yet this is part of the ABC of the Gospel. How essential it is to teach and train young Christians in the realities of their possessions in Christ as well as their responsibilities as Christians. J. Oswald Sanders makes this point clearly and emphatically:

> Discrimination should be made between the gifts and the fruit of the Spirit. Between the two, there are several clear contrasts. A gift may be imparted from without, and may remain separate and distinct. Fruit, however, is not an extraneous addition to a tree, but is the issue of the life of the tree and is produced from within. Fruit is a quality of character which is common to all, but not so with gifts. They are special, and are distributed as the Spirit wills. There is no several distribution of fruit. Scripture records that He gave some to be apostles, prophets, teachers, etc., but there is no parallel passage that He gave to some, joy, to some, peace. Gifts are in the plural, but the fruit is set forth in the singular number, for the fruit is the product of the whole man. [1]

That is a very definite statement of the difference. Fruit is the manifestation of the life of God in the soul of man. There is no

---

[1] J. Oswald Sanders, *The Holy Spirit of Promise* (Fort Washington, Pennsylvania: Christian Literature Crusade, n.d.), p. 114.

truer or better way of manifesting that we belong to God and that the Holy Spirit indwells us. Let the fruit be seen. Let our lives be like Christ. Let Him be seen in all our work. Let Jesus Christ be the sole objective of our labor and praise. And let us show forth His love not only with our lips but in our lives. "You will know them by their fruits," Christ said. "Do men gather grapes of thorns, or figs of thistles?" (Matt. 7:16). Ultimately, the only true evidence that we are servants of Jesus Christ is His image in us.

The call of Christ to His disciples was first of all "that they should be with him, and that he might send them forth to preach" (Mark 3:14); but there was something more than that in the Lord's ordination of the Twelve. Christ said: "I have chosen you, and ordained you, that you should go and bring forth fruit, and that your fruit should remain" (John 15:16). They were to be not only preachers; they were to be fruit-bearers. Out of their lives they were to radiate the loveliness of Christ. Through their testimony they were to manifest the graciousness of Christ. In all their life together, they were to show to one another the grace of their Lord Jesus Christ.

This is what is meant by the lovely little hymn that has come to be sung everywhere in the 1970s — "They'll Know We Are Christians by Our Love." How else will men know whose we are and whom we serve? Love is the key. Love is surrender to the will of God. We are known as children of God by the love we bear to all men and especially to the household of faith.

A service of love

"A new commandment I give to you, that you love one another; even as I have loved you, that you also love one another (John 13:34 RSV). This was repeated by Christ. "This is my commandment, that you love one another as I have loved you" (John 15: 12 RSV). The Kingdom of heaven is a Kingdom of love. By love we show the faith we hold. As Kagawa, that noble son of Japan, once wrote for the *Christian Century:*

> Like Christ who bore our sins upon the Cross,
> I, too, must bear my country's sins and dross;
> Land of my love! Thy sins are grievous to be borne,
> My head hangs low upon my form forlorn. [2]

---

[2] Toyohiko Kagawa, from his poem "To Tears."

It is to a service of love that the Holy Spirit leads us. This is what Paul was saying when he wrote to Rome and pleaded, "Now I beseech you, brethren, for the Lord Jesus Christ's sake, and for the love of the Spirit, that you strive together with me in your prayers to God for me" (Rom. 15:30). The love of the Spirit is the quality of love that is in the Holy Spirit. It means "the love the Spirit shows." That love calls us on to do service in the Kingdom of our Lord in the power of His everlasting love.

We cannot, of course, do this in our own strength. As we have so constantly noted, it is by the aid of the Holy Spirit that we can further the cause of Christ in His world. And His cause? The manifestation of a love divine, all loves excelling. When the Spirit of love fills our lives, then we see all men in a new way. We identify with others in a way that formerly we could not do. We learn to suffer with them when they suffer and to rejoice with them when they rejoice. We cannot encompass all the need of the whole world. We are wholly finite. But the Holy Spirit causes special objects of love and concern and tender responsibility to arise in the immediate foreground of our lives. These we love. On them we pour out part of the total cosmic love of God that fills the deep heavens around us. By the Holy Spirit we learn to relove those we have known best and come to take for granted. In the curriculum of the Spirit no one is taken for granted. The love of Jesus is shown through us by the Holy Spirit to that fragment of human need that faces us — you in your small corner, and I in mine.

The ministry of love

Why does the Holy Spirit do this? Because He is love. Because there is no greater work that we can do than manifest the love of God to men who do not know it, who perhaps have never heard it. We are sent out to preach, to proclaim, to teach the everlastingness of the love of God. For the great objective of the Holy Spirit is that they too may make the greatest of all discoveries, that they too may find God, that they too may learn that God is, may be found of Him, may learn the wonder of the Eternal breaking in upon them and making their lives to become living instruments of the eternal Life. God grieves over prodigal sons. We know that, for Jesus told us so. But wherever a heart has tasted the father-love, there again will that heart become a shepherd-heart yearning over sheep not having a shepherd, not knowing where the green pastures are, not even aware that there are green pastures anywhere.

This is why missions will never die where the Holy Spirit is moving men and women to see a world without the love of God. He will thrust them forth into the harvest fields and they will rejoice when they find that He has gone before them and prepared hearts to hear the tidings they bring. A true missionary is one whose heart has been broken by the things that break the heart of God and who has then in love, impelled by the Spirit of love, gone out to tell how "God so loved the world that he gave his only begotten Son, that whosoever believeth in him should not perish but have everlasting life" (John 3:16). A missionary is a love-intoxicated being. The call of the everlasting love is on him and he cannot say it nay. The decline of missionary interest and the loss of that holy concern which our fathers knew and which they called "concern for a world of lost souls," will also in our day mark a Church that has lost its first love and from which the candlestick has been removed. I know, of course, that there is a type of missionary work that can be carried forward in the energy of mere mind and money. I know also that there is Christian missionary activity inspired by a desire to show statistics of lives that have been brought under the wing of a church. Let that grow until the harvest. The Lord of life knows them that are His. But I am only thinking now of the real work of those who, like cosmic mothers, have heard the whisper of the eternal Love and have opened their hearts to let that mighty river of God flow through them to the deserts of the world. We need a revival of all such ministry and may God grant it soon.

This is the ministry of love to which the eternal Spirit draws us. Our Lord told His disciples that it was vital for them that He should leave them, for if He did not so, the Comforter would not come (John 16:7). That was a hard saying which they found difficult to understand. But when Pentecost came, they knew the reason why their Lord had departed. He had gone in order that He might be with them in a closer intimacy than ever before.

And when the Holy Spirit came, it was in order that Christ's ministry might be extended and deepened. The Spirit came to fulfill the ministry of Jesus, which was always a ministry of love. But can that ministry be fulfilled in lives that are unclean? When Christ came, a Body was prepared for Him. When the Spirit comes to dwell within the temple of our body, too often the temple looks like a desecrated shrine, unkempt, unclean. The Holy Spirit, however, is infinitely patient. He may be grieved by our questionable behavior: love is sensitive; it shrinks from rejection and any lack of trust. Yet the Holy Spirit waits to use us, waits to make us His instruments of mercy to men. How much longer can we deny Him His rightful place in our hearts?

Learning the art of self-emptying

If we wish to know the fullness of the Holy Spirit, we must be prepared to empty ourselves of everything that grieves Him. Literally, this means that we must learn to "die daily" to self, to "reckon [ourselves] to be dead indeed unto sin, but alive unto God" (Rom. 6:11).

When this happens, we abide in Him. "Hereby know we that we dwell in him, and he in us, because he hath given us of his Spirit. . . . God is love; and he that dwelleth in love dwelleth in God, and God in him. Herein is our love made perfect, that we may have boldness in the day of judgment: because as he is, so are we in this world. There is no fear in love; but perfect love casteth out fear: because fear hath torment. He that feareth is not made perfect in love" (1 John 4:13, 16-18). Do you notice two phrases that stand out plainly here? They are "hereby know we" and "herein is our love made perfect." Love is created and fulfilled in us by the Spirit of love, God the Holy Spirit. What is needed of us is that we present ourselves empty. When that happens, God fills us. It could be put in a very simple way like this: What I give, God takes. What God takes, He cleanses. What God cleanses, He fills. What God fills, He uses. What God uses, He uses more and more. For growth in the Kingdom of God is in accordance with our surrender to His will and acceptance of the divine provision He has made for us. If we are sincere in our motive of serving Christ, there is nothing He will not do. Miracle will become commonplace to us. We shall expect the unbelievable because God is with us. But all too often God has to wait almost our whole life long before we are ready for Him to act. And then we are often too tired or too burdened with years to do much for Him. Yet His promise remains: "I will restore to you the years that the locust has eaten" (Joel 2:25). This is the everlasting mercy. He gives us another chance of doing what we have failed to do.

Perhaps it is for this that you have been waiting. Open *now* your heart to the inflow of the love of the Spirit of God. He will take nothing from you except for your good. In place of what may be taken, He will give you the waters gushing from the rock. Your soul will be "like a watered garden, like a spring of water, whose waters fail not" (Isa. 58:11). God grant it for His glory and the reaching of multitudes with the bread of life.

11

The Holy Spirit and Conscience

*I say the truth in Christ, I lie not, my conscience also
bearing me witness in the Holy Spirit* (Romans 9:1).

CONSCIENCE OCCUPIES A LARGE PLACE in the New Testament. It
is very important that we note the work of the Holy Spirit in human conscience.

The subject is crucial, for the voice of conscience is well known.
"Trust that man in nothing who has not a conscience in everything." [1] Benjamin Franklin called a good conscience "a continual
Christmas." Shakespeare, as we might expect, being not only our
greatest dramatist but also a supreme psychologist, refers frequently
to conscience. "Conscience makes cowards of us all" mutters
Macbeth.

Or hear his Richard III:

> My conscience hath a thousand several tongues,
> And every tongue brings in a several tale,
> And every tale condemns me for a villain.

In another mood, he shows the opposite experience when conscience is clear:

> . . . I feel within me
> A peace above all earthly dignities;
> A still and quiet conscience.

---

[1] Laurence Sterne, *The Life and Opinions of Tristram Shandy, Gentlemen*,
first published in 1759 (New York: Odyssey Press), bk. 11, ch. 17.

Karl Barth goes so far as to say, "Conscience is the perfect interpreter of life."[2] From two thousand years earlier we can find corroboration of Barth's thought in the words of Polybius, a historian of the second century B.C.: "There is no witness so terrible, no accuser so dreadful, as the conscience that dwells within the heart of every man."[3] Clearly conscience is of great importance in any psychoanalysis of human personality. Equally clearly, the Holy Spirit must have some special relationship to man's conscience when He begins indwelling the temple of his body.

But we must be more specific for a moment. What is conscience? It has been variously explained by moralists, philosophers, theologians, and psychiatrists. In the history of ethics, it has been regarded as the rule of a divine power expressing itself in man's judgments. It is an innate sense of right and wrong and is found among the most primitive of tribes. Psychologists differ greatly in their views of conscience. For some theorists, conscience is merely the accumulated consciousness of the tribe or community in which a person lives — this community consciousness determines what will be regarded as the right or wrong thing to do. In this sense, there is nothing of any absolute essence in the voice of conscience. It is a condition largely imposed by the environment in which we are fated to be born, and as such is only a characteristic of a certain race or cultural group at a given time in world history.

Can we accept such a superficial definition of conscience? In classical Greek, the word is *syneidesis* — and quite definitely it means there a knowledge of right or wrong, especially in relation to God. It is in this sense that I understand it; and I believe this is the New Testament sense. When man fell, God left within him a remnant of his primary state, and conscience is the remains of God's image in man. It is the nearest approach to the divine within him; it is the guardian of the honor of God amid the ruins of the fall. The universal fact of this inner voice is all-important to our assessment of the essence of conscience. That universally there is such a voice — "a thousand several tongues" in Shakespeare's phrase — dividing between truth and error, right and wrong, is

---

[2] Karl Barth, *The Word of God and the Word of Man* (Edinburgh: T. and T. Clark, 1957), p. 243.

[3] Polybius, *History,* bk. XVIII, sec. 43.

inescapable. For this reason alone, I feel we must accept conscience as being an awareness of the divine and a consciousness of a divine law. Unless man is utterly depraved (a condition which happens only after many refusals to listen to the voice of conscience), we must accept that conscience is indeed an abiding rule of divine power within the judgment of man. This means that when we plead with a man to follow Christ, we have an ally already within that man's breast — his conscience. In every case, obedience to the voice of conscience will coincide with an acceptance of the revealed will of God in the Scriptures.

Now, as we have already said, the New Testament has much to say about conscience and all of it essential. John records the story of the woman taken in adultery and the action of our Lord. "He that is without sin among you, let him first cast a stone at her." Then He stooped and wrote on the ground. What happened? "They which heard it, being convicted by their own conscience, went out one by one, beginning at the eldest, even unto the last" (John 8:7-9). Even within the venomous breasts of these Pharisees there was a conscience that condemned them. They were *convicted* by their own conscience. Paul the theologian becomes Paul the anthropologist in Romans 2 when he writes of the Gentiles outside the pale of divine revelation. "When Gentiles who do not possess the law carry out the precepts of the law by the light of nature, . . . they display the effect of the law inscribed on their hearts. Their conscience is called as witness, and their own thoughts argue the case on either side, against them or even for them" (Rom. 2: 15, 16 NEB). Later on, while discussing the place of Israel in the sovereign plan of God, he says, "I am speaking the truth as a Christian, and my own conscience, enlightened by the Holy Spirit, assures me it is no lie" (Rom. 9:1 NEB). This statement implies Paul's recognition that discerning truth necessarily involves obeying the will of God and accepting the voice of conscience and the testimony of the Holy Spirit. Indeed, we cannot escape the impression that Paul is stating here that the testimony of our conscience and the inner voice of the Holy Spirit become, in the course of Christian maturity, one and the same. Conscience is thereby restored to its high position originally ordained of God. It becomes the very voice of God.

Therefore Paul urges Timothy to "fight gallantly, armed with faith and a good conscience"; and further, to ensure that all appointed as deacons should be "men who combine a clear conscience with a firm hold on the deep truths of our faith" (1 Tim. 1:19; 3:9 NEB). He can do so naturally, for he himself serves God "with a clear conscience" (2 Tim. 1:3 RSV) and consequently has great liberty in his constant prayers for him. His counsel to Titus is equally emphatic. "Don't hesitate to reprimand them sharply," he says, "for you want them to be sound and healthy Christians . . . Everything is wholesome to those who are themselves wholesome. . . . But nothing is wholesome to those who are themselves unwholesome and who have no faith in God — their very minds and consciences are diseased" (Titus 1:13-15 *Phillips*). This is what happens in a Christian when any sin is unconfessed and unrejected. The stain remains, the conscience is defiled, because the light given by both conscience and the Holy Spirit has been refused.

How the Holy Spirit works on our conscience

1. The Holy Spirit cleanses the conscience. This is a wonderful fact. The cleansing is needed by every believer.

No man comes to Christ without a warped and unclean conscience. This is inevitable. Living in sin means that conscience is defiled. The condition of men who abandon the faith is terrible. They "allow themselves to be spiritually seduced by teachings of demons, teachings given by men who are lying hypocrites, whose consciences are as dead as seared flesh" (1 Tim. 4:2 *Phillips*). The sole hope for men in such a state is to let God cleanse their conscience.

He does so. He is able to do so because Christ has died for sin. So the writer of Hebrews says in a passage of singular beauty and forcefulness: "For if the blood of bulls and of goats, and the ashes of an heifer sprinkling the unclean, sanctifieth to the purifying of the flesh; how much more shall the blood of Christ, who through the eternal Spirit offered himself without spot to God, cleanse your conscience from dead works to serve the living God?" (Heb. 9: 13, 14). There is no other solvent to the stain of sin. The blood of Christ, the Lamb of God, reaches the conscience, answers all its questions and allays its fears. Then the love of God floods the soul. Then there need be "no more *conscience* of sins" (Heb. 10:2). Our hearts are "sprinkled from an evil conscience" (Heb. 10:22).

This is the privilege of every child of God. The power of the blood of Jesus is mighty. Where all else fails, His blood can penetrate to the very heart of our conscience and deliver us from the guilt sense and feeling which a sin-laden conscience till then has created.

2. The Holy Spirit reveals God's holy law. He is the Spirit of truth and He brings the truth to shine upon the conscience. When He does so, the conscience becomes a fully informed conscience. God's law is perfect. As the perfection of the law of God shines on the conscience of man, there is evoked a response, a full agreement with the revelation of the will of God. This is very simple and direct, for, as Martin Luther loved to say, the Holy Spirit is the plainest teacher of all. That is true — when He is welcomed. We do not need again to rehearse the steps by which the Holy Spirit enters the life of a penitent. He comes when Christ is claimed as Savior and Lord. He comes to glorify the Son of God and He does so by allowing the truth of God, all of which centers in and upon Christ, to play upon the conscience with tremendous effect. The grace and truth that came by Jesus Christ are seen to be the very heart of the Gospel, and to all that the conscience says *Amen.*

Take an illustration. You have lied to a friend. Your conscience has condemned you. You are unhappy. You feel guilty and never more so than when you are in the company of that friend. But God's law is revealed to you. You read Ephesians 4:25: "Finish, then, with lying, and tell your neighbor the truth" *(Phillips).* The Holy Spirit brings this to your conscience, reinforces the truth that you have sinned, and brings you to the place where you are willing to admit to your friend what you have done. You go and confess and make restitution if that is necessary. What has happened? The Holy Spirit has attested God's law within you. You have obeyed. You have confessed. Your sin is forgiven. Your conscience, in the great words of Scripture "is cleansed from dead works." Joy is restored. Love reigns. You enter into the peace of God that passes all understanding. And it is all done by God the Holy Spirit working in you both "to will and to do of his good pleasure" (Phil. 2:13).

3. The Holy Spirit strengthens our conscience and deepens faith. It is essential that we walk with God. We must be content with nothing less than Paul's thrilling testimony: "Our rejoicing is this,

the testimony of our conscience, that in simplicity and godly sincerity . . . by the grace of God, we [behaved ourselves] in the world" (2 Cor. 1:12). What an amazing word we have here — "the testimony of our conscience"! Here is real cause for glorying in God. If God can do that, then anything is possible. The life of faith is possible, for the Holy Spirit, as we ask Him, will maintain a good conscience in us day by day. And we should be satisfied with nothing less than this. Go to the Westminster Abbey of the New Testament in Hebrews 11; read again the exploits of the men and women of faith; like Abel, they "had this testimony that [they] pleased God" (Heb. 11:5). We may be "strengthened with might by His Spirit in the inner man" and when this happens, Christ does indeed dwell in our hearts by faith and we are firmly "rooted and grounded in love" (Eph. 3:16, 17).

When we are experiencing this kind of life, we shall find ourselves more and more looking to the blood of Christ to keep on cleansing us daily, yea even moment by moment, from all sin. The blood that has sprinkled our conscience is mighty. It is the glory of highest heaven. We walk in the light with Him and, as we do, we discover that "the blood of Jesus Christ, [God's] Son, cleanseth us from all sin" (1 John 1:7).

A good conscience

We must be content with nothing less. God certainly wills that we should know only this — "love which springs from a clean heart, from *a good conscience,* and from faith that is genuine" (I Tim. 1:5 NEB).

There are side effects of failing to maintain a good conscience, as noted in 1 Timothy 1:19: "It was through spurning conscience that certain persons made shipwreck of their faith, among them Hymenaeus and Alexander" (NEB). Shipwreck through spurning conscience. Dangerous indeed are the effects of failing to maintain a good conscience, failing to walk in humility and faith with our Lord by His Holy Spirit. We may overcome this tendency only by the action of faith — as Paul says later in the same letter to Timothy: "Holding the mystery of the faith in a pure conscience" (1 Tim. 3:9). A pure conscience is maintained when we learn and keep our Lord's commandments. It is then that we prove the blessedness of abiding in Christ and in childlike faith claim all the promises of God. Can we do that if our conscience condemns us? Never!

We begin to see how large a place conscience takes in the life of sanctification. Perhaps you had not realized until now how great is the importance that God lays on our conscience. But it is essential that we know the truth. The answer of a good conscience, an untroubled conscience, a conscience that knows itself cleansed by the infinite purification that God alone can give and thus made sensitive to the slightest whisper of His will — all this is a hallmark of true holiness.

And let us never forget! It is by the Holy Spirit that this comes to pass. He gives us a strange sense of disquiet when we are in danger of sinning. He makes us hate sin as God hates sin. He makes us fear sin as we realize that sin will separate us from fellowship with God. As Charles Wesley sings,

> Ah give me, Lord, the tender heart
>   That trembles at the approach of sin;
> A godly fear of sin impart,
>   Implant, and root it deep within,
> That I may dread Thy gracious power,
> And never dare offend Thee more.

A godly fear of sin impart! God grant this prayer.

Maintaining a good conscience

"I say the truth in Christ, I lie not, my conscience bearing me witness in the Holy Spirit" (Rom. 9:1). To maintain a conscience void of offence is our high calling. The rules are simple but absolute. They are detailed and clear; but they are not for bargaining. Obedience is the test. To maintain a good conscience before God, I must:

1. Confess every sin as soon as it is recognized;
2. Be content with nothing less than walking in the light with Christ;
3. Be faithful to conscience as a lesser light and to the truth of the Spirit as a greater light;
4. Bow before every reproof of conscience;
5. Search out the sins that are peculiar to myself, allowing the Holy Spirit to reprove and condemn, confess them, and find forgiveness and cleansing in Jesus' blood;

6. Remember that only obedience — i.e., the acceptance of the laws of Jesus Christ — can demonstrate surrender to Him;

7. Walk the Calvary road; by that I mean, learn to die daily to all known sin;

8. Be willing to be taught and be certain that the Holy Spirit will teach;

9. Pray that the witness of my conscience and the witness of the Holy Spirit may increasingly become one;

10. Believe that I may serve God "unto all pleasing" as my conscience is in full and vigorous action.

The witness of conscience as to what you are doing will be met by the witness of the Holy Spirit as to what Christ is doing and will do. There is no debate possible when an enlightened conscience speaks. Keep your inner vision clear and you will surely possess "a conscience void of offence toward God, and toward men" (Acts 24:16).

12

The Holy Spirit and the Subconscious

Casting down imaginations, and every high thing that ex-
alteth itself against the knowledge of God, and bringing
into captivity every thought to the obedience of Christ
(2 Corinthians 10:5).

HOW HARD IT IS for us to know ourselves! We can be totally blind
to errors and abrasiveness in our walk, conversation, and character
while others see them very clearly. If our friends were utterly
honest with us, they would tell us. And if we were truly taught
by the Holy Spirit, we would accept their testimony as from Him
and make the alterations needed.

There is another area, however, on which I feel we must dwell
and this is hid not only from ourselves but from all who are near
to us and see us constantly. It is an area into which we must
bring the Holy Spirit in all His sovereignty and love if we are going
to know real cleansing in depth. I am thinking of what the psychologists call the realm of the "unconscious" or the "subconscious."
It is that part of our mental life that is not within the immediate
coverage of our conscious mind and from which we cannot always
summon at will the things we would wish. In these hidden byways
of our personality, the Spirit of God must be placed in control.
Otherwise, we may well suffer in a multitude of ways for things for
which God never meant us to suffer.

Paul speaks of "bringing into captivity every thought to the
obedience of Christ" (2 Cor. 10:5). Here is a tremendous theme.
What a conquest this will be if into our lives the blessed Holy
Spirit brings such victory that even our most secret thoughts —

134

the hidden motives that control so much of our actions — will be conformed to the will of Jesus Christ our Lord. Anything less than this is less than God has promised. We must claim all that God has promised. One of the things that He has promised to do is to cleanse us "thoroughly," that is, to leave no part of our total personality unwashed by the precious blood of our Redeemer. For this we pray in the hymn:

> Search me, O God, my actions try,
> And let my life appear
> As seen by Thine all-searching eye:
> To mine my ways make clear.
>
> Throw light into the darkened cells,
> Where passion reigns within;
> Quicken my conscience till it feels
> The loathsomeness of sin.
>
> Search all my thoughts, the secret springs,
> The motives that control;
> The chambers where polluted things
> Hold empire o'er my soul.
>
> Search, till Thy fiery glance has cast
> Its holy light through all,
> And I by grace am brought at last
> Before Thy face to fall.
>
> (Frank Bottome, 1823-1894)

This is a prayer that the whole realm of the subconscious will be purified.

A great deal of nonsense has been bandied about concerning the subconscious. Freudian disciples regularly teach that negative and undesirable behavior of anyone can be excused because it was determined by something in the past history either of himself or his parents. Viewed in this light, there is no need for a person to feel guilty about anything. Bad behavior must never be classified as blameworthy. We are products largely of our subconscious selves. And in the hidden realms of our subconscious, there are a thousand causative factors of illness, sickness, and disease. For none of them are we responsible. The superego or the conscience is largely the product of social mores and the opinion and motivations of others. Others are therefore responsible for socially unacceptable behavior.

We are not to be blamed for what we had no responsibility in creating. We become neurotic if the delicate fabric of our individuality is fractured through someone else foolishly jeopardizing our security. Transgressors are really victims of others' transgressions; e.g., most unwed mothers are victims of their parents' problems. This reduces man to an irresponsible pawn. The sense of sin in a true biblical sense is never admitted.

If such views were right and our sense of guilt one vast mistake, then we should be living today in a very happy society. Permissiveness is everywhere. So joy should be unconfined and happiness shared in by all. But this is not so. Divorce rates soar. Suicides multiply. Broken homes are increasing. Marijuana and contraceptives have not brought peace and joy to the girls on campus. Heroin and speed are lethal. Liquor is taking stronger grip on young and old and is still our number one addictive drug. The plain fact is that in spite of what Freud and others have said, sin is a fact; guilt is a fact; responsibility to the law of God is a fact. And buried deep in our subconscious, that vast depth of our personality over which we have so little control, there are forces of evil that can drive us to terrible sin.

This is clearly recognized in the Bible. As David says, "Behold, thou desirest truth in the inward parts. . . . Hide thy face from my sins and blot out all mine iniquities" (Ps. 51:6, 9). Ezekiel knew much about this, for he was taught of God. One day God came to him and said,

> Son of man, dig now in the wall: and when I had digged in the wall, behold a door.
> And he said to me, Go in, and behold the wicked abominations that they do here.
> So I went in and saw; and behold every form of creeping things and abominable beasts, and all the idols of the house of Israel, portrayed upon the wall round about.
> And there stood before them seventy men of the ancients of the house of Israel, and in the midst of them stood Jaazaniah the son of Shaphan, with every man his censer in his hand; and a thick cloud of incense went up.
> Then said he unto me, Son of man, hast thou seen what the ancients of the house of Israel do in the dark, every man in the chambers of his imagery? for they say, The Lord seeth us not; the Lord hath forsaken the earth (Ezek. 8:8-12).

This phrase "what they do in the dark" is terrifying in its implications. Its meaning is not strictly "the subconscious" of Freudian terminology; but it is nonetheless a fact that in hidden realms of our personality, the imagination can take over and we find ourselves involved in a thousand things that we would blush to mention to our neighbor, or even to our husband or wife. Jesus said, "Out of the heart proceed evil thoughts, murders, adulteries, fornications, thefts, false witness, blasphemies. These are the things which defile a man" (Matt. 15:19, 20). There is a principle of evil at the heart of us all. It is there, hidden down deep "in the dark" and if we are to walk with God, something must be done about it.

Help from above

This help is the ministry of the Holy Spirit. Into the depths of our subconscious selves He will move and begin to bring the cleansing, fiery flame of divine holiness. He will purify what is impure. He will give us purity of heart, that purity of heart that "sees God." He will wholly purify the temple of our bodies even as our Lord cleansed the temple of the moneychangers and the seats of them that sold doves, saying, "It is written: My house shall be called the house of prayer, but you have made it a den of thieves" (Matt. 21: 13). Cleansing is our supreme need. None but the Holy Spirit can bring to us the cleansing that will permit us to stand before a holy God.

> O how shall I, whose native sphere
>   Is dark, whose mind is dim,
> Before the Ineffable appear,
> And on my naked spirit bear,
>   That uncreated beam?
>
> There is a way for man to rise
>   To that sublime abode:
> An offering and a sacrifice,
> A Holy Spirit's energies,
>   An Advocate with God. [1]

Here is a way of cleansing and power. The Holy Spirit applies to the realm of our subconscious the blood of Christ and purifies us with the infinite purification of the blood of the cross. Thus, "though

---

[1] From "Eternal Light" by Thomas Binney (1798-1874).

[our] sins be as scarlet, they shall be as white as snow; though they be red like crimson, they shall be as wool" (Isa. 1:18).

What must we do to enjoy this kind of blessedness? What are disciplines we must face? It is a necessary question. A negro spiritual expresses it well:

> You won't get to heaven on a rocking chair,
> My Lord don't want any lazybones there. [2]

Viewed from the perspective of eternity, the most important need of the age is for men and women of Christian conviction to return from their Babylonian captivity and begin to glorify the name of God once more. Too long have we lingered on in a dim twilight of commitment. Far too long we have been content with much less than God's best. But the darkness of the hour is too black, God's sorrow is too great, man's need is too vast for us to be content with anything less than wholehearted obedience. We must rediscover what it means to walk with God "in holiness and purity all the days of our lives." To that divine life we must cling. In that abiding and energizing grace we are all made one. In that current we must bathe. For the heart of a truly Christian life is in its commitment, in its worship, and not in reflection and theory.

Throw light into the darkened cells

It is unfortunately true that much of our twentieth-century Christianity is of ersatz stock. It is not pure. The gentleness we show is not the wisdom that cometh from above which is "first pure, then peaceable, gentle, and easy to be entreated, full of mercy and good fruits, without partiality, and without hypocrisy" (Jas. 3:17). How often have we gone to another and said to him genuinely, "I'm sorry"? Yet, if we claim to be Christian and can continue being unforgiving, hard, and cold, we have not even begun to think about the meaning of the Christian oneness the world must be able to see. To effect this, the Holy Spirit must do His work of grace deep in our subconscious.

If this does not happen, God's purposes are thwarted in us. Then, rightly

---

[2] From the negro spiritual "You can talk about me as much as you please, I'll talk about you down on my knees."

Weep, weep for those
Who do the work of the Lord
With a high look and a proud heart.
Their voice is lifted up
In the streets, and their cry is heard.
The bruised reed they break
By their great strength, and the smoking flax
They trample.
Weep not for the quenched
(For their God will hear their cry
And the Lord will come to save them)
But weep, weep for the quenchers.

For when the Day of the Lord
Is come, and the vales sing
And the hills clap their hands
And the light shines
Then shall their eyes be opened
On a waste place,
Smouldering,
The smoke of the flax bitter
In their nostrils,
Their feet pierced
By broken reed-stems. . . .
Wood, hay, stubble,
And no grass springing,
And all the birds flown.

Weep, weep for those
Who have made a desert
In the name of the Lord. [3]

We must suffer the Holy One to fulfill all His holy purposes of
grace deep down in those hidden parts of our souls. By quiet, persistent practice we must turn all our being to the light. Mental
habits of divine orientation must be established. Even as you read
these words, begin now to offer yourselves wholly to God, not only
the things you know, but also that great, uncharted deep of your
unconscious self. Keep contact with God. Plead with Him that
His Spirit will teach you daily the hidden mysteries of heavenly love.
Pray for the beauty of the Lord to rest upon you. Let inward prayer
be your last act before you sleep and your first as you awake. Make

---

[3] Evangeline Paterson, "Lament" in *Deep Is the Rock* (Ilfracombe, England:
Arthur H. Stockwell Ltd., n.d.).

your bed an altar on which you give yourself over to the will of Him whose will is always perfect and complete, and demand in faith that "all that is not holy, all that is not true" will be cast away from you.

Allow the subconscious to work

One of the very remarkable things about our subconscious selves is a capacity for working even while we sleep. Have you ever experienced a problem being resolved for you while you slept? I have, times without number. I find it wise, if some problem appears intractable, to turn it over definitely to God and as often as not I will wake in the morning and see quite clearly what is the right thing to do. God Himself works in our souls, in their deepest depths, taking increasing control as we are progressively willing to be prepared for His wonder. But we must cease trying to be dictators, with God only the listener. We must learn the art of joyfully committing to Him the problems of our minds and hearts and wonderingly watching Him work them out. He is the Master who does all things well.

This applies also to dreams. Here is a realm in which the psychologists have loved to dabble. But I am prepared to counter every suggestion they make regarding dreams if they do not bring God into them. If we allow God to possess our total selves, the conscious and the subconscious, He will watch over our dreams. The presence of Christ will fill our bedroom as we fall asleep. The glory of Christ will filter through in glory with the morning light.

When we allow God to control the subconscious, He will prove Himself able to remind us of what is important. I could not number the times when, in situations that made it impossible to take note in writing of something important — a face, a name, a verbal promise — if I instantly committed the need to Him, He has brought these things to remembrance on time. I cannot think of a single instance when this has not proved true. Learn, then, to commit your way to Him. His promise is "The meek will he guide in judgment; and the meek will he teach his way" (Ps. 25:9).

The open secret of the subconscious

Thomas Kelly tells how he began to cultivate the life of the Holy Spirit within his subconscious self by simply saying over and over again through the day, "Thine only, Thine only."[4] Does that seem too absurd? Try it. I tell you it works.

In our deepest hearts, and at the moments when we are at our best, we really want to see God glorified and His Kingdom come among us. How shall this be? What can we, as very ordinary Christians, do to bring in the Day of the Lord? The answer I offer may not seem profound. I certainly appeal to no law of the subconscious, no occult knowledge possessed by only a few. The secret is a very open one that any wayfaring man can read. I once heard A. W. Tozer very quietly mention this but it seemed as though all eternity hung upon the words he spoke. The secret is simply the age-old counsel "Acquaint now thyself with [God]" (Job 22: 21). What is the result? Peace. The peace of God that passes all understanding. The peace that comes from an opened heaven and the ever-transforming view of God.

The God we seek must be the God of the ends of the earth, the God of glory, the God whom angel and archangel glorify. He is the God who sits upon the circle of the earth, bringing out His starry host by number and calling them all by their names through the greatness of His might. This means a bold repudiation of every false thing this fallen world has to offer and the closing in with the offer of mercy that the God and Father of our Lord and Savior Jesus Christ provides. As the majesty of God fills our vision, we shall find that the subconscious is gradually brought into a divine balance. Purity of heart is the great balancer of personality. Our whole being is filled with God when the Holy Spirit fills our subconscious selves. Our witnessing, singing, praising, praying, preaching, and writing all center around one mighty Person — Jesus Christ our Lord. Let us see to it that our lives bear witness only to Him.

Every thought captive to Christ

While we have stated that much nonsense has been bandied about in psychological circles regarding the subconscious, it remains a fact that where formerly *consciousness* was looked upon as the characteristic feature of psychic life, studies in depth psy-

---

[4] Thomas Kelly, *Testament of Devotion* (London: Hodder and Stoughton, 1943), p. 53.

chology in recent years have offered a very different picture. In fact, forces quite different from the rational faculties of knowledge and will are often in control. In their warfare with the higher levels of understanding and freedom, the lower forces of the instincts use a secret strategy; and while it may seem to the individual that the rational forces of his personality normally gain the victory, in actual fact the instinctive tendencies always gain their objective. They govern our conduct. They are the real motive force behind all our behavior. And this is done behind the screen of conscious life.

Now we are not writing a manual on the psychology of the subconscious. We are not studying psychoanalysis or depth psychology. What we are interested in is discovering the areas of our total personality over which it is necessary for the Holy Spirit to gain control if we are to know the freedom of the true children of God. There has been very strong reaction against Freudian concepts — rightly so, in many cases. Yet it is incontrovertible that hidden behind the facade we show our neighbors and friends, there is another self governed and controlled by libidos and desires. It is in this realm we encounter "high things that exalt themselves against the knowledge of God" (2 Cor. 10:5), and it is in this area that the victory has to be won if God is to be honored and exalted within us. Paul has just been speaking about the "weapons of our warfare" and has been stating that to the Christian there have been given "spiritual weapons not carnal." These spiritual weapons are able to cast down every evil imagination and to bring every thought into captivity to the mind of Christ. The phrase "casting down imaginations" is fascinating. Phillips translates, "Our battle is to bring down every deceptive fantasy and every imposing defence that men erect against the true knowledge of God." Now if it be true that in the hidden areas of our personalities there are tremendous forces that can control our spirits, then clearly these are the areas wherein the devil will operate with all his ingenuity and subtlety. It is within this realm that every thought must be "brought into captivity to the mind of Christ." It is at this sublevel of conscious knowledge that we must plead for the victory of God and the total overthrow of all that would assert itself against the kingdom, power, and glory of our Lord.

13

The Holy Spirit and Missionary Work

Now there were at Antioch, in the Church that was there,
prophets and teachers. . . . And as they ministered to the
Lord and fasted, the Holy Spirit said, Separate me Bar-
nabas and Saul for the work whereunto I have called
them. Then, when they had fasted and prayed, they laid
their hands on them, and sent them away. So they, being
sent forth by the Holy Spirit, went down to Seleucia
(Acts 13:1-4, translation mine).

THE CHURCH AT ANTIOCH was founded by the faithfulness of an
unknown missionary. We do not know to whom was given the
honor of first preaching Christ on the streets of Antioch. What we
do know is that the church at Antioch became one of the most
flourishing churches in apostolic times and that it was from Antioch
the first great missionary journey began.

Antioch was, of course, a very busy seaport and travellers from
all over the Mediterranean would at one time or another visit there.
It was a thriving city with great natural advantages and it is surprising that of all the letters by the apostles, none that was sent to
Antioch is preserved. The Church was founded in days of persecution. After the persecution that arose when Stephen was martyred,
there was a massive exodus to outposts of the Roman Empire;
and to Antioch came many Jews who in the beginning spoke about
Christ only to the Jews. But that soon changed. Men of Cyprus
and Cyrene followed hard on their heels and they spoke quite
openly to the Gentiles, telling them that Jesus Christ was Lord.
The result? A flourishing congregation of tremendous zeal. So
great indeed was the eagerness shown by the believers there that

143

tidings reached the elders at Jerusalem who sent forth Barnabas, a good man, full of the Holy Spirit and of faith. When he came, he recognized the unmistakable marks of genuine faith and exhorted the believers there that with purpose of heart they should remain faithful to the Lord. The whole story is told in Acts 11.

One thing that impressed Barnabas when he was there alone was that someone must be brought who could with consistency and diligence preach the truth of the Lord to them. He thought of Saul. Immediately, we read, he set off for Tarsus to look for Saul and found him there in his home city. He persuaded him to return with him to Antioch and we are told that "for a whole year they assembled themselves together and taught much people" (Acts 11:26).

The mark of a Christian

There must have been something altogether distinctive about the Christians in Antioch, for it was there that the Christians were first called by that name. They came to be known as bondslaves of Jesus Christ. They belonged to Him body and soul. This soon became very evident, and in the most natural way the name of Christ became associated with the followers of Christ.

What are the marks that identified the Christians? It would take a book in itself to recount them. But there was a spontaneity of life, a depth of joy running like a silver vein through their days, a carefreeness about financial security, a willingness to go wherever their Lord commanded them, an acceptance of suffering and testing as a sign of God's trust, and a set purpose of heart to cleave to Christ without hesitation or fear. The people of Antioch saw this. They noticed the difference in the men and women whom they had formerly known. So they coined a name for them. "The disciples were called Christians first in Antioch" (Acts 11:26). Here for the first time we see this wonderful name — Christian! Christians were marked persons, marked by the distinctive qualities of the Holy Spirit. Whenever they witnessed, they talked about the Christ; and gradually the name of Christ and that of Christian became inevitably latched together. As they walked through the city of Antioch, they carried with them the fragrance of One called the Christ. So they were called Christians — the servants of Christ, the bondslaves of Jesus Christ.

In this way the Holy Spirit was fulfilling His ministry. As we have so frequently seen, His great office is "to glorify Christ." This He was doing in the hearts and lives of the believers in Antioch. Of them it could clearly be said that men saw in them "none but Jesus only." It has been rightly said that the book we call the Acts of the Apostles could just as correctly have been called the Acts of the Holy Spirit. It is the work of the Spirit of God that we see in these Christians at Antioch. It is through the faith He had given them that they were able to believe in Christ. And it is through His power that we follow their steps in further pursuing missionary activities. Great missionary motives filled the minds of these Christians. Beyond the horizon, they thought of "those other sheep" of whom Christ had spoken, and they longed to preach the good news to them.

All this is the mark of a Christian. If any of these marks are lacking, then something fundamental has been dropped from the categories of the Christian life. Faith, hope, and love; patience, endurance, and peace; rest, serenity, and joy; a forgiving spirit and a contrite heart — and with all these things, a missionary mind. These were the hallmarks of the Christians at Antioch; and all of them we too should covet.

Mission — the goal of the Incarnation

When we think of the missionary task of the Church, we go naturally to the time of the birth of the Savior. Why was He born? He was born that He might die. He came in order to offer Himself up on the cross. He was born in Bethlehem, the "House of Bread," and He was given to be the Bread of Life to the whole wide world.

Bethlehem is therefore junction point for Calvary. Naturally yet miraculously Jesus came among us to fulfill the law of God and make it honorable, and then to offer Himself as a "ransom for our sins" (Matt. 20:28). But when He hung upon the cross, and as His eyelids closed in death, we verily believe that He saw His Church, the whole company of believers from every age, and out of every country, tribe, and nation. He saw them, coming from the North, the South, the East, the West and sitting down with Abraham and Isaac and Jacob in the Kingdom of His Father (Matt. 8:11). He saw His servants crossing land and sea, passing across mountain and plain, seeking the lost and bringing them to the eternal fold of their Lord. Mission would be the climax of His work in their hearts.

If this is true, it follows that no believer has truly fulfilled the commandment of his Lord if he is not committed to the missionary passion of the Church of Jesus Christ. He promised His servants that they would be His witnesses everywhere: "You shall receive power after the Holy Spirit is come upon you, and you will be witnesses unto me both in Jerusalem, and in all Judaea, and in Samaria, and unto the uttermost parts of the earth" (Acts 1:8). He sent them forth. "Go ye into all the world and preach the gospel" (Mark 16:15). Only in the fulfillment of this divine commission would they reveal themselves as Christians indeed. The one supreme aim of the gift of the Holy Spirit by the ascended Christ is to equip His disciples to be witnesses to the uttermost parts of the earth. The whole world is their parish. A whole Christ is their life. A total mission to all the world is the goal of the Incarnation and the crown of God's plan of redemption.

Missionaries incognito

It is wonderful to think of the establishing of the Church at Antioch. We do not know who was the first to make the great proclamation of salvation through the Savior's name on the streets of Antioch. The Church there was founded through the faithfulness of an unknown missionary. In this fact is a source of tremendous encouragement to many a missionary today.

We rightly extol the names of great servants of God who have built churches in lands across the seas. We honor a William Carey for his untiring labors. We celebrate an Adoniram Judson for the way in which he spent himself for the cause of the Gospel. There is good reason for praising God for the gift of a man like C. T. Studd and many others who left homes of cultured ease because the love of Christ constrained their hearts. "If Jesus Christ be God and died for me, then no sacrifice that I can make for Him is too great." [1] Right! In the great period of missionary expansion from the early decades of the nineteenth century there is a host of names that should be inscribed in letters of gold on all our hearts. We

---

[1] Norman Grubb, *C. T. Studd, Cricketer and Pioneer* (Worldwide Evangelization Crusade), p. 141.

honor them. We follow them insofar as they followed their Lord; or we *should* follow them.

Yet, while that is true, it is likewise true that the greatest number of missionaries are the men and women to whom the world has paid scant heed. They have given themselves and have not counted the cost. They have fought the good fight and not heeded the wounds. Known only to a few, in comparison with the total numbers of the universal Church, they live and die, their bodies are buried in peace, but otherwise they have no memorial. Known to the Lord are all their works for "His eye seeth every precious thing" (Job 28:10); but their work is unsung among the churches. They want it so. They are men and women who, having found the pearl of great price, want to give it away to others. This they have done. They would have it no other way.

The first person to cross the mighty Andes mountains on muleback was a woman. Do you know her name? Not many do! This is as she would wish it. I know a missionary who is now an invalid at home with heart trouble. Why? Because for many years she lived at an altitude of ten to eleven thousand feet in Bolivia and her heart was inevitably affected in the course of time. One could go on listing people who have given themselves for missionary goals and in the way have suffered mortal wounds. They are God's incognitos in the great army of His saints. And should these lines ever be read by some of you who are toiling faithfully through the years for your Master and your work never makes the headlines, what of it? He knows. If you are faithful to Him, fruit will grow that you never dreamed possible and some day you will stand in God's presence and say, "Behold, I and the children whom the Lord hath given me" (Isa. 8:18). One day a missionary in a Moslem land asked me: "When are you going to send us reinforcements?" I was dumb. In the good providence of God, reinforcements were sent. But not in time. Later, I stood beside her grave on the hill overlooking the city which she had loved and in which she had labored long, and I vowed again that I would spend myself in sending others out to the mission fields of the world.

The missionary heart

The missionary heart cannot be manufactured. It cannot be copied. It is part of the fruit of the Holy Spirit. Witnesses spend their strength in vain unless empowered by the Holy Spirit. The guidance of God in separating special people for particular assignments is a ministry or office of the Holy Spirit. He is the Spirit of mission. This emerges very clearly in the passage at the head of this chapter. Previously, we have had records of individuals preaching and doing missionary work — Philip ministered in Samaria and Peter at Caesarea. A significant difference is apparent in Antioch. Special men were still chosen, Saul and Barnabas, but they were chosen by the local congregation under the guidance of the Spirit of God. Acts 2 may naturally be considered the commission of the Church for home mission work; Acts 11 and 13 are of no less importance from the standpoint of the Church's task in foreign mission work.

"Separate me Barnabas and Saul." This is how the Holy Spirit spoke to the men who were God's leaders in the church at Antioch. They were all men of the missionary heart. Possibly many of them had come from other lands themselves and now the vision of the world's need and the growing compulsion of the Holy Spirit brooded upon them. They fasted and prayed. They asked for guidance and it was given. They were asked by God to give their best — Barnabas and Saul. They could have been asked for no greater gift than this. But, after fasting and praying again (one almost gets a sense that they doubted the guidance first given) they knew beyond the shadow of a doubt that it was the will of the Holy Spirit that these two men should go on a missionary journey — the first ever contemplated by the early church. It is to the everlasting credit of the leaders in Antioch that, once they were persuaded of the will of God, they offered no opposition. "Whate'er my God ordains is right." That was their motto and to that they gladly yielded themselves. God's will is best. Therefore they sent Paul and Barnabas forth. This is the missionary heart. It has quieted forever all the voices that would clamor for self-praise. It is poised and eager to go with the good news wherever the doors open wide. Its ear is pierced by the lance of the Holy Spirit so that the voice of God is heard unerringly. On their heart there lies the burden of a world in terrible need. To meet that need they go with God.

Now, to be in the place where the Voice speaks and the Spirit enables hearing is a sign that the hearers are "watching" and waiting on God, having known glad response to all His earlier promptings. Sad to tell, in many churches today there is no such preparation of heart, no watching and waiting, nothing therefore of voice or hearing.

A friend of mine spoke recently in a church and answered a host of questions at the end of his talk. Among the questions most frequently asked were ones like this: "Why do you take Christianity which is essentially a Western religion and ram it down the throats of other people, multitudes of them from the East, who have religions of their own?" He had the answers; but he told me that he felt little success in persuading the group before him that Christianity is for all and that the commandment resting on the Church is still the eternal commandment: "Go ye into all the world and preach the gospel to every creature" (Mark 16:15).

The heart that is taught by the Spirit of holiness will not be troubled by that kind of doubt. The Holy Spirit is the Spirit of mission. When He fills us and when He fills the Church with Himself, you can be very sure that His call is going to be heard and immediate response made.

> See o'er the world wide open doors inviting:
> Soldiers of Christ arise and enter in;
> Christians awake! Your forces all uniting,
> Send forth the gospel, break the chains of sin.
>
> (James McGranahan, 1840-1907)

The person with the missionary heart trembles before God because of the need of others who have not heard the name of Christ. An intolerable craving is in him, a clarion vibrates through him like a trumpet call. And the urge is to save men from perdition and bring them to the one fold and the one Shepherd.

The Church with fire at its heart

One of the great symbols of the Holy Spirit is fire. On the day of Pentecost cleft tongues of fire appeared to rest on every head. As churches were formed across different parts of Asia Minor, fire was kindled on the altar of worship when the Holy Spirit took control. We see this in Antioch. The elders there fasted and prayed. Theirs was a spirit of separation from the world around. They fasted. Self-sacrifice was rigidly practiced. They prayed together and they prayed alone. The result was that there were zeal and ardor, fervor and enthusiasm, passion and power in their response to the claim of the Holy Spirit. The leaders "laid their hands on them [and] sent them away" (Acts 13:3).

I know of no other way to produce Christian missionaries. You can shape them in a certain mold; but then the Spirit of fire is not there. The anointing and ordination of the pierced hand are needed. It is usually the case that when spiritual devotion fades, ritualism takes its place. Earth-kindled fires burn fiercely but they soon go out. God is dethroned when we turn to men for our inspiration. The sanctuary becomes a secularized club when we look to the world for power. Such congregations may produce learned and dedicated humanists. But if the fire of God is unknown, the missionary spirit is unknown.

John the Baptist spoke of the One to come and said, "He will baptize you with the Holy Spirit and with fire" (Matt. 3:11 RSV). Our Lord, speaking of His own ministry, said: "I came to cast fire on the earth" (Luke 12:49 RSV). The fire of the Holy Spirit is an intense zeal that possesses the believer with a passion for God. The love and holiness of God become our master passion. The spirit of cold obedience is driven from us and in its place there arises, phoenixlike from the ashes of our dead past, a flame of eager devotion. We find ourselves possessed with a fervent dedication to the will of the Father. His holy passion for righteousness and His consuming love for the lost souls of men burn up all the dross of base desire. We find ourselves illumined in mind, energized in every faculty, and impassioned with the spirit of the compassion we see in the good Samaritan.

The Christians at Antioch knew themselves to be saved "so as by fire" (1 Cor. 3:15). Men so ablaze are invincible. This is our greatest need today. We have everything except this fire of God. We have lovely sanctuaries, air-conditioned chapels, gorgeous vestments, great organs — but no fire. Here is the agony and the heartbreak of the Church today.

We are all His missionaries

It was a very personal statement of our Lord to the disciples before He ascended on high: "You shall be my witnesses." He singled them out; and as we watch them one by one, as reports are given of their various activities, it becomes clearer and clearer that He, the Holy Spirit, had a specific task for each of them to do. That was made clear to Ananias when he was sent by the Spirit to Saul in the street called Straight. "Go thy way, for he is a chosen vessel unto me, to bear my name before the Gentiles, and kings, and the children of Israel; for I will show him how great things he must suffer for my name's sake" (Acts 9:15, 16). Saul of Tarsus was singled out for a specific work. But in that he is no different from the rest of us. God has His chosen place for us to labor. He will make it very clear where He wants us to go and what He wants us to do. There is no jingoism, there is only joy, in the quatrain:

> I'll go where you want me to go, dear Lord,
> Over mountain, or plain, or sea:
> I'll do what you want me to do, dear Lord;
> I'll be what you want me to be.

It is very natural, therefore, that when the fire of God sweeps the altar of our hearts, we are given divine assurance of His perfect will. Fire is the best defense against corruption. When the disciples saw the Lord cleanse the temple, they remembered words from the Old Testament: "Zeal for thy house has consumed me" (Ps. 69: 9 RSV). If we would be safe, we must be likewise clothed with zeal as with a garment. It is fire that prevails.

Charles Wesley has few peers in expressing genuine Christian doctrine and truth. Hear him in this context:

> O Thou who camest from above,
>   The pure celestial fire to impart,
> Kindle a flame of sacred love,
>   On the mean altar of my heart.
>
> There let it for Thy glory burn
>   With inextinguishable blaze,
> And trembling to its source return
>   In humble prayer and fervent praise.

That is not all. There is still one note he wants to stress:

> Jesus, confirm my heart's desire
>   To work, and speak, and think for Thee;
> Still let me guard the holy fire,
>   And still stir up Thy gift in me.

(Charles Wesley, 1707-1788)

Yes indeed! We must stir up the holy fire. We must "stir up the gift of God" that is in us (2 Tim. 1:6). Destitute of fire, nothing counts. Nothing else really matters in the absence of the fire of God. How we may receive and retain it is the most urgent question of our time. One thing we know: it comes only with the gift of the Spirit of God, Himself the Spirit of fire. God alone can send the fire from Heaven. It is His Pentecostal gift.

Our Lord — God's missionary

The saying is old — but true: "God had only one Son and He made Him a missionary." He sent forth His Son to be the Savior of the world. And this wonderful ministry the Lord continues by the Holy Spirit. Barnabas and Saul were sent forth from Antioch "by the Holy Spirit." It was when it seemed right to the Holy Spirit and to the assembled leaders of the church that these two brothers were dispatched on a mission that was to open up Asia Minor to the Gospel. The Church had an important part to play. It still does. It is quite wrong for Christians to go forth at their own behest. I believe that the scriptural pattern is very clear. The Holy Spirit speaks to the Church concerning some member or members of the fellowship. The Spirit says, "I want him or them out in a particular area to do service for their Lord." The Church prays. The message is confirmed by signs and assurances. Then follows the missionary farewell. They go forth, sent by the Holy Spirit and by the Church. This is the New Testament pattern. This is a normal relation. We go under the commandment of the Holy Spirit. When He, the Spirit of fire, has burnt away all the things that hold us back from seeing the real glory of our Lord and hinder us from hearing His Word, then we are ready to act. We are ready to go.

We therefore follow our Lord when we go forth as His missionaries. We follow in the footprints of Him who was Himself a missionary, and in them we plant our own. "As my Father hath sent me, even so send I you" (John 20:21). This familiar verse, which has inspired one of the greatest missionary hymns ever written, is an undergirding and strong support for the missionary anywhere. Far from home and loved ones, often working with incompatible people, strained and drawn with tension and at times with fear, the missionary of Christ nonetheless knows that the Holy Spirit, who is the mighty power of God, is with him; the work is His and He will complete it.

Can you really imagine a Christian who is not a missionary at heart? It seems a plain contradiction in terms. Every true believer in Christ should be a director, a supporter, a helper, a contributor, and above all else a praying heart on behalf of those who have gone forth into the vineyard of the Lord.

He still sends disciples forth. It has been my joy through the years to send many forth in the name of the Lord. But it has been possible only because the Spirit of holiness and power, the Spirit of mission, was in it from the beginning. In the church where I am presently a minister, there is a plaque donated by the Manchurian Christians in remembrance of Jonathan Goforth. He was one of our fellowship. Clearly he was set apart to be God's missionary — and equally clearly was his wife Rosalind. Let me quote from their farewell.

> Of that wonderful farewell meeting words fail me to describe. On January 19, 1888, the old, historic church of Knox was filled to capacity. The gallery was crowded with students from Knox and other Colleges. Among those on the platform were the Hon. W. H. Howland, then Mayor of Toronto, one of the most honoured and loved Christian workers Toronto has ever known, Principal Caven and Professor McLaren of Knox College, Rev. Dr. Henry Martyn Parsons, Minister of Knox Church, and Goforth's closest friend, Rev. William Patterson.
>
> The train was due to leave at midnight from the Old Market Station half a mile distant from the Church. Soon after 11 o'clock, hundreds started for the station, Principal Caven with his professors and students.
>
> Toronto probably never witnessed such a scene as followed. The station platform became literally packed. Then hymn after hymn was sung. As the time drew near to start, Dr. Caven, standing under a light in the midst of the crowd, bared his head and led in prayer. A few minutes more and the train began to move. As it did, a great volume of voices joined in singing Onward Christian Soldiers — then they were gone. [2]

Is there any wonder that this sending forth was the harbinger of tremendous days of revival in Manchuria and elsewhere?

---

[2] Rosalind Goforth, *Goforth of China* (Grand Rapids: Zondervan Publishing House, 1937), pp. 65, 66.

Yes, the Holy Spirit is the Spirit of mission. It was "through the eternal Spirit" that our Lord was prepared, came, witnessed, died, and rose again. It is the same Holy Spirit who endows today.

God help the missionary who has not been truly "sent forth" by the Holy Spirit! The quicker he returns home, the better.

14

The Spirit of Guidance

As many as are led by the Spirit of God, they are the sons of God (Romans 8:14).

THERE IS NOTHING MORE wonderful than the guidance of God.

Twice in the twenty-third Psalm the phrase "He leadeth me" is found. The two instances are in very different contexts. One context is beside the still waters of rest where the surroundings are pastoral and all nature seems hushed to hear the voice of its Creator. The other is in the paths of righteousness, where life is militant and temptation is very near. Yet God leads His people wherever they may be. The Christian life is a guided life. "As many as are led by the Spirit of God, they are the sons of God" (Rom. 8:14). Divine guidance is a seal of divine sonship. God's methods vary, but His goals are always the same. "The Lord shall guide thee continually and satisfy thy soul in drought" (Isa. 58:11).

Some time ago I stood with a friend on the shore of the Gulf of Mexico and watched the sun drop like a ball of fire into the sea. It was warm and we lingered through the twilight into the darkness of the southern night. Presently the heavens above were sprinkled with stars, glowing and sparkling, and the silver arc of the moon traced a pathway to our feet across the waveless sea.

We talked about the majesty of God.

We agreed together that our generation was marked by a tragic loss of the sense of the majesty of God, His transcendence, His sovereignty; and that this loss lay like a blight across the life of the Church today.

155

The night grew darker. Presently my friend said, "The whole concept of the divine majesty has dropped from the popular religious mind; and in its place we have bred a race of self-confident worshipers."

As the mysterious wonder of the night deepened around us, I said, "Our generation hasn't time to look at a sky like that — if they had, they would think more of the majesty of God."

"True," he replied. "No time to be still and know that God is God."

We were silent for a while. Then he said, "But look at that sky — stars by the billions, galaxies now being reached by radio telescope that are at least five billion light years away. Yet every one of them moving in perfect synchronization, not one split second out of time.

"What's more," he added, "I believe that when we come to the end of life's road and we have a chance to look back on the finished story, we'll see that God has interwoven His purposes through our choosing more perfectly than He guides the stars in the heavens."

On the way home he told me some of the ways in which the Holy Spirit had guided his own life. There was no put-on in what he said, nothing pedantic. It was all very real. Instance after instance proved with greater emphasis the miraculous reality and intimacy of the guidance of the Holy Spirit. Finally he said: "I can only say that for me one of the greatest verses in the Bible is Romans 8:14: 'For as many as are led by the Spirit of God, they are the sons of God.'"

God's guidance is a tremendous reality. The God of the Bible is a guiding God. The people of God are a guided people. The whole Bible is the story of how God led His people from age to age. There is a kind of secret stairway down which the Holy Spirit comes and communicates His will to the glory of God. The guidance is always in accordance with the Word of God written and it is unmistakable when it comes. In big things and little things the Holy Spirit directs. The more we know of the communion of the Holy Spirit, the more easily do we see the guidance of our Lord in even the smallest detail. His divine designs are recognizable everywhere. His timing is a never-ending surprise. His providence is a daily delight. Gerhardt Tersteegen leads the Church in joyful praise when he sings,

> Let Him lead thee blindfold onwards,
> Love needs not to know;
> Children whom the Father leadeth
> Ask not where they go.
> Though the path be all unknown,
> Over moors and mountains lone.
>
> Give no heed to reason's questions —
> Let the blind man hold
> That the sun is but a fable
> Men believed of old.
> At the breast the babe will grow;
> Whence the milk, he need not know. [1]

"I will guide thee with mine eye" (Ps. 32:8). This is the Spirit's holy office.

Sanctification — the key to guidance

It is seldom noted that the Holy Spirit can lead only holy people. Immediately before that key passage in Romans we read, "If by the Spirit you put to death the deeds of the body you will live" (Rom. 8:13 RSV). This verse is followed by the verse on guidance and is introduced by the word "for." The guidance of the Holy Spirit is to holiness, as we have already seen. Now this means that He guides us to this mortifying or destroying of the deeds of the body. Those who are so led are manifestly the sons of God. The Holy Spirit is the Spirit of the holy life we see in Christ Jesus.

When we are led of the Holy Spirit, we are never led into sin. We are never led into the paths of the ungodly. We are never led into the haunts of evil men. No! He leads in the paths of righteousness, always. Thus, to be led by the Holy Spirit implies having committed ourselves to His loving direction. In guiding us to holiness, He gives us spiritual perception. Sometimes we are prone to speak of God's guidance merely in terms of the sphere in which He wants us to serve. It is more important, however, that we be the right kind of people for serving Him. It is to this holy estate that the blessed Holy Spirit leads. He is the Spirit of holiness and He can lead us into nothing else than the very holiness of God.

It is possible for an unholy mind, an unsanctified mind, to teach the truths of the Bible as far as they can be humanly learned.

---

[1] From "The Blessed Journey," published by James Nisbet & Co., London.

But there is a place to which the unsanctified mind cannot go. There are hidden recesses of the heart, deep down in the unseen laboratory of the human life, where the Holy Spirit dwells and where He teaches us right decisions and sanctified purposes. It is in this hidden laboratory of the inner life that the Holy Spirit takes up His residence and there He moves and impels us to become filled with the knowledge of God's will in all wisdom and spiritual understanding. Spiritual understanding comes only with the growth of the spiritual person. One who wishes to know the leading of God must yield himself completely — mind, heart, will, imagination, personality — to the dominion of the Holy Spirit; he must open up his life to the infilling of the Spirit of holiness and power.

Led by the Spirit into temptation

We are told by the evangelists that our Lord "was led by the Spirit into the wilderness to be tempted of the devil" (Luke 4:1). Mark uses an even stronger word. He says, "And immediately the Spirit driveth him into the wilderness; and he was there in the wilderness forty days, tempted of Satan" (Mark 1:12, 13). A saying like this appears at first sight almost incredible. Was Jesus really led by the Spirit to be tempted of the devil? Well, that is what the Bible says. Our Lord was guided into temptation. But by the same Spirit He was led back into Galilee with great power: He "returned in the power of the Spirit into Galilee" (Luke 4:14), and He began His ministry in Nazareth with the words "The Spirit of the Lord is upon me" (Luke 4:18).

The Christian is taught by the Holy Spirit that temptation is a necessary part of his spiritual education and growth in grace. He learns that assaults by the enemy of souls will be inescapable. Bitter temptation will be his lot. But temptation in itself is not sin. Our Lord was tempted yet He was "holy, harmless, undefiled, separate from sinners" (Heb. 7:26). He was tempted as none other has ever been, yet He did not sin. We must never forget this. Sin occurs only when there is true consent of our will with the allurement to sin. To be tempted to sin is not sin. To yield to temptation is sin.

When we are walking with the Spirit, we shall find that our temptations are ordered and even engineered by Him. It was in the timing of the Holy Spirit that Christ Jesus was led into the wilderness to be tempted by the devil. Leadership must be tested. Christ must be perfected through the sufferings of infinite temptations. This is what happened in the wilderness. But, as we have noted, He returned in the power of the Spirit. And so may we. This is the wonder of God's promise to us. "Sin shall not have dominion over you" (Rom. 6:14). "There hath no temptation taken you but such as is common to man; but God is faithful who will not suffer you to be tempted above that you are able, but will, with the temptation also make a way to escape, that you may be able to bear it" (1 Cor. 10:13). This promise we can claim. God is faithful. He will deliver us from the burning, fiery furnace. At times when we are being led by the Holy Spirit into temptation, it is good to know that our temptations are being superintended by Him. They are actually timed by the Holy Spirit. We can therefore pray confidently: "Lead us not into temptation without at the same time giving us a guarantee of complete deliverance from evil" (cf. Matt. 6:13).

Guidance through the holy Scriptures

"All scripture is given by inspiration of God" (2 Tim. 3:16). This statement is emphatic and unequivocal. In the Scriptures God speaks. They are His Word written. They were written as "holy men of God spoke as they were moved by the Holy Spirit" (2 Peter 1:21).

It is natural, therefore, that in the leading of God's child, the Holy Spirit will use the Scriptures He has Himself inspired. These Scriptures were given to train and direct God's people. They are still the principal instrument He uses. He will guide through circumstances, through the counsel of Christian friends, through the worship of a believing fellowship, through the inspired utterance of a preacher, and through many other ways. But the classic mode of direction is still through the holy Scriptures. Through the knowledge of the Word of God we are "guided" into righteousness, we are "led" into the full knowledge of the purposes of God. The Scriptures should therefore be read regularly, systematically, thoughtfully, reverently, expectantly, and humbly. We ought to be businesslike in our study. We should follow the rules that John Wycliffe gave his evangelists —

It shall greatly helpe ye
To understande scripture,
If thou marke,
Not only what is written or spoken,
But of whom,
And to whom,
With what words,
At what time,
Where,
And to what intent,
With what circumstances,
Considering what goeth before
And what followeth.

Guidance is given through the Scripture as the Spirit breathes upon the Word. Over all the great areas of life, the areas that deal with morality, truth, integrity, righteousness, compassion, and the like, God has spoken. He has revealed His will. There is no need for further instruction or revelation. He has given all we need to know. He has revealed all that is sinful and therefore forbidden: adultery, fornication, theft, evil-speaking, sexual indulgence of any kind, murder. And as we allow the Holy Spirit to teach us His will, we learn what is right in the sight of God and we do His bidding. It becomes our joy to follow the scriptural revelation and to permit God to cleanse our ways as we take heed to His most holy Word.

Guidance through closed and opened doors

In Paul's second missionary journey, it was apparently his intention to strike north and then go east through Asia Minor. There is no evidence at the beginning of that journey that he would land in Europe. But the doors to the north and the east were closed tightly. We are not told how. But he was sure that he was "forbidden" of the Holy Spirit to preach the Gospel there (Acts 16:6). "They assayed to go into Bithynia; but the Spirit suffered them not" (Acts 16:7). The only road that was left was to the west; so westward he went with his companions. Ultimately, he found himself at Troas, and Troas was the end of the road. Ahead, there was the blue Aegean sea. Can we doubt that he at times doubted the guidance he was being given? Surely he must have asked repeatedly for fresh assurance that he was on the right road. The assurance was given. There in Troas, Paul in a vision of the night saw a man of Macedonia crying to him and saying, "Come over into Macedonia and help us." What then? This is what we read: "So after he had seen the vision immediately we endeavoured to go into Macedonia *being absolutely certain* that the Lord had called us to preach the Gospel there" (Acts 16:10, translation mine). Little had he guessed it, but God was planning the opening of new continents to the Gospel. Great doors and effectual were opening before him. God was taking him across the great continental barriers of Asia and planting his feet firmly in the western world.

Closed doors? We hate them. We turn from them with distaste. We shrink from the failure that they proclaim. But God is able to take the closing of these doors and make them signposts to new worlds. Thus God performs His miracles still. We planned to go to college — and then mother fell ill. We wanted some special promotion — and another got it. We hoped to complete some deadline — but other things pressed in from which escape was impossible and the deadline passed without our winning through. There was an engagement we simply had to meet — but there was a breakdown of power on the subway and we missed our appointment completely. So it goes, year by year, day by day. Doors shut in our face and we wonder why.

For Paul the door closed in order that a greater might open. It was as simple as that. And is this not a fixed principle of the Christian life? "All things work together for good to them that love God" (Rom. 8:28). Surely this means that the unexpected barriers and the unwanted vetoes of our treasured plans are part of a merciful Providence leading us on to greater things. The Holy Spirit controls. We may not understand at the time. We may very likely question the guidance being given us. But God makes no mistakes. "The Lord alone did lead him, and there was no strange god with him" (Deut. 32:12). Even in the days when the shadows seem darkest, God by His Holy Spirit is silently planning in love for His own.

David Livingstone wanted to go to China. But the door was closed and he reached Africa instead. The China Island Mission was formed to evangelize many parts of China, and God most wonderfully blessed there. Then came the communists and the door to China has been closed for more than a generation. But while we sorrow over the silencing of faithful witnesses to the Gospel in that great land, we nonetheless marvel at what has happened since. Hundreds of missionaries have been released for service elsewhere and some of the greatest movements of revival are being seen today in lands to which these missionaries went.

> Deep in unfathomable mines
> Of never failing skill
> He treasures up His bright designs,
> And works His sovereign will.

Doors close that others may open — great and effectual doors. This is just another of the abounding surprises of God. He is always doing the unexpected.

> E'en the hour that darkest seemeth
> Will His changeless goodness prove;
> From the mist His brightness streameth:
> God is wisdom, God is love.

It may be that some door has closed on you today. Perhaps your dreams this very moment are lying a crumpled heap around you, and you are asking the everlasting question "Why?"

But be assured. God is not helpless when things seem out of control. His purposes will ripen fast, unfolding every hour. He is always worthy of trust. Leave it all quietly with Him.

The Holy Spirit and the upper room

Our Lord sent the disciples back to the upper room. There they prayed. They waited through ten long days. And on the fiftieth day after His resurrection they were gathered there. Then the Holy Spirit came. It was when they were praying that the Spirit came. Even as it was with our Lord. While He was being baptized by John, He was praying and the Holy Spirit descended like a dove. I feel that the Holy Spirit has loved the upper rooms of the saints of God since that day with a special love. Out from that upper room He led them. He gave them utterance in other tongues. He led and inspired their speech. He made them evangelists within an hour.

He still waits for us to pray. How shall we pray? In the name of Jesus, for He has said, "Whatsoever ye shall ask the Father in my name, he will give it to you" (John 16:23). We must ask believingly and without ceasing. We should pray alone and pray together. True prayer is always thanksgiving and should be offered with the utmost sincerity. We must pray with a forgiving spirit and must acquire the habit of submitting everything, every detail and desire, to the direction of the blessed Spirit. Prayer is not bound by circumstances. The men of faith we see in the Bible pray at all times and in all places — evening and morning and noonday — in the lions' den and on their bed at home, on a rooftop or in the temple, on the side of the mountain slopes or by the edge of the sea. Prayer is the Christian's vital breath, his native air. And it is as we pray that we are led by the Holy Spirit.

Prayer is revealed in meekness and David tells us in the 25th Psalm that God guides the meek with judgment. A true Christian delights to pray, for he is living in the presence of the God by whose love he has been redeemed. As he lives in the atmosphere of prayer, he lives also in the realm of daily miracle, for the God in whom he has come to believe is One who "alone doeth wondrous things."

This we too may learn, for there is no restriction in the school of Christ. There will be many barriers to be overcome if we set ourselves to see God in earnest, humble prayer; but we will learn, as William Cowper did, to push these aside:

> What various hindrances we meet
> In coming to the mercy seat!
> Yet he who knows the power of prayer,
> Longs greatly to be often there.

Learn to take your problems to God in prayer. The Holy Spirit will teach you. Learn to cast all your care on Him as you pray. Learn too the holy art of committing everything to Him in prayer.

> For what is prayer when it is prayer indeed?
> The mighty utterance of a mighty need.
> That man is praying who doth press with might
> Out of his darkness into God's own light.
>
> (author unknown)

Thus you will be guided by the Holy Spirit to pray. As you pray, you will find Him leading you deeper and deeper still into the "more and more" of the love of Jesus Christ.

Back to the beginning

This takes us right back to sanctification, the secret of guidance. The leading of the Spirit is inseparable from the sanctifying of the

Spirit. Begin at the beginning. Obey the commandments of God as you know them. "If any man's will is to do his will," said Jesus, "he shall know whether the teaching is from God . . ." (John 7: 17 RSV). Obey. Follow. Believe. Give up every sin. Give up all to the voice of conscience. Mortify the deeds of the body. Reckon yourself dead to sin and alive to God. As His child, place yourself completely at the disposal of the Spirit of God. Then the Holy Spirit Himself, this same Spirit by whom Christ offered Himself to God, this same Spirit to whom you yield your members, will bear witness with you that you are born of God. With a joy and power hitherto unknown, you will be assured by the Holy Spirit of God that you enjoy all the privileges of a child within the redeemed family of God.

Could anything be more wonderful? No! Let the Holy Spirit then control you wholly. You will enter joyfully into the life of the sanctified. You will also gratefully and with undying praise know His leading in God's perfect way.

15

Walking in the Spirit

This I say then, Walk in the Spirit and you shall not fulfil the lust of the flesh (Galatians 5:16).

THE CHRISTIAN WALK is one of the most frequent themes of discussion in the New Testament. "We are his workmanship, created in Christ Jesus unto good works, which God hath before ordained that we should walk in them" (Eph. 2:10). When Paul prayed for the Christians in Ephesus, his petition was "I therefore, the prisoner of the Lord Jesus, beseech you that you walk worthy of the vocation wherewith you are called" (Eph. 4:1). In the great prayer for the Colossian Christians there occurs what many have thought to be the supreme petition ever offered by the apostle: "For this cause we also, since the day we heard it, do not cease to pray for you, and to desire that you might be filled with the knowledge of his will in all wisdom and spiritual understanding; that you might walk worthy of the Lord unto all pleasing, being fruitful in every good work, and increasing in the knowledge of God" (Col. 1:9, 10). The emphasis is on the "walk" of the Christian. The verb is a very direct one meaning exactly what it implies — "walking around." It is this Greek word, *peripateo,* that is used most frequently, and indeed is used in the verse that is at the head of this chapter. It is one of the most common Greek words for "walking," though it is interesting to note that it subsequently came to be used for "living."

That in itself is not surprising. For "walking" is a natural corollary of "living." "Walking in the Spirit' and "living in the Spirit" are really the same thing. The activeness of "walking" is certainly implied by the apostle when he uses it in this connection. But the real meaning is to have one's conduct, conversation, and character molded by the indwelling life of the Holy Spirit. When we "walk in the Spirit," we are in a place of security, safety, and scope. The "walk" of the believer is his life, his liberty, his activity, his creativeness, and his guidance under the controlling power of the Holy Spirit.

The liberty of the Spirit

The Christian walks in freedom. "Where the Spirit of the Lord is, there is liberty" (2 Cor. 3:17). Our Lord says in John 8:36: "If the Son therefore shall make you free, you shall be free indeed." Freedom is one of the great emphases of the New Testament. "Stand fast therefore in the liberty wherewith Christ hath made us free, and be not entangled again with the yoke of bondage" (Gal. 5:1). The salvation that we receive in Christ gives us freedom from the power of Satan (Mark 3:27; John 12:31-36), freedom from the dominion of sin (Rom. 6:17), freedom from the law (Gal. 4:21-31), and freedom from the fear of death (Heb. 2: 15). To be a member of the redeemed family of God means that we are introduced into the freedom of God's family — or, into God's family of the free. Creation itself will be set free from its bondage to decay, Paul says, and will obtain "the glorious liberty of the children of God" (Rom. 8:21). "The law of the Spirit of life in Christ Jesus" has freed us from "the law of sin and death" (Rom. 8:2).

This can be viewed from different angles. In one sense we are made free from the power of sin; sin is dethroned; our deepest desires come to be to serve, love, honor, and obey the Lord our God. In another sense we are made free from the outward compulsions of the law — that is, we are no longer bound to obey the law of God in all its inexorable demands. We never could meet the demands of that law at any time. But we were bound by them, until we saw Christ who fulfilled all the law of God. Now, having seen the sin-bearer Savior Christ, we are delivered from the bondage to the law that unforgiven sinners always labor under. When we set these two great realities together, we see that by freeing us from the condemnation of the law and by freeing us also from the power of inward, inbred sin, Christ is straightening out the twists and distortions of our nature, those marks of Satan that are so discernible in the life of the unregenerate. We know the freedom of the regenerate (John 3:3ff.); we rejoice in the freedom of the resurrection life (Col. 2:12-13); we share the new creation in Christ (2 Cor. 5:17); and we are renewed in the spirit of our mind by the Holy Spirit who indwells us (Titus 3:5).

The liberty is distinguished, however, in one very exceptional way. George Matheson describes it for us:

> Make me a captive, Lord,
> And then I shall be free;
> Force me to render up my sword
> And I shall conqueror be;
> I sink in life's alarms,
> When by myself I stand;
> Imprison me within Thine arms
> And strong shall I withstand.

In other words, this freedom is the freedom of the bound. Paradox? Not really. It is just the only way in which the Christian life can be described. It is like two lovers who feel absolutely free in each other's love and company. They know themselves to be one with each other. But they know also that this is possible only because they are "bound" by cords of love. They would lay down their lives for each other. And the freedom of the Christian is the freedom of the servant who acknowledges a master to whom he has committed himself totally. Paul speaks of himself regularly as a *doulos* — a "bond-slave" — of Jesus Christ. He is Christ's freeman. Yet he is bound to Him. He would have no other tie than this. He wants to be His servant forever.

Christian freedom in the Holy Spirit is marked by the same dedication as the Spirit's dedication to glorifying the Son of God. Without this kind of complete commitment, there is no real unity in Christ or with Christ. Freely, wholeheartedly, voluntarily, the Christian gives himself over to the enslavement of the Son of God and rejoices in the fetters that bind him to such a glorious One. To be free in Christ means that you are bound to everything to which Christ is bound — to righteousness, to holiness, to love, to service, to self-forgetfulness. So the Christian is a freeman, yet bound. To quote Matheson again:

> My will is not mine own,
> Till Thou hast made it Thine;
> If it would reach a monarch's throne,
> It must its crown resign.
> It only stands unbent,
> Amid life's crashing strife,
> When on Thy bosom it has lean't
> And found in Thee its life.

This does not mean that we are free to do what we like; it means that for the first time in our lives we are free to do what we ought. That is a very different thing. We reveal our love for Christ by doing His will. We are those who live henceforth no longer "unto themselves, but unto him who died for them and rose again" (2 Cor. 5:15).

The Christ we serve is the giver of freedom. "If the Son therefore shall make you free, you will be free indeed" (John 8:36). We maintain our freedom as we serve Him only. But we must be very sure that the Christ we serve is indeed the Christ of the Bible. We have heard preachers speak of Christ as One who will help in any or every circumstance. He will help the big-league pitcher to get the right curve on the ball when he is in a clutch situation. He is One who will help a young Christian at school to win the high jump if only sufficient intercession is made for this kind of success. He is One, we have heard time and again, who is able to help a business man pull off a big deal even though it meant he undermined a competitor by undercutting his bid for a contract and thereby procured the discomfiture of someone else. Sometimes one has heard testimonies of the "God runs my business" variety that have the appearance of giving license to anything under-the-counter if only the desired objective is secured.

Against all that kind of petty thinking about Christ we must steel ourselves. We serve no utilitarian Christ. He is a very present aid in the time of trouble to those who are His own. That we never deny. But to say that we manipulate our Lord is to affirm the impossible. This is not Christian freedom. This is worldly folly.

Legalism or obedience

There is a form of "walking in the Spirit" that very closely resembles a type of slavery. Certain acts become essential. Certain religious routines become for us a condition of standing well before

God. In other words, we use our means of grace either as status symbols or as assembly lines for creating a good standing in the sight of God.

This is pure legalism. It is a reversal to the bondage of the law. Where Christ has redeemed us from the curse and bondage of the law, we slip back too easily into it by feeling that there are certain things we must do, certain rituals we must perform, certain services we must carry out. In this way we lose the true freedom that is in Christ and which He has given us lavishly.

It is very pathetic to see a Christian to whom all the fullness of Christ has been given by the Holy Spirit trying to increase that by so-called works of merit. You find it in almost every level of Christian experience. The Christian minister determines he will cover so many visits in a week. The Christian evangelist feels he must show his ability by producing so many decisions for Christ in every campaign or crusade he conducts. The Christian song leader is unsatisfied if he cannot make a congregation sing louder than they have ever sung before. The Christian Sunday school teacher tries to outdo others in making his class grow and will use any means to achieve his end. The Christian journalist apes the standards of the popular magazines, even descending to levels that the worldling would scarcely countenance. The Christian business-man must be seen in the forefront of action in community affairs, and that not for the glory of his Lord, but to be seen of men.

All this is legalism. It binds. The Holy Spirit does not come to lead us into this kind of life. He comes to set us free. He comes to clothe us with the freedom of the children of light. He gives us a freedom that is joy and full of happiness. He gives us freedom that is unrestrained and unconfined because it is unclouded with subtle selfishness. This is the mission of the Holy Spirit and we may all know the power of that freedom. We must guard it. We must "stand fast" in it. We must refuse to become entangled again with the poverty-stricken elements of the world.

Over against this legalism is the spirit of true obedience. Obedience is freedom. When we obey our Lord we are walking with Him in perfect liberty. It is only in the pathway of obedience that the truly active co-operation of the Holy Spirit is discerned and experienced.

So many Christians are bound in legalistic fetters because they have refused to accept the commandments of their Lord. They are not obedient to the heavenly vision. They resist, they grieve, they quench the Spirit by whom they are sealed. There is only one true answer to this spirit of legalistic bondage. It is a full and glad obedience to the claims of the eternal Christ. One of the German mystics once wrote, "There are plenty who will follow our Lord halfway, but not the other half. They will give up possessions, friends and honors, but it touches them too closely to disown themselves." Is this where the problem lies with the Church today? Are we unwilling to say one great NO to ourselves? Well, let us heed the wise words of Thomas Kelly:

> It is the astonishing life which is willing to follow Him the other half, sincerely to disown itself, this life which intends complete obedience, without any reservations, that I would propose to you in all humility, in all boldness, in all seriousness; I mean this literally, utterly, completely, and I mean it for you and for me — commit your lives in unreserved obedience to Him. [1]

There is a revolutionary explosiveness in this kind of life. For when God finds a man who is willing to obey Him completely — an Abraham, for example — He breaks through that life in amazing miracle. World-renewing forces of divine power are released. History changes.

This dynamo of life is utterly different from what we generally think of as the religious life. Perhaps the word "religion" itself has become a hindrance and drag on our minds. It may be that we are unwilling to let go the mudholes of our own dire selfishness. And because of this we do not experience the thrilling wonder of God's miracles. Our church assemblies are full of respectability. But there are few who show the marks of the good Samaritan. There are too many among us like the elder brother who was "angry and would not go in" (Luke 15:28). But when God moves us to our depths, then there begins a passionate quest for the whole bread of life. This is what is rightly called an imperative God-hunger; and with it you will always find a life that is astonishing in its completeness. The prophets and apostles knew nothing else but this quality of life; and they summon us to Him who alone

---

[1] Thomas Kelly, *The Testament of Devotion* (London: Hodder and Stoughton, 1943), p. 47.

can recreate us in the image of God the All-lovely, and thereby begin to send currents of reviving power into this tottering western culture and renew us as a fellowship of creative, heaven-led souls.

Liberty or unlimited license

Jude warns his readers against perverting "the grace of God into licentiousness" (v. 4 RSV). If we are to "walk in the Spirit," we must learn what pitfalls are around us on every hand. Sinful self-indulgence is all too often found in Christians. Victorious life in Christ is impossible unless we yield our members as "instruments of righteousness unto God" (Rom. 6:13). Though dethroned in us, sin is still with us; but sin shall not have dominion over those who are upheld through the renewing and quickening power of the Holy Spirit. Never forget that God's promise to His child is that "the law of the Spirit of life in Christ Jesus has made [him] free from the law of sin and death" (Rom. 8:2).

For illustration, take marriage. Marriage is a holy state of life which God instituted in the beginning. Now this law is unalterable. It is a divine absolute. A Christian will seek God's will in this. He will believe that the Holy Spirit can keep him pure from sinful acts such as extramarital sex. There is no question about this being the will of God if we take the Bible as our guide. In marriage we see that the basic unit of creation is man-woman in a God-given unity. If we see only the sanction of social custom, the lure of financial gain, or any other kind of pragmatic convenience in this holy institution of marriage, then we are missing God's clearest teaching. If you follow this pragmatism through to its logical conclusion, you find yourself in the company of Dr. Robinson, Bishop of Woolwich. In *Honest to God* he avers that there is no unalterable image of Jesus, that therefore Christian ethics can be changed to situational ethics.[2] As a result of this, Dr. Robinson had little difficulty with such views as those of D. H. Lawrence, set forth in his *Lady Chatterley's Lover*. Lawrence believed in natural forms of evolution and change from the absolute rigidity of an unchanging ethic. But that is not what God tells us in the Bible.

Fidelity within the marriage bond is the unchanging Christian ethic. This is biblical teaching that is constantly reiterated by

---

[2] John A. Robinson, *Honest to God* (Philadelphia: Westminster Press, 1963).

prophets and apostles. The fidelity of which we speak is exemplified best by the love Christ has for His Church. For her He died. His love is changeless as the everlasting hills. His love remains the same. The marriage bond is a human and earthly symbol of the relationship between Christ and His Church. Luther in *Table Talk* says, "There is no more lovely, friendly and charming relationship, communion or company, than a good marriage."

When we "walk in the Spirit" we tenaciously hold to this truth of revelation. We refuse to see any other taking the place of the one to whom we are joined in the most sacred of bonds. And this is liberty. There is no greater freedom of personality than that found by the Christian man and maiden who love and know their love is returned, that love is deepening day by day, and that their love for each other is blessed and owned of God their Father. In such unions, there is no place for license. Licentiousness would destroy all that is lovely and good and true in the Christian home. There-fore we "walk in the Spirit" — we refuse to indulge and "fulfil the lust of the flesh" (Gal. 5:16). The new morality has no place in such areas of life. Christ by His Spirit guides us "in the paths of righteousness" and we want nothing more.

A renewed mind in conflict with evil

"Be not conformed to this world, but be ye transformed by the renewing of your mind, that you may prove what is that good, and acceptable, and perfect will of God" (Rom. 12:2). When by the grace of God we find our minds being renewed by the Holy Spirit, then we experience a new understanding of the nature of evil and how vital it is that we combat it seriously. Evil is all around us. It is within us, too, as we have so frequently noted. The world, the flesh, and the devil will contest every forward step we take. But a renewed mind, being created in righteousness and true holiness will tenaciously and toughly war against all that God hates.

Satan will never cease opposing us. He is very cunning. Pride is always at our elbow wanting to assert itself within us. If we are to overcome, we must continually put on "the whole armour of God" and then listen to the counsel of John in his first letter (1 John 2: 15-17 *Phillips*):

Never give your hearts to this world or to any of the things in it. A man cannot love the Father and love the world at the same time. For the whole world system, based as it is on men's primitive desires, their greedy ambitions, and the glamour of all that they think splendid, is not derived from the Father at all, but from the world itself. The world and all its passionate desires will one day disappear. But the man who is following God's will is part of the permanent and cannot die.

We are summoned to "mortify" or to "crucify" the flesh (Rom. 8:13; Gal. 5:24). In *The Spirit Within You,* a wonderful little book on the Holy Spirit, created by the joint writing of two Anglican clergymen, A. M. Stibbs and J. I. Packer, there is a paragraph that expresses tersely but sternly the type of warfare we face.

Self-denial can hurt, and the temptation to draw back from the ultimate in discipleship is strong. Moreover, the temptation recurs; we never say goodbye to it till we leave this world. If it ceases in one form it starts up in another. Thus the Christian constantly finds himself opposed, distracted, enervated, assaulted as he seeks to go forward with God. The Christian life has its low moments as well as its high spots. It is conventional in many quarters today to play down this grimmer side of Christian living, but such a policy is the reverse of wise. The man who gets into the way of assuming, or pretending, that his foes are not there is asking to be ambushed; sooner or later he will find that his spiritual life has become a second Glencoe. The only man who is safe is he who knows his enemy, and is able to detect his approach and to counterattack. [3]

One of the greatest safeguards is worship within a renewed fellowship of Spirit-filled believers. The Holy Spirit comes to give us this joy. We share Christ's life with many others and are strengthened thereby. The enjoyment of our spiritual heritage is never full if we do not know we are intended to live and function in active fellowship, not only with God, but with our brothers and sisters in Christ. Life in the Spirit is known at its most glorious when it is life shared daily with others of like precious faith.

Walking in the Holy Spirit is living a life of glory, joy, and praise — a life transparent in its beauty. And, best of all, it is the very life of Christ Himself which He gives to us by the Holy Spirit. By the Holy Spirit we are baptized into one body — Christ! In all

---

[3] A. M. Stibbs and J. I. Packer, *The Spirit Within You* (London: Hodder and Stoughton, 1967), p. 56.

the trials we face in life, Christ is with us to comfort and uphold. Has He not said, "I will never leave you nor forsake you"? In His strength we overcome.

> I cannot do it alone;
>   The waves run dark and high,
>   And the storm beats loud and nigh,
>   While the stars go out in the sky;
> But I know that we two shall win in the end,
>   Jesus and I.
>
> Coward and wayward and weak,
>   I change with the changing sky;
>   Today, so eager and bright,
>   Tomorrow too weak to try;
> But He never gives in, so we two shall win,
>   Jesus and I.

(anonymous)

16

The Spirit of Prayer

> *The Spirit of God not only maintains this hope within us,*
> *but helps us in our present limitations. For example, we*
> *do not know how to pray worthily as sons of God, but*
> *his Spirit within us is actually praying for us in those*
> *agonizing longings which never find words. And God,*
> *who knows the heart's secrets understands, of course,*
> *the Spirit's intention as he prays for those who love God*
> (Romans 8:26, 27 *Phillips*).

THE HOLY SPIRIT has many offices. Of them all, possibly the most remarkable is the work He executes as the Spirit of prayer.

We pray to the Father who gives to all men liberally and never reproaches (James 1:5). We pray through the Son. He taught, "If you will ask anything in my name, I will do it" (John 14:14). And we have further the Holy Spirit in whom we pray — "praying always with all prayer and supplication in the Spirit, and watching thereunto with all perseverance and supplication for all saints" (Eph. 6:18). The Holy Spirit draws us to prayer. As He does so, He is praying in us with such inexpressible longing that even God the Father has to search our hearts to know what is the mind of the Spirit. There is mystery here, of course, but we cannot deny the plain letter of Scripture. Charles Wesley speaks of this in his own characteristic manner:

> He is the Advocate on high;
> Thou art the Advocate within;
> Oh, speak the truth, and make reply,
> To every argument of sin.

What we must infer is that even as Jesus Christ is our great High Priest who intercedes on the throne on high for His servants, so the Holy Spirit intercedes within the temple of the body of the believer and this intercession of the Spirit *within* is as divine and effective as is the intercession of the Son *above*.

Prayer is work. A brief review of the activity of the Holy Spirit from the first of time will show how mighty His operations have been. "The earth was without form, and void; and darkness was upon the face of the deep. And the Spirit of God moved upon the face of the waters" (Gen. 1:2). Through the energizing activity of the Holy Spirit life and light and fruitfulness came to the dark chaos of the primeval deep. When man was formed, God "breathed into his nostrils the breath of life; and man became a living soul" (Gen. 2:7). Again, it is the mighty Spirit of God who works this miracle of creating man in the divine image. Similarly, when our Lord came to earth, a body was prepared for Him within the womb of the Virgin Mary. How? "The Holy Spirit shall come upon thee, and the power of the Highest shall overshadow thee; therefore also that holy thing which shall be born of thee shall be called the Son of God" (Luke 1:35). Our Lord was "declared to be the Son of God with power, according to the Spirit of holiness, by the resurrection from the dead" (Rom. 1:4). Even so shall our mortal bodies be quickened in the day of resurrection of the dead — by the Holy Spirit.

We must never confuse the offices of the Father, the Son, and the Holy Spirit. Equal in power and Godhead, each Person of the blessed Trinity has a specific ministry to fulfill. God the Father is the Father almighty, Author of all. God the Son reveals the Father; in Him the perfect image of God is revealed, brought near to us, made manifest; He is the form of God and He fulfills the perfect will of God in the redemption of the world. God the Holy Spirit is the indwelling God, inhabiting the temple of our bodies when we believe in God through Jesus Christ. What the Father has purposed, and what the Son has procured, can be appropriated only through the activity and power of the Holy Spirit.

In intercessory prayer, then, the Father is the Giver, the Son is the Teacher, and the Holy Spirit is the Helper. As we go to prayer, the first thing we should do is with bowed head and uplifted heart call on the Holy Spirit to aid us as we pray. Remember, "the Spirit helps us in our weakness" (Rom. 8:26 RSV). Have we a greater weakness than our prayer life demonstrates? If we are honest with ourselves, I think we shall all immediately say that prayerlessness is one of our greatest sins. But the Holy Spirit helps. In Paul's first letter to the church in Corinth, he says, "Eye has not seen, nor ear heard, neither have entered into the heart of man the things that God has prepared for them that love him. But God has revealed them unto us by his Spirit; for the Spirit searches all things, yea the deep things of God. For what man knows the things of a man, save the spirit of man which is in him? Even so the things of God knows no man, but the Spirit of God" (1 Cor. 2:9-11). When we kneel to pray, let us be certain to ask the aid of this blessed Holy Spirit of God.

Praying in the Holy Spirit

"But beloved, building up yourselves on your most holy faith, praying in the Holy Spirit, keep yourselves in the love of God, looking for the mercy of our Lord Jesus Christ unto eternal life" (Jude 20, 21). That is no impossibility. What God tells us to do, we can do. Therefore we can "pray in the Spirit." That means that all our requests will be made known to the Father as we are guided by the Holy Spirit. All our thanksgiving will be harmonized by the Holy Spirit. All our confession of weakness will be with the kind of meekness that is the fruit of the Holy Spirit. All our supplication for our own growth in grace will be in dependence on the Holy Spirit. God reveals to us by His Spirit the things that we most need, as well as the ways in which we can most surely glorify the Father. All our dependence ought therefore to be on the Holy Spirit when we kneel to pray.

When Paul writes of the reconciling work of Christ, He stresses that we experience this through the mediation of the Holy Spirit. "By His sacrifice," he writes, "he removed the hostility of the Law, with all its commandments and rules, and made in himself out of the two, Jew and Gentile, one new man, thus producing peace. . . . Then he came and told both you who were far from God and us who were near that the war was over. And it is through him that both of us now can approach the Father *in the one Spirit*" (Eph. 2: 15-18 *Phillips,* italics mine). It is, as we have emphasized, "in the one Spirit" that we draw near or have access to God our Father.

The same emphasis is found when Paul is speaking about the true circumcision. He says, "We are the circumcision which worship God *in the spirit,* and rejoice in Christ Jesus, and have no confidence in the flesh" (Phil. 3:3, italics mine). It is as we worship *in the Spirit* that we offer the sacrifices that are worthy of God. As the Father seeks those who will worship Him in spirit and in truth, so do we seek the daily anointing of the Spirit that will liberate us from all the bondage to our carnal natures and lift us into the realm of "worship in the Spirit."

It is a wonderful day in any Christian's experience when he really learns to pray in the power of the Holy Spirit. I do not intend to go back to material that we have already exhaustively analyzed in chapter 5, but it is right that we should recall that this kind of praying in the Spirit need in no way be associated with speaking in tongues. Those to whom this gift is given will find it most natural to do so. For others, praying in the Holy Spirit will mean another form of expression. It will mean for all who truly pray in the Spirit an understanding of the will of God, the praying of prayers that have been born in heaven — and these are really the only prayers that God answers — and also the ability to claim the name of Christ and all the powers associated with that name as we pray. No one can really pray in the name of Jesus except under the sovereign direction of the Holy Spirit.

Seek then to be filled completely with God's Holy Spirit as you pray. You will discover thereby a liberty, a joy, an exuberance, an uplift such as you have never known before. Pray in the Spirit. Pray expectantly. Pray the prayer of faith. Pray with joy.

> Pray as if on you alone
>   Hung the issue of the day;
> Pray that help may be sent down;
>   Watch and pray.

(Thomas Hughes, 1823-1896)

When we are filled with all the fullness of God, we begin to pray for what cannot be expressed, and our only comfort then is that the Holy Spirit is praying with us and in us with groanings that cannot be uttered. The God, however, who searches the hearts understands the language and vocabulary of the Spirit and answers in power.

Praying with the understanding

When Paul wrote to the Corinthian church, he said, "I will pray with the Spirit and I will pray with the understanding" (1 Cor. 14:15). The Corinthian Christians were apt, under the influence of charismatic gifts, to neglect their understanding. We are liable to fall into the opposite extreme. We are often liable to pray with the understanding but not in the Spirit. Yet, can one really pray with understanding unless he prays also in the Spirit? I do not think so. We must give due place to the two great areas of the Spirit's dominion — one, the Word of God: it must dwell in our hearts richly; and two, the innermost recesses of our heart where the Spirit should be in control. Then He will not only illumine us with the light from the holy Scriptures, He will instruct and guide us on through fervent prayer to the throne of God where it is the delight of the Father to answer abundantly the cry of our heart. As the Holy Spirit becomes more and more real to us, we shall also recognize the greatness and the hunger of the Holy Spirit with which He draws our hearts to heaven.

We must never undervalue the mind in our Christian experience. Too often this imbalance has occurred — always with tragic results. When Paul speaks of "praying with the *understanding*," he uses the little Greek word *nous* which means "mind" — that part of our personality with which we think. And Paul says that "the mind" must play an important part in our prayer life and that it should be totally under the direction of the Holy Spirit. Yet, it is quite demonstrable that in the twentieth century the Christian Church has largely abdicated the Christian authority that the informed mind should hold in every sphere of life. The further descent to mental secularism is easy and uninterrupted. Christians, for the most part, expect their minds to be governed by human values and to work within a frame of reference that reflects wholly secular standards. We have not allowed the Holy Spirit to saturate our minds with Christian truth. We have allowed the world, instead, to govern and control our thinking to such a degree that there is scarcely any apparent difference between a Christian and a non-Christian.

Is there any escape? The answer can only be that the Holy Spirit will "renew our minds" if we are prepared to allow Him to do so. The apostolic mind was under the control of the Spirit. The great fact of the redemption of Christ tinges all that is considered. If Paul is speaking about the "eating of meats," he immediately adds the principle: "Destroy not him with thy meat for whom Christ died" (Rom. 14:15). If he has occasion to rebuke the impure and the unclean, he does so with the shadow of the cross resting on his judgment: "You are not your own; you were bought with a price" (1 Cor. 6:19, 20 RSV). When he portrays the ideal marriage of husband and wife, he sets this in the light of Calvary: "Husbands, love your wives, even as Christ also loved the church and gave himself for it" (Eph. 5:25). And if he is encouraging his hearers to be liberal in all their lives, he surrounds his words with allusion to the sacrifice of Christ Himself. "You know the grace of our Lord Jesus Christ, that, though he was rich, yet for your sakes he became poor" (2 Cor. 8:9). Everywhere and in all circumstances, life for Paul is seen through the tremendous realities of the love of God and the redemption of the world through our Lord Jesus Christ.

We too can allow the Holy Spirit time and opportunity to think through us. We can think God's thoughts after Him. Let the mind of Christ be in us as we pray. Thus will we pray with wisdom and true understanding.

This resolve must be very practical. There are hosts of ways in which we can fill our mind with those things that will help us as we pray — a prayer calendar of missionary friends, needs, events, travels, and crusades; a list of verses on prayer that contain some of God's wonderful promises to those who pray; the use of some hymnbook where we can share the life of thousands who have blessed the Church with gracious verse; the fellowship of other minds and other personalities — these give us opportunities to "grow in grace and in the knowledge of our Lord and Saviour Jesus Christ" (2 Peter 3:18). And all these help us to pray "with the understanding."

Praying in the name of Christ

There is nothing more wonderful than praying in Christ's name.

To enter into a life of prayer where we are able to claim the power of the name of our Lord is the summit towards which we should continually be striving. Our Lord has promised, "If you will ask anything in my name, I will do it" (John 14:14). To pray in the name of Jesus means that we pray in entire dependence on all that Christ is and on all that He has done. If I can show the signature of some wealthy friend on a letter stating that he will stand surety for me at the bank up to any sum that I might indicate or desire, the bank manager will have no hesitation in giving me what I ask. So it is with the name of Jesus. I go to the throne of God. I present my supplications over the signature of the name of Jesus, and the Father immediately grants me my request.

I will not, of course, ask anything in the name of Jesus that is contrary to the will of my Lord. That would be absolutely wrong. But as the Holy Spirit assures me of the fullness of His love and the unbreakableness of the ties that bind me to Him, I go with ever-increasing boldness to the Father and I ask Him to supply all my need. But better than that is the word that we are learning from the Scripture that heads this chapter. The Holy Spirit prays within us. "We do not know how to pray worthily . . . but his Spirit within us is actually praying for us in those agonizing longings which never find words." What comfort is here!

When we do not know how to pray, there is One who does. We can stand aside therefore at that time to allow Him to take over complete control. The mighty Intercessor within us is pleading our cause before the throne of God. He prays in the will of God. Therefore His prayers are heard and answered. Gradually we learn to trust Him more. Bit by bit we come to understand what it is to place our confidence in Him and to plead the strong name of the Son of God. Armed with this might, we approach our God, behold the face of the Father, and are blessed with all spiritual blessings in heavenly places in Christ Jesus.

I recall one dark and foggy night in the month of November. The roads were muddy and the dampness wrapped itself around, chilling us to the bone. We were on our way to evening church, knowing that there would be only a handful of people present because of the inclement weather and also because an epidemic of influenza was raging just then. I must confess to being dispirited. But just at that moment, around the foot of the hill on which the church stood, there came the Springburn Salvation Army Band and they were playing

> Take the Name of Jesus with you,
>   Child of sorrow and of woe;
> It will joy and comfort give you,
>   Take it then where'er you go.

It was all so sudden. And at once the fog seemed to vanish and the murk and mire to disappear.

> Precious Name, O how sweet!
>   Hope of earth and joy of heaven;
> Precious Name, O how sweet!
>   Hope of earth and joy of heaven.

Something of the same experience was Matthew Arnold's. He was in Bethnal Green in London in August. He tells the story:

> 'Twas August; and the fierce sun overhead
>   Beat on the squalid streets of Bethnal Green;
> And the pale weaver, through the window seen,
>   Looked deep dispirited.
>
> I met a preacher there to whom I said;
>   "Ill and forspent, how fare you in this scene?"
> "Bravely," he said, "for lately I have been,
>   With thoughts of Christ, the living Bread,
>   been nourished." [1]

When we pray "in the Name of Christ" the shadows do scatter and the west winds play, while all the windows of our heart are opened to the day.

But if this is to be, the Holy Spirit's unquenched indwelling must be our care. The Holy Spirit works on in our hearts, lifting them continually to the throne of God, as in faith we hold God's promise, and as, in the entire surrender of the flesh to the death of the cross, we yield ourselves to our beloved Lord, that He may fill us with His Spirit to the overflow.

---

[1] From the poem "Bethnal Green."

17

Filled With the Spirit

They were all filled with the Holy Spirit (Acts 2:4).
Be filled with the Spirit (Ephesians 5:18).

WHEN THE EARLY FATHERS of the Church wrote their statement of
faith, they boldly included the strongest affirmation of the deity and
power of the Holy Spirit.
In the opening chapter we noted some of their statements. But
it would be good to recall at this point the particular emphases they
made. Firmly they declared that every quality belonging to almighty God is everywhere in the Bible attributed to the Holy Spirit.
Without hesitation, without compromise, without doubt, they attested that the Holy Spirit, given by the Father and the Son to the
Church on the day of Pentecost, was "very God of very God." The
Nicene Creed affirms this:

> And I believe in the Holy Spirit,
> The Lord and Giver of life,
> Who proceedeth from the Father and from the Son;
> Who with the Father and Son together
> Is worshipped and glorified.

Even more emphatic is the Athanasian Creed, where the statement concerning the Holy Spirit is made with a sweep and com-
prehensiveness, a definition and precision, incomparable in any
literature.

> There is one person of the Father, another of the Son, and an-
> other of the Holy Spirit.
> But the Godhead of the Father, of the Son, and of the Holy Spirit
> is all one: the glory equal, the majesty co-eternal. . . .

183

And in this Trinity none is afore, or after another; none is greater, or less than another.

But the whole three persons are co-eternal, and co-equal.

So that in all things, as aforesaid, the Unity in Trinity and the Trinity in Unity is to be worshipped.

The three Persons of the Godhead work together. They are one in substance. They are one in operation. God the Father is never present in any one place without the Son and the Holy Spirit. Yet, in office they are distinguishable. The Father is the Father Almighty, Maker of heaven and earth. The Son is the Revelation of the Father and the Redeemer of men. The Spirit is agent of the Godhead and He is the indweller of the life of the child of God, his guide into all truth, the glorifier of the Son of God. It is axiomatic for us to say that all things come from the Father, through the Son, by the Holy Spirit.

In the perfect plan of God, the Holy Spirit was not fully known until after the ascension of Christ to the right hand of God the Father. He had told His disciples it was expedient for Him to go away. If He did not depart, the Comforter would not be able to come. "But if I depart, I will send Him unto you." (John 16:7). When He ascended on high, He prayed the Father for the gift of the Spirit; and the Father, whose delight it is to glorify the Son, granted His request. All the excitement of this is focused in Paul's glowing words to the Ephesians (4:8-13), proclaiming that the glorified Christ, having ascended far above all heavens that He might fill all things, gave His Holy Spirit and with Him all the gifts of the Spirit. This was Pentecost. On that unforgettable day, the coming of the Holy Spirit signified the absoluteness of the victory of Christ over death, Satan, and evil of every dimension. And this was sealed to those who belonged to Christ by their "being filled with the Holy Spirit."

All the fullness of God

When Paul prayed for the church at Ephesus, he included this request of God:

For this cause I bow my knees unto the Father . . . of whom the whole family in heaven and earth is named, that he would grant you, according to the riches of his glory, to be strengthened with might by his Spirit in the inner man; that Christ may dwell in your hearts by faith; that you, being rooted and grounded in love, may be able to comprehend with all the saints what is the breadth and length and depth and height; and to know the love of Christ which passeth knowledge, that you might be filled with all the fulness of God (Eph. 3:14-19).

To be filled with the Holy Spirit means to be filled with "all the fullness of God." This means that if the Holy Spirit is infilling my life, then, should I sin, I sin in the presence of the Holy Spirit. To sin, of course, would mean that I was not filled with the Holy Spirit; for the Holy Spirit makes us free from the law of sin and death. It is when we are faithless and turn from the indwelling and infilling Spirit of God that we are prone to temptation and liable to fall into sin.

But the infilling of the Holy Spirit is granted us in order that we might not sin. This is what John means when he speaks of the victorious life: "Whosoever abideth in him sinneth not" (1 John 3:6). To abide in Christ is to dwell under the power of His Holy Spirit. We are filled with the Spirit. Therefore we do not live "after the flesh." By the power of the indwelling Spirit we are kept from plummeting down into sin and falling before all manner of temptations.

John adds in the same chapter (1 John 3:9): "Whosoever is born of God doth not commit sin." That is, he does not make it his habit to continue in sin. If we are habitually drawn into sin, we are plainly evidencing that the Spirit of holiness has not taken His dwelling within us. To be filled with the Spirit surely demands that we "walk after the Spirit and not after the flesh." And surely this is why, after the passage we have quoted above from Ephesians 3, Paul breaks out into doxology, into praise of the One who is able to do far more than we can ask or think. Look again at these amazing words:

> Now unto him that is able to do exceeding abundantly above all that we ask or think, according to the power that worketh in us, unto him be glory in the church by Christ Jesus throughout all ages, world without end. Amen (Eph. 3:20, 21).

This is the spontaneous song of them that are "filled with the Spirit." They rejoice with the joy of the Lord.

A continuous experience

Years ago I noted some words of Dr. Charles Inwood when he spoke at the Keswick Convention in England on the theme "The Infilling of the Holy Spirit." I cannot recall the passage he spoke from; nor can I find the message in any of the published annual reports. But my notes carry this unique statement from him and they have burned their way into my heart and mind:

> There is no such thing as a once-for-all fullness. It is a continuous appropriation of a continuous supply from the Lord Christ Himself. It is a moment-by-moment faith in a moment-by-moment Saviour, for a moment-by-moment cleansing and a moment-by-moment filling. As I trust Him, He fills me; the moment I begin to believe, that moment I begin to receive; and as long as I keep believing, praise the Lord, so long I keep receiving.

This is an all-important fact. There is no such thing as a permanent filling. There is no such thing as a once-for-all filling. The reverse is the truth. I come in my emptiness to the Lord today with the prayer that I may be filled with His Spirit. He answers that prayer. He fills me. As the day goes on, I continue making the same prayer. And as the days pass by, another miracle happens. I find that I have an increased capacity for fullness. It is in this way that we grow in grace and in the knowledge of our Lord and Savior Jesus Christ.

This infilling of the Spirit is always associated with a deep longing for it. "Blessed are they who hunger and thirst after righteousness: for they shall be filled" (Matt. 5:6). Likewise with thirst. "He that drinketh of the water that I shall give him shall never thirst" (John 4:14). Thus did our Lord speak to the woman of Samaria by the well of Jacob. He went on: "The water that I shall give him shall be in him a well of water springing up into everlasting life." On another occasion He emphasized the same truth: "He who believes in me, as the scripture has said, 'Out of his heart shall flow rivers of living water'"; and John adds this comment: "This he said about the Spirit, which those who believed in him were to receive; for as yet the Holy Spirit had not been given, because Jesus was not yet glorified" (John 7:38, 39 RSV).

We know from the subsequent history of our Lord's life, death, resurrection, and ascension, that the Holy Spirit was given when Christ was glorified, taking His place at the right hand of God the

Father Almighty. Yet it is also true in daily experience. If Jesus is not glorified, the Spirit will not fill us. It is only when we acknowledge Jesus Christ as Lord of all and work in accordance with that fact that the Holy Spirit fills and possesses us to the uttermost. Blest indeed are they that know this truth, glorify Christ continually, and are filled with the Spirit!

From the Old Testament there comes the word "I will pour water upon him that is thirsty, and floods upon the dry ground" (Isa. 44: 3). The fullness of the Holy Spirit is an accompaniment of such thirst. Jonathan Goforth tells us in his journal:

> I began to experience a growing dissatisfaction with the results of my work. Restless, discontented, I was led to a more intensive study of the scripture. Every passage that had any bearing on the price of, or the road to, the accession of power became life and breath to me. If Finney is right, I vowed, then I am going to find out what these laws are, and obey them no matter the cost. [1]

That is true thirst. God satisfied Goforth. The revival fires that broke out as he blazed a trail for God in the Orient were not of his creating. They were the evidence of the infilling of the Holy Spirit of one man's life totally dedicated to God. For such thirst we must pray. The Achilles' heel of our spiritual life is lack of desire. We have not, because we desire not.

Emptied of self

It may seem a simple truism that God can fill only that which has first been emptied. Yet we fail so often here. We ask for fullness; but we are already full — of ourselves. To be full of self means to be full of sin. And God cannot pour His Spirit into that which is unclean. "Grieve not the Holy Spirit of God, whereby you are sealed unto the day of redemption" (Eph. 4:30). That is Paul's counsel to believers who wish to be "filled with the Holy Spirit." Around that verse he has grouped a series of things from which the believer will separate himself. "Neither the immoral nor the dirty-minded nor the covetous man . . . has any inheritance in the kingdom of God. . . . Steer clear of the activities of darkness; let your

---

[1] Jonathan Goforth, *By My Spirit* (Minneapolis: Bethany Fellowship, 1942), ch. 4.

lives show by contrast how dreary and futile these things are. (You know the sort of things I mean — to detail their secret doings is really too shameful" (Eph. 5:5, 11, 12 *Phillips*). From such things we must be delivered. We must empty ourselves of all double-mindedness, greed, love of money, envy, anger, ease, or unclean-ness. It is the emptied vessel, purified by the blood of the Redeemer, which the Holy Spirit will fill.

Out of the heart of the Ruanda revival came the following story. A Ruanda pastor, with whom the Holy Spirit had been striving for many months over certain things in his life which he knew were not pleasing his Lord, dreamed a dream. In his dream he saw a long, narrow room in which was a table prepared for a meal with dishes for food and cups from which to drink. The table was cov-ered with a spotless cloth of white. Suddenly, into the room Christ came. He carried in His hand a chalice with which He approached the table and began to pour into the cups as though in preparation for guests who would soon appear. But there were some cups by-passed and into them He poured nothing; then, having gone com-pletely around the table, He vanished as quickly as He had come. From his watch-stance, the Ruanda pastor rose, for he wondered why it was that Christ had not filled all the cups. Slowly he crept to the table; and when he reached it and looked within the cups that were still empty, he saw that they were altogether unclean.

Unclean? Yes, indeed! Into a heart that is harboring unclean thoughts and evil imaginations, Christ will never pour His Spirit. If we would know the fullness of God and be filled with the im-measurable fullness of God, then we must empty ourselves of all that grieves the Spirit of purity and grace.

The Spirit without measure

In John 3:34 we read, "He whom God hath sent speaketh the words of God; for God giveth not the Spirit by measure." In the Authorized Version, the words "unto him" are added; but they are not in the original text. Doubtless it is true that our Lord exem-plifies preeminently the life filled with the Spirit, the life in which the Spirit is found "without measure." But in the age of the Holy Spirit this is also true of every believer. Without measure He is given to us. We may have all of the Holy Spirit we desire to have if we are prepared to meet God's conditions — purity of heart, hunger and thirst after righteousness, yearning for God. Where these things are found, there the Holy Spirit is given "without measure."

All this is of grace. It is never of merit. We do not qualify for it by some unusual excellence of gift or ability. No! We receive this as we manifest the broken and contrite heart, which the Lord never despises. "The sacrifices of God are a broken spirit; a broken and a contrite heart, O God, thou wilt not despise" (Ps. 51:17). God always fills those lives with His Spirit who eagerly seek for this. When He does so, He presents us also with some of the gifts and powers of the Spirit so that we can go forth and tell others about the wonderful salvation we have found in Christ. Witnesses are never lacking when the Holy Spirit is given within His Church "without measure."

Some wonderful words of John Wesley may fittingly be quoted here. He has been speaking about the witness of the Holy Spirit in the heart of the believer and is proceeding to show the effects of this Spirit-filled life.

> He is no longer under law but under grace. He has received the Spirit of Adoption whereby he now cries, "Abba, Father." He has cried unto the Lord in his trouble and God delivers him from all distress. His eyes are opened in quite another manner than before, even to see a loving, gracious God. While he is calling, "I beseech Thee, show me Thy glory!" — he hears a voice within his inmost soul, "I will make all My goodness pass before thee and I will proclaim the name of the Lord; I will be gracious to whom I will be gracious, and I will show mercy to whom I will show mercy." And it is not long before "the Lord descends in the cloud, and proclaims the name of the Lord." Then he sees, but not with eyes of flesh and blood, "The Lord, the Lord God, merciful and gracious, longsuffering, and abundant in goodness and truth; keeping mercy for thousands, and forgiving iniquities, and transgressions, and sins."
>
> Heavenly, healing light now breaks upon his soul. He looks on "Him whom he pierced"; and "God, who shineth out of darkness, shines within his heart." He sees the light of the glorious love of God in the face of Jesus Christ. He has a divine "evidence of things not seen" by sense, even of "the deep things of God" and overpowered with the sight, his soul cries out, "My Lord, and my God." [2]

---

[2] Sermon 9, "The Spirit of Bondage and Adoption," from *Forty-Four Sermons*.

This passage would be worth quoting even if it were for nothing else than demonstrating that Wesley quoted so copiously from Scripture, and how the Scripture was indeed woven into the very texture of his thoughts and speech. But there is a further reason than that. Here is manifest the life of the Holy Spirit poured forth without measure upon all believers. And in that "without measure" you and I may share.

A divine commandment

We must not forget that when the apostle Paul gives us his teaching regarding the fullness of the Holy Spirit, he uses the imperative mood: "Be filled with the Spirit" (Eph. 5:18).

In other words, it is a commandment. It is a duty. The verb is imperative. We are commanded to be "filled with the Holy Spirit." We are expected to have the Holy Spirit in free and uninhibited power within our personalities. We should constantly be allowing Him to have His own way, for in no other way will Christlikeness be known in us. The Christian life is a supernatural life and can be lived only from supernatural resources. There are no powers latent within ourselves that will help us live the Christian life. No matter what our disposition may be, it is essentially hostile to the Lord. We must therefore obey the commandment given us. Even as an officer in any army will give the order and expect it to be obeyed, so must we obey the commandment of our Lord: "Be filled with the Spirit."

And our Lord said, "If you love me, keep my commandments" (John 14:15). His commandments are not grievous. That is, they are not hard to follow or obey. Indeed, there is a sense in which we know the true liberty of the children of God only when we serve and obey Him. In following Christ and in doing His bidding, we are freed from bondage to lesser things and can go forth in the energy of the Holy Spirit to mount new offensives for the Kingdom of God. The commandment He imposes is not a key to some form of Christian luxury nor the admittance form to an establishment where we are in a kind of spiritual lotus land. No! His commandments demand our total attention, our undivided concentration. But they can be fulfilled through the strength that He supplies.

When Christ commands, He enables. The commandment is by itself a covenant promise. When we are entreated to be "filled with the Spirit," we are offered all needed grace to fulfill the command-ment. When God directs, He enables. His commandments are covenants of promise. So it was with the disciples when He told them to "tarry in the city of Jerusalem, until you are endued with power from on high" (Luke 24:49). They tarried. Through the ten long days of waiting they sought the throne invisible; and when the day of Pentecost came, they were together "with one accord" and there, when the cloven tongues as of fire lighted upon them, "they were all filled with the Holy Spirit" (Acts 2:1-4). Similarly, the promise of Christ "You shall be my witnesses in Jerusalem and in all Judaea and Samaria and to the end of the earth" (Acts 1: 8 RSV) was fulfilled to the very letter. The commandment was His enabling. He does not ask of us anything that He will not enable us to perform. So, when He summons us to "be filled with the Spirit," He guarantees that He will do what He is commanding us to do. There may be conditions attached to the commandments He gives. Often there are. Even so, He delights to fulfill them on our behalf. He will never leave us in the lurch. He will stay close by and through the Holy Spirit will indwell and support us all the way through.

A God-glorifying life

We should at this point stress once more that only through the infilling of the Holy Spirit is there any possibility of our glorifying God. It is from the Spirit-filled life that the fruit of the Spirit comes — love, joy, peace, longsuffering, gentleness, goodness, meekness, faith, self-control. All these signs of the life of the Holy Spirit are indicators of the very life of Christ. If you wanted to describe the life of Christ, you could do it in no more perfect way than by de-fining the fruit of the Spirit. And when the Spirit fills us to the uttermost, then we can be sure that He will bring forth fruit that will glorify our wonderful Lord.

The Holy Spirit within us glorifies Christ. He makes the Savior wonderfully real and precious. Christ becomes the altogether lovely One, the fairest among ten thousand to our souls. We have our life and being in Christ. He becomes our chief desire and sole end. Holiness is perfected in us through the power of the divine Spirit. And all our needs are met when He controls.

The chief need of our lives is to be filled with the Holy Spirit.

We need wait not a moment longer, for the Spirit is waiting to take over control. Let us pray for Him to cleanse us of all impurity and then enter and abide with us forever. This He will do. He will not be untrue to His promise. And this too is the chief need of the Church. We may as a church have a great program, lovely music, a magnificent organ, a lovely sanctuary, and gifted and eloquent preaching. But all of this will be only a kiss of death if the Holy Spirit is not energizing the whole. More and more we must pray:

> May the love of Jesus fill me,
> As the waters fill the sea;
> Him exalting, self abasing,
> This is victory. [3]

---

[3] From the hymn "May the Mind of Christ, My Savior," by Kate B. Wilkinson (1859-1928).

18

Suffering and the Help of the Holy Spirit

He hath also sealed us, and given the earnest of the Spirit in our hearts (2 Corinthians 1:22).

Likewise also the Spirit helpeth our infirmities (Romans 8:26).

SELDOM ARE YOU far distant from the problem of pain in the Bible. Job stands before us in all his manly grandeur as one who suffered greatly and that by the good intent of God. The saints of God in the Bible suffered. "They were stoned, they were sawn asunder, were tempted, were slain with the sword; they wandered about in sheepskins and goatskins; being destitute, afflicted, tormented (of whom the world was not worthy) they wandered in deserts, and in mountains, and in dens and caves of the earth" (Heb. 11:37, 38). Our Lord Himself was made "perfect through suffering" (Heb. 2:10). And there are very few Christians who reach the land of endless day without passing through the desolation and desert of great pain. Sorrow will meet us on our path. Bereavement will be our lot. Suffering in body and mind will be our portion. There is no escape.

The Christian and suffering

It is the high privilege of every child of God to be entrusted with suffering. That may seem a very hard thing to say. Yet it is true. Suffering is one of the great hallmarks of God's trust in us. Job, as we have seen, suffered. Out of a clear blue sky the thunderbolt came. His wife came to him and said, "Curse God and die." But Job could not do that. "The Lord gave, and the Lord hath taken away; blessed be the name of the Lord. . . . Shall we receive good at the hand of God and shall we not receive evil?   In all this Job did not sin with his lips" (Job 1:21; 2:10). He worshiped the Father of lights "with whom is no variableness, neither shadow of turning" (James 1:17). Rising early, he prayed for his children. Waking late, he sought God's blessing upon them, lest they had erred from the way and sinned. He was a just and upright man; yet God made him experience suffering greater than any other man apart from our Lord Jesus Christ.

And God ordains that His children will suffer. How foolish are those that say God will never send pain to His child. Pain can become a ministry of grace. All our joys are touched with pain. Thorns hedge us around when we walk in the way of His blessed will.

> Lord Jesus, King of pain,
>   Thy subject I;
> Thy right it is to reign:
>   O hear my cry,
> And bid in me all longings cease
> Save for Thy holy will's increase.
>
> Thy right it is to reign
>   O'er all Thine own;
> Then, if Thy love send pain,
>   Find there Thy throne,
> And help me bear it unto Thee,
> Who didst bear death and hell for me.
>
> Lord Jesus, King of pain,
>   My heart's Adored,
> Teach me eternal gain,
>   Is Love's reward:
> In Thee I hide me, hold me still
> Till pain work all Thy perfect will. [1]

From a fragrant book by Miss Clarkson whose poem has just been quoted I cull a few lines:

> Pain for you may be physical, or it may be one of the countless forms of suffering. Your illness may have been diagnosed as inoperable cancer. Death may have robbed you of one you loved more dearly than life, or its dread shadow may be hanging over

---

[1] E. Margaret Clarkson, *Grace Grows Best in Winter* (Grand Rapids: Zondervan Publishing House, 1972), p. 54.

such an one. Your baby may have been born a mongoloid or with a hopelessly deformed body. The one to whom you have joined yourself in the bonds of what you thought would be a truly Christian marriage has proved unworthy of the trust. Your child may have rebelled against God and deliberately turned aside to walk the ways of sin. The savings of a lifetime may have been swept away or your means of livelihood suddenly cut off. You may be compelled to watch a dear one undergo long years of physical or mental torment and be helpless to assuage his grief. You may have fallen into a deep depression, undergone a nervous breakdown, even total mental collapse, and doctors have been unable to do much to assist you in your struggle to regain emotional stability. The horror of suicide may have invaded your home or your circle of friends, or you yourself may walk daily in its spectral shadow. Human suffering wears a thousand guises, and in gathering them together under the single term "pain," I include all types of mortal ills. Whatever your sorrow, whatever constitutes God's hedge of thorns for you, His grace alone is sufficient to make you stand. [2]

Does this seem farfetched? Surely not to those who have passed through life and known its multiplied testings. There is no temptation that God may not ask us to pass through. But He is faithful. In the midst of the storm, when the waves beat high and we feel ourselves going under, His hand will stretch forth and save us.

Suffering — a means of grace

"Beloved, think it not strange concerning the fiery trial which is to try you, as though some strange thing happened unto you; but rejoice, inasmuch as you are partakers of Christ's sufferings, that when his glory shall be revealed, you may be glad also with exceeding great joy" (1 Peter 4:12, 13). In verse 19, Peter says, "Wherefore let them that suffer according to the will of God commit the keeping of their souls to him in well doing, as unto a faithful Creator." What is the way by which suffering becomes a means of grace? In the acceptance of God's good and perfect will lies our peace. Therefore, let us commend our souls to Him as to a faithful Creator.

How wonderfully God made suffering become a means of grace to Paul. Paul wrote, "I knew a man in Christ above fourteen years ago (whether in the body I cannot tell, or whether out of the body

---

[2] Ibid., pp. 55-56.

I cannot tell; God knoweth); such an one caught up to the third heaven. . . . He was caught up into paradise and heard unspeakable words, which it is not lawful for a man to utter. Of such an one will I glory; yet of myself I will not glory, but in my infirmities. . . . And lest I should be exalted above measure through the abundance of the revelation, there was given to me a thorn in the flesh, the messenger of Satan to buffet me, lest I should be exalted above measure" (2 Cor. 12:2, 4, 5, 7). What a picture! Here was Paul blessed with revelations that none other had ever known. But, lest he should become boastful or presumptuous, God gave him pain — a thorn in the flesh, as he describes it. Then he added, "For this thing I besought the Lord thrice, that it might depart from me. And he said unto me, my grace is sufficient for thee, for my strength is made perfect in weakness" (2 Cor. 12:8, 9).

It has been said that grace grows best in wintertime. And countless Christians have proved this true. There is no sorrow that God cannot take and sanctify by the glory of His presence. There is no difficulty that He cannot make to become a means of grace, a stimulus to spiritual growth. God is able. He never leaves us to our own devices. He is always planning secretly for His own. And often you may see God's saints battle-scarred and weary with the heaviness of the way. They may be experiencing what Bunyan called "many a brunt upon the way." But the God of all grace is able to make His grace abound towards us. That sickness! That financial loss! That heartache! He knew all about it. And that success that almost drew you under and far away from God, He knew about that also; and He planned that something would touch you at a tender spot; something would hinder and hold you back. What then? "All things work together for good to them that love God, to them who are the called according to his purpose" (Rom. 8:28). This is His promise. And He cannot lie.

Suffering can lead us to a deeper prayer life than could ever have been possible without it. Even as pain can be a way of knowing God, so suffering in all its mystery can lead us to reiterate the blessed name of Jesus in such a way that He becomes nearer than breathing, closer than hands and feet. Our cry may even be wordless. We may be too exhausted to phrase thoughts into words. Yet at times like these it is possible for us to know the true communion of the Holy Spirit. As George Macdonald says so poignantly, "Never wait for fitter time or place to talk to Him. To wait till thou go to church or to thy closet is to make Him wait. He will listen as thou walkest."[3]

In ways like these, suffering becomes a means of grace, training us for future and eternal service of the King of kings. Through pain we enter into the mystery of the sufferings of the Son of God like Paul, who was willing to complete in his flesh "what is lacking in Christ's afflictions for the sake of his body, that is, the church" (Col. 1:24 RSV). As Bengel comments in his *Gnomon of the New Testament:* "The Church's measure of sufferings was fixed. The more of them therefore that Paul endured, the less is left for himself and others; the communion of saints produces this effect."[4] The reference to the communion of saints partaking in the sufferings of Christ is most significant. Suffering is the hallmark of them that follow the suffering Savior. Through suffering we too are perfected. In the midst of suffering we may know the joy of our Lord "who, for the joy that was set before him, endured the cross" (Heb. 12:2). Suffering ripens for glory.

Our limitations and the help of the Spirit

As Paul thinks of these things in Romans 8, he thinks of the whole creation suffering as a result of the fall of man and the entrance of sin into the estate of God on earth. He sees the entire creation standing, so to speak, on tip-toe, waiting for the manifestation of the saints of God. Creation that was so abruptly brought under universal travail as a result of man's sin, believes that it will be liberated from the tyranny of change and decay and again share the magnificent liberty that can rightly belong only to the children of God. "We who have the foretaste of the Spirit are in a state of painful tension, while we wait for that redemption of our bodies which will mean that at last we have realized our full sonship in him." Paul writes further of this hope and then dramatically he breaks out in one of the greatest passages of all the Bible: "The Spirit of God not only maintains this hope within us, but helps us in our present limitations" (Rom. 8:23, 26 *Phillips*). Citing one

---

[3] C. S. Lewis, *George Macdonald: An Anthology* (London: Geoffrey Bles, 1946), p. 94.

[4] J. A. Bengel, *Gnomon of the New Testament* (Philadelphia: Perkinpine & Higgins, 1860).

example, our inability to pray as we ought to pray, he demonstrates that in this area the Holy Spirit prays within us with agonizing longings that cannot find words.

Once again, therefore, we see something of the unique and unparalleled work of the blessed Holy Spirit. "He helps us in our present limitations." "Limitations" is a unique word. It can be translated by words such as "disease" or "infirmity" or "sickness" or "weakness." But the essential root meaning is clear. It is a disability from which all sinful humanity suffers. And in the midst of this disability, this weakness, this pain, the Holy Spirit helps.

We are weak Christians. We fail our Lord seventy times a day and more. But the Holy Spirit helps us. We lack hope. But in our state of hopelessness the Holy Spirit comes and renews our hope. Bunyan's analysis of the human heart is exact when he describes how Christian found Hopeful. When passing through the town of Vanity Fair, he had refused with his comrade Faithful to buy the wares set forth before them, declaring, "We buy the truth." Then, when Faithful was martyred, Christian sallied forth alone along the way leading to the eternal city; and on the way he met Hopeful. This is the ministry of the Paraclete, the other Comforter. He renews within us the hope that is "undefiled and that fadeth not away" (1 Peter 1:4). He witnesses with our spirit that we are born of God and that "whatsoever is born of God overcometh the world" (1 John 5:4).

Groanings that cannot be uttered

In chapter 16 we wrote of the work of the Holy Spirit and of the way in which He leads us to pray. We are taught by the Spirit; and when we don't know how to pray, the Holy Spirit prays within us according to the will of God.

All that is very precious. But there is another note in these lines of Paul that we deliberately kept unstressed until this point. For one of the great services of the Holy Spirit is to support us in the midst of our suffering. It is by His power that we light a torch in the darkness of our tribulation. It is through His holy upholding that we are enabled to endure when it seems as though our foot had well-nigh slipped. "He helps us in our limitations." That is, He supports us through the valley of the shadow, guides us to our temptations, and makes us victors on the field. He is constantly reminding us of the promises of God and enabling us to take these promises for our own help and support. With agonizing longings that are too great for mere words, He lends us his aid. He intercedes. He prays for us.

This is something that every mature Christian ought to know. The Holy Spirit is never inactive. He is a mighty ocean force. He is an energizing sea of fire. He is ever strengthening us as we walk in the light with God and bringing to our side the allies we need so desperately. His thoughts defy expression in human language. Within us, the intercommunication of the Holy Trinity takes place and we are delivered from all our fears.

Suffering therefore can be understood as part of the will of God for us only when we recognize that the Holy Spirit is pledged to support us all the way through. Without this kind of pledge, suffering even when set against the glory of heaven hereafter could in many cases seem meaningless and even callous. But the point that is constantly being stressed by the apostles in their interpretation of the issues of suffering is that God undertakes never to leave nor forsake us. He is with us to the end. "For I the Lord thy God will hold thy right hand, saying unto thee, Fear not; I will help thee. Fear not, thou worm Jacob, and you men of Israel; I will help you, saith the Lord, and your Redeemer, the Holy One of Israel" (Isa. 41:13, 14). This is His promise. It is made by the God and Father of our Lord and Savior Jesus Christ — the Father of lights, with whom there is never the slightest variation or shadow of inconsistency.

Constantly within us the Holy Spirit pleads and prays. Even as our Lord prays and intercedes for us at the throne on high, so the Spirit pleads and supplicates within the temple of our mortal bodies in which He dwells. Wesley's words are again so apt:

> He is the Advocate on high;
> Thou art the Advocate within;
> Oh, speak the truth and make reply
> To every argument of sin.

This the Holy Spirit loves to do. He helps us in our infirmities.

Bearing the cross in the Spirit's power

There is another sense in which we have to understand the word "infirmity" — namely, our hesitation in taking up the cross and following the Lord. Like Peter, we all would like to turn away from the cross. "Be it far from thee, Lord: this shall not be unto thee." But our Lord rebuked him severely. "Get thee behind me, Satan; . . . thou savourest not the things that be of God but those that be of men" (Matt. 16:22, 23). How prone we are to want a crossless Christ. How willing we are to accept His ways of salvation if they leave us undisturbed and able to follow our own deliberate ways. Jacob knew all about this when he tried for twenty years to live a life without a witness for God, to live for himself, to forget the wrongs that he had done. He forgot that if he was ever to receive from God the fullness of His blessing he must make things right with his brother whom he had so grievously wronged. But then God allowed Jacob to so engineer his ways that he found himself alone with God by the brook Jabbok. There Jacob died. By the power of the eternal Spirit he faced himself — Jacob — and what he saw was not a pleasant sight. He saw the selfishness, the egotism, the grasping, greedy nature of his life. There, the first time for many a day, he really prayed. Charles Wesley has expressed most beautifully the kind of prayer that he probably prayed:

> My strength is gone, my nature dies;
>   I sink beneath Thy weighty hand;
> Faint to revive, and fall to rise:
>   I fall, and yet by faith I stand;
> I stand, and will not let Thee go,
> Till I Thy Name, Thy Nature know.
>
> Lame as I am, I take the prey;
>   Hell, earth, and sin, with ease o'ercome;
> I leap for joy, pursue my way,
>   And as a bounding hart fly home,
> Through all eternity to prove,
> Thy Nature and Thy Name is love.

Jacob could never have done this apart from the aid of the Holy Spirit. By Jabbok's brook, Jacob learned that "the Spirit also helpeth our infirmities."

Have we died to sin? Is the cross a reality within our lives? Until this happens, we are in great danger of falling before the strengthening onslaught of our own carnal nature. Moral imprudence pursues us. Only when God conquers us and we are prepared to allow Him to have His own way, are we really safe.

Yet how many there are who think that the Christian life can be lived without the cross! It was by the cross, Paul said, that he had been crucified to the world (Gal. 6:14). The cross where the Savior died became likewise the site of the crucifixion of the apostle. All the loss, the shame, the reproach, the rejection, and the wounding belong both to the Christ and to His servants. There are not two crosses. To die to sin, to die rather than sin, was the choice of Christ. To all of carnality and this world's empty show He died. And shall not we who are named by His Name? Yet, as we have said, there are many Christians who covet a life without a cross, following after publicity-hunting leaders, evangelical carnality, worldly reputation. Let me quote from A. W. Tozer:

> The old cross slew men; the new cross entertains them.
> The old cross condemned; the new cross amuses.
> The old cross destroyed confidence in the flesh; the new cross encourages it.
> The old cross brought tears and blood; the new cross brings laughter.
> The flesh, smiling and confident, preaches and sings about the cross; before that cross it bows and towards that cross it points with carefully staged histrionics — but upon that cross it will not die, and the reproach of the cross it stubbornly refuses to bear. [5]

It is in this context ultimately that we have to interpret the words "groanings which cannot be uttered." For the Holy Spirit is determined to make us holy and to make us pure as God is pure. The Holy Spirit has come to glorify Christ and He will not rest content until He sees the image of our wonderful Lord expressed clearly within and upon us. Therefore He intercedes wordlessly. The cry of the Holy Spirit of God within us is one that only a God of purity can hear and answer. And in that cry of infinite supplication that we might all be conformed to the likeness of God as seen in Jesus Christ, God's Son, there is all the heart-rending plea that we shall give heed and follow the way of holiness without which no man shall see the Lord.

It is at this point that we see the true union of human suffering and spiritual crucifixion. In the truest sense, they are one. God

---

wants to lead us on into His own life of His Spirit — love, joy, peace, longsuffering, gentleness, goodness, meekness, faith, self-control. But this cannot happen until we are ready to die to all that sin and self mean. The graving tool of human pain has sometimes to be employed by the Lord in order to lead us to the place of death. Likewise, God will use our own sinful folly, as He did in the case of Jacob, to corner us and bring us to the place where we see and abhor ourselves. When this happens, the prayer of the Holy Spirit rises on high. "And he that searcheth the hearts knows what is the mind of the Spirit, because he maketh intercession . . . according to the will of God" (Rom. 8:27). With "groanings which cannot be uttered" He pleads our cause before the throne. If our hearts are truly longing after God, be assured that prayer will be abundantly and instantly answered.

19

Witnessing in the Power of the Holy Spirit

You shall receive power when the Holy Spirit has come upon you; and you shall be my witnesses (Acts 1:8 RSV).

THERE IS NO MORE exciting adventure than being a witness for Jesus Christ. When He called His disciples to follow Him, He said, "Follow me, and I will make you fishers of men" (Matt. 4:19). On the eve of His departure in ascension to the right hand of the Father on high, He repeated this great promise: "You shall receive power when the Holy Spirit has come upon you; and you shall be my witnesses in Jerusalem and in all Judaea and Samaria and to the end of the earth" (Acts 1:8 RSV). So they were commissioned for their lifelong task. Witnesses for Jesus! Nothing greater could be asked of them. Nothing greater could be conferred on them.

This is the task of every Christian. Christ means him to be a witness. Not to be a witness for God is to deny the faith by which we are saved. We are called to be witnesses.

Yet there are very few Christians who are really witnessing for Christ. It has been estimated that it takes a thousand laymen and six pastors to win one soul to Christ every year. Incredible? Yes, indeed; but true! Why should this be? No doubt there are many reasons, but there are supremely two reasons why there are so few Christians witnessing. The first is that the average Christian is simply not living a full, mature Christian life. He has not learned the secret of victory through the blood of Christ. The second reason is that the average Christian has not been taught how to communicate his faith. But the really joyful Christian cannot help himself. He will give himself to this all-important task and will learn from whatever source he can the ways by which he can effectively share his faith with others.

Fortunately, in this decade of the seventies in the twentieth century, God has been raising up a number of organizations that are doing nothing else but teaching the way to communicate the faith. The Navigators have been wonderfully used in this work. Think, too, of the effect of the ministry of Campus Crusade for Christ International. Dr. Bill Bright and his wife gave themselves to work on the campus of the University of California twenty-one years ago; and from that modest beginning there has sprung a great army. The method used is to reproduce reproducers. It is in obedience to the great commission of our Lord to "go . . . and make disciples of all nations" (Matt. 28:19 RSV). A long list could be compiled of dedicated men and organizations given over to the task of witnessing the Word of life to this generation. But probably one of the great climaxes was reached at Explo '72 in Dallas, Texas. There nearly one hundred thousand came together for no other purpose than to learn how to communicate more effectively the faith they possess. To see the Cotton Bowl at Dallas filled to overflowing night after night by eager young people wanting to learn more of the faith they possessed and to learn also how they might more ingeniously and comprehensively tell others about that faith was an unforgettable and unforgotten sight.

Bible study and fellowship with other Christians, private and corporate prayer, are all necessary in the full-orbed Christian life. But there is a sense in which the most important element of all is to tell others about your faith and share with them all that God has done in Christ for you. True joy is known only by those who are witnesses in the power of the Spirit; it is this joy we must seek as we witness daily to the glory of our divine Savior. We must strive and seek and refuse to yield to any pressure that would set us back, in order that we may become the better witnesses for God. Christ gives us many encouragements along the way. He tells us that He will make us "fishers of men." He also says that when the Holy Spirit has entered our life, we shall become true witnesses for Him. What then hinders?

Be sure you are a Christian

Would anyone ever want to witness for Christ who was not a Christian? It is a good question. In answer, we may well note that John Wesley was a missionary to the Indians in Georgia before his heart was strangely warmed and he found peace with God. Many people have come to training sessions to learn how to communicate their faith, only to discover that they had no faith to communicate. In the study sessions they saw their own inefficiency and their lack of love for Christ.

In the very beginning, therefore, it is all-important that we stress the need to be a totally dedicated Christian. We must know the meaning of the new birth that our Lord taught Nicodemus at the heart of the night. We need to learn that full commitment to Jesus Christ means that we belong to Him, body and soul; that our brain and heart and will are altogether given over to the service of our Lord. Only a true Christian can witness to the Christian faith.

Becoming a Christian means receiving the life of God. In this act, God raises the soul from the death of sin to the life of righteousness. By the power of the Holy Spirit, the heart of man is created anew in the likeness of Jesus Christ, renewed after the image of God in righteousness and true holiness. All that was lost in the fall is recovered when the Holy Spirit enters and we are ransomed, healed, restored, forgiven. When this great change takes place, the love of the world is changed into the love of God. Pride gives place to humility. Passion is overthrown by meekness. Hatred, envy, and malice give way to the entrance of a sincere and disinterested love for mankind. In a word, it is that change whereby the earthly, sensual, and devilish mind of the natural man is transformed into the mind which was in Christ Jesus. So is everyone that is born of the Spirit.

How essential, then, to be born anew of the Holy Spirit! In no other way is Gospel holiness stamped upon the heart. Being born of the Holy Spirit, we discover that our whole mind is fashioned after the image of Jesus Christ, the Son of God. And if we are ever going to be true witnesses for Jesus Christ, this great change must take place within us. We must be born again of the Spirit. We must become like Jesus. A good life of moral integrity is no substitute for the new birth. Regularity in church attendance is no substitute for the new birth. Copying the example of Jesus Christ is not the new birth. No! The new birth is that act of God whereby we receive His life, as we accept Jesus Christ as Savior and Lord. In that moment, the Holy Spirit enters and we are "adopted into the family of God" and are able to call God "our Father in heaven."

Once this great change has taken place, you will find that there is a natural desire to share your faith with others. This is Christian witnessing. This is the inevitable expression of the life of God within the soul of man. God is a God of communication. His children likewise become communicators of the truth of God. The joy of the Lord is known by those who speak forth His praise.

Confession of sin and the fullness of the Spirit

At many points in the New Testament we are commanded to "confess our sin" in order that we may know the joy of fellowship. "If we confess our sins, he is faithful and just to forgive us our sins and to cleanse us from all unrighteousness" (1 John 1:9). And again: "If we walk in the light, as he is in the light, we have fellowship one with another, and the blood of Jesus Christ his Son [keeps on cleansing] us from all sin" (1 John 1:7). Sin always hinders a Christian from experiencing a life of joy. Sin also makes it impossible for a Christian to show forth the fruit of the Spirit. We must learn, therefore, the practice of saying no to sin and confessing it whenever it has been committed.

True confession of sin means agreeing with God that sin is wrong. God has shown us in His Word and in Jesus Christ His Son the real nature of a holy life and, correspondingly, the real nature of sin. "If I regard iniquity in my heart, the Lord will not hear me" (Ps. 66:18). Sin is anathema to God. His child must turn from sin.

True repentance becomes a reality in the life of the believer. Repentance recognizes sin for what it is and turns from it. Repentance sees that all sin was dealt with at the cross, believes that any particular sin for which forgiveness is sought was dealt with at the cross, resolves to have nothing more to do with that kind of sin, and asks the aid of the Holy Spirit to overcome it. True repentance is always made with Calvary in view, for the child of God who is asking for pardon and cleansing will learn that all sins — past, present, and future — have been dealt with at the cross. Because of the sacrifice of Christ for sin at Calvary, there remains no more atonement for sin. In other words, there is no plus to the cross.

You cannot add anything to the infinite nature of the sacrifice made on Golgotha's hill. True repentance believes that "there is therefore now no condemnation to them that are in Christ Jesus" (Rom. 8: 1). "He is the propitiation for our sins" (1 John 2:2).

The fullness of the Holy Spirit is enjoyed by all who have truly confessed and renounced their sins. We have seen already that we are commanded to be filled with the Holy Spirit. The fullness of the Holy Spirit is always experienced by those who have fully repented of their sins and are walking in the light with their Lord and Savior. We must therefore believe all that God has said about the total nature of the sacrifice of Christ. "There remaineth no more sacrifice for sins" (Heb. 10:26). And we must equally believe all that God has said to us about the infilling and fullness of His Holy Spirit. These promises we claim by faith as all the promises must be claimed. Then, filled with the Spirit's power, we launch out to witness for Christ. Through the same eternal Spirit by whom our Lord offered Himself to God, we offer ourselves for the service of our Master. We go out to witness to Him and to Him alone. "We proclaim not ourselves," says Paul so definitely, "but Christ Jesus the Lord" (2 Cor. 4:5).

To summarize, we must be very sure we are true Christians; we must repent of every sin and turn resolutely from sin; and we must be filled with the Holy Spirit. Now what follows?

Sharing our faith

We come to the real heart of the matter at this point. The Christian's highest duty as well as his greatest joy is to be a witness for Jesus. All the essential presuppositions for this task have been outlined and underlined. What must we do next?

Well, first of all, we must be prepared to share our faith with others. When the Holy Spirit indwells us, He also overflows from us; and in doing that the overflowing cup of our faith tells that the Spirit within us is the Spirit of Jesus Christ. There is a sense in which we share our faith without speaking a word. Our very bearing demonstrates whose we are and whom we serve. Love should be manifest in all our actions and if this is not so, we are not truly sharing our faith with others. But there is more to our sharing than that. If we are really going to share our faith with others, if we are really going to witness for Christ to others, then in some way we must verbalize our faith. We must become vocal. We must, in the truest New Testament sense of the term, prophesy. Prophecy means both "fore-telling" and "forth-telling." It is the latter connotation that is dominant here. We must learn to tell forth our faith to others. This is witness.

Now, witnessing can be learned. Indeed, without making light of this ministry in any way, it is undoubtedly true that a normal person can learn, through a few hours of effective study or training, to communicate effectively with others. There are many ways in which this can be done. But it will require some careful thought and preparation. Sometimes, the Holy Spirit will prompt you to speak words that you could never have imagined. At other times, He will guide you to prepare the ways in which you can best begin a conversation about Christ. Nothing great is ever learned easily. Witnessing, being one of the supreme ways in which the Church of Christ grows, is obviously a great art. It must be studied. And we have countless examples of how it can be done.

Take, for one, the example of our Lord. He sits by the well of Sychar, wearied with His journey. Along comes a woman at mid-day, seeking water, and very naturally He asks for something to drink from the well. That was the beginning. But it was a beginning that led to one of the greatest conversions in the history of the Church. It led also to the evangelization of a city of Samaria — one of the towns in which Christ did not usually operate or preach. Or think of Him another time when He met with Zacchaeus. Christ knew where this hated man was and when He came to the place, He stopped right under the tree and said, "Zacchaeus, make haste and come down; for I must stay at your house today" (Luke 19:5 RSV). Could anything be more explicit? He literally invited Himself to supper in the home of Zacchaeus and eternity alone will reveal all that happened there.

As a general plan, we should be quite definite, direct, and explicit in talking with others about the faith. This is really far more effective than the use of some special technique. Be sure to emphasize all that Christ has been to you, all He has done for you. You see, in a court of law, when you are called as a witness, you are not asked your opinions about certain things. You are asked to give definite witness to what you have seen or heard. So it is also in witness for Christ. Listen to John! "We are writing to you about something which has always existed yet which we ourselves actually saw and heard: something which we had opportunity to observe closely and even to hold in our hands, and yet, as we know now, was something of the very Word of life himself" (1 John 1:1 *Phillips*). He was writing about what he had actually seen. That is witness. Anything less than this is not witness. It may be reporting; but it is not direct testimony. And it is direct and definite testimony for which the world waits.

It is good when talking with friends to tell them about specific changes that have been wrought in you by the power of Christ. Those who are closest to you and who know you best will see most definitely the change in your life. It is very important that you tell them about it. As I write, I think of a young girl from a very wealthy home in Toronto who found Christ. The change in her life was so dramatic, it proved impossible for her parents not to realize that their daughter had been "taken with religion." Her father offered to send her to the greatest universities of Europe. But stubbornly, though graciously, she refused and went instead to the Ontario Bible College. Graduating from there, she went overseas as a missionary where she still is. For directness and unequivocality I have never seen anything quite so clear. She was unerring and unchanging in her confidence in God. He was her all in all and for Him she spoke with continual joy.

In witnessing, you must see to it that you do not separate yourself from non-Christian friends. How are you ever going to reach them if you are separated from them? It is here that so many Christians fail. They believe in living a life of separation, and rightly so. But there is a separation that is in actual fact insulation from life. Becoming a Christian should make you a better friend to them than you were before. Even though they may not understand and even though there may be some tendency to ridicule, still hold on. Tell them of Jesus, the mighty to save. You will sometimes find that God has actually prepared the heart of those beside whom you sit to hear what you have to say. I was kept waiting for six hours in an airport in the Maritimes recently and could not understand the reason why. But I had no sooner taken my seat beside my fellow-traveler than I knew. For five hours I had the opportunity of witnessing to him; though I must in all honesty say that it was he who gave me all the openings I needed.

There may be special groups with whom you want to associate and to whom you feel you have a word of witness. Seek out the best way of meeting them. It may be in your own home. It may be in their home. But a true Christian should at all times in his life be seeking ways and means of making contact with others — by letter, by phone, by "house visitation" — and of telling them how great God is and what a wonderful Savior is Jesus, our Lord. You may meet with atheists (so-called) or with agnostics, and it will be your responsibility to witness. In witnessing to them, tell them directly what Christ has done for your soul. Leave no stone unturned to try to show them that Christianity is the only true faith, that Jesus Christ is the only Lord of the universe, that the Scriptures are true and trustworthy, and that the Holy Spirit can enter their lives in the same way as He has entered yours.

You may find yourself witnessing to people of various cults. This is difficult. But never shy away from them. Treat each one you meet as a person. Tell them of the greatest Person you know and tell them again and again where God has placed Him — at the right hand of the throne of the majesty on high. Ultimately, there is only one major question: "What think ye of Christ?" (Matt. 22:42). And if God has given Him a Name far above all, then can we ascribe any lesser position to Him? This is the major point to stress when dealing with the cults.

You may sometime have opportunity to witness to Jewish friends. In order to do so wisely, be sure that you are acquainted with Jewish holidays, history, customs, and culture. Ask them if anyone has ever explained Christianity to them and ask them to discuss openly with you your own beliefs as contrasted with theirs. Refer to Jesus as Messiah rather than Christ; they will appreciate this all the more coming from a Christian. Be friendly with them. Participate as you are able in things they do and make a point of honoring their special days through some small gift or a special greeting. All this is witness. These are tactics you are employing in order to reach the strategic goal of winning them to your Savior and Lord. Tell them what it means to be a "complete Jew." There are some excellent articles written on this theme and related themes. Use them. Keep them near you if you think there is any chance of your meeting with a Jewish friend. There is simply no limit to what you can do if you are determined to do it.

In doing house to house visitation — and this is still one of the most effective ways of reaching a community — you are going to meet with an infinite variety of people. You should carry a kit of gospels in different languages, some pieces of literature directed towards the cults of our modern age; and never leave without giving an invitation to the church from which you have gone. This may be the most effective thing you can do. However great the ministry of personal witnessing is, and it is very great, preaching is still one of God's supreme methods of saving men. If you can bring even one soul within the walls of a church, you have won a major victory.

Witnessing and prayer

There are some great promises of God linked with prayer that every witness should carry with him and claim before going out to speak with others. For instance, it is right that we remember that God is "not willing that any should perish, but that all should come to repentance" (2 Peter 3:9). We should remember also that "if we ask anything according to his will, he hears us" (1 John 5:14). Now these are tremendous promises. They are given so that we will place our faith firmly upon them and ask God for His answer. God is more concerned about the person we are to speak to than we will ever be. And God has covenanted that if we truly pray and keep on praying, then souls will be aroused from the dull sleep of sin and begin to listen to the voice of the Holy Spirit. "This is the confidence that we have in him," says John (1 John 5:14).

In such confidence, make up your own prayer list. Now I know as well as anyone how difficult it is to maintain constant prayer for people on a prayer list. Some people are methodical. Some are not. I have found for myself that it is one of the most difficult things to be constant and faithful in prayer for specific people and undertakings. Yet I know that I have been the recipient of countless prayers of others who have been more tenacious and persistent than I have been for them. The late Tom Rees, whose evangelistic ministry meant so much to so many, and who was called home to heaven while sitting quietly alone in a hotel room in New York, prayed for me on my birthday every year for twenty-five years. Over and over again he prayed on other occasions. But that was a special day on which he remembered me before the throne of grace. How is it with you? Are you disciplined? Should you not be asking the Lord to discipline you and to teach you more of what it means to be faithful in prayer? I am convinced that the beginning of all effective witness is in a place alone with God. He hears and answers prayer.

Sally forth with expectancy

We are commanded to go. "Go ye into all the world." That is our commission, our battle orders. At no place are we told that the world will come to us. The orders under which we serve are "Go," "Search," and "Find."

Our Lord has sent us out into all the world with His Gospel and He has told us to "make disciples of all nations" (Matt. 28:19 RSV). The great commission has never been revoked. Yet so often and tragically we fail. We become lethargic, indifferent, and apathetic. We allow problems to block and undercut us. We make endless promises and as many evasions for ourselves. We lack the will to win. How can we so forget that our Lord triumphed at the cross and that He has sent us forth to be His ambassadors empowered by His Holy Spirit? We must discover or recover this spirit of great expectancy; for our Lord has sent us forth from the place of victory to plant the flag of victory over unreached lives and lands. So often we fail in faith because we lack the Spirit's gift of vital expectancy. The true Christian witness, by the grace of the Holy Spirit, ought to be ready, curious, eager, inventive, foreseeing, always anticipating that God will break through and work miracles. Witness for God ought to be carried out in expectation of some mighty deed that God will do. One of the saddest facts of the Christian life is that between the great commission and the divine policy implied therein there so often lies a terrible gap whitened by the bones of failure and futile efforts. That kind of thinking or acting has no real place in the mind of the Christian who is determined to be one hundred percent for God. He believes God has a plan and that God will reveal that plan to him as he stubbornly bears the cross and moves forward to work and witness. As he does so, suddenly, like secret ink becoming visible, God's plan emerges into view and, equally suddenly, the right words are given to convey all that God is saying.

Our priorities must be so arranged as to allow time for witnessing. The Holy Spirit will help us to do this if we will only take time to review everything prayerfully in His presence. It is a true saying that, though prayer takes time, prayer also makes time. Assuming that you have some person or persons in mind during prayer, the next step is to plan the day in such a fashion that you will be prepared to meet them should they pass your way, and you will have God's word for them. Don't be discouraged if they rebuff you. What is success in witnessing? I have never heard a better definition than that given by Dr. Bill Bright of Campus Crusade, International: "Success in witnessing is simply sharing Christ in the power of the Holy Spirit and leaving the results to God." But make no mistake about this. Men in our time want to hear about God. It is still true today that "the fields are white unto the harvest" (John 4:35).

> Men die in darkness at your side,
>   Without a hope to cheer the tomb;
> Take up the Cross and wave it wide,
>   Its beams will light men's deepest gloom.
>
> Toil on, faint not, keep watch, and pray,
>   Be wise the erring soul to win;
> Go forth into the world's highway,
>   Compel the wanderer to come in. [1]

The great commission has neven been withdrawn. Our task is clear. Our duty is unmistakable. Let us not fail Him who has called us with a holy calling and still awaits that day when all "his enemies be made his footstool" (Heb. 10:13).

---

[1] From the hymn "Go, Labour On, Spend and Be Spent" by Horatius Bonar (1808-1889).

20

The Surprises of the Holy Spirit

When he, the Spirit of truth, is come, he will guide you into all truth: for he shall not speak of himself; but whatsoever he shall hear, that shall he speak: and he will show you things to come (John 16:13).

THE SILENCE OF THE HOLY SPIRIT about Himself is one of the Bible's great surprises.

One would naturally have expected that He, who is the agent of the Godhead, would be loud in His own acclaim. But it is not so. "He shall not speak of himself." Our Lord quite simply yet definitely states that the role of the Spirit will be to bear witness to Him — to Jesus Christ alone. "He shall glorify me." We have noted this already but it cannot be noted too often. Whatever begins with the Holy Spirit always ends with Jesus Christ. Thus, as He teaches the disciples to be true and faithful disciples, He is silent concerning Himself. He has one great and glorious theme — Jesus Christ. One portrait alone is drawn by Him and on a cosmic scale. It is the heavenly portrait of the Savior of the world.

A Spirit like this is alien to our natural, carnal nature. We love to draw attention to ourselves. By nature we are proud, conceited, egotistic, vain, and overweening. We show this in a thousand ways. By the clothes we wear. By our pursuit of distinction. By our unwillingness to listen to others. These are marks of our vanity. We dream dreams of greatness. We presuppose that we are better than others. So we allow the conversation to circle around ourselves and we pursue the arts and crafts of selfishness. This is man — arrogant and vainglorious. It is as Henry Mencken says in his third series of *Prejudices:*

> Nine times out of ten, in the art as in life,
> there is actually no truth to be discovered,
> there is only error to be exposed. [1]

We know this to be true of ourselves. That is, if we dare to be honest with ourselves.

Our Lord condemned the spirit of the Pharisees for the way in which they sought such self-glory. "Woe unto you, scribes and Pharisees, hypocrites! for you devour widows' houses and for a pretence make long prayer: therefore you shall receive the greater damnation" (Matt. 23:14). The same emphasis is found in the verse immediately following. "Woe unto you, scribes and Pharisees, hypocrites! for you compass sea and land to make one proselyte; and when he is made, you make him twofold more the child of hell than yourselves" (Matt. 23:15). The scribes and the Pharisees boasted as much of the goodness of their works as of the orthodoxy of their teaching, and expected to be justified by them. Yet the very things they boasted about were an abomination in the sight of God.

So is it true of all men. Apart from the grace of God, they cannot help praising themselves and their works. But this is not the way of the Holy Spirit. "He shall not speak of himself; but whatsoever he shall hear, that shall he speak." In other words, He is the tongue of the Father and the Son. He hides Himself.

Surprising guidance into all truth

Can there be anything more surprising? The Holy Spirit indwells us in order to lead us into every facet of the truth of God — all truth. How comprehensive is this saying. Not just into a part of the truth but into *all truth*. This means that He leads us into the truth concerning God. We know God as the Holy Spirit reveals Him to us. It is true that Christ is the Revealer of the Father. But it is "through the eternal Spirit" that He gives this revelation. Nothing can ever happen in the actions of God without all three persons of the Godhead being present. Yet their functions are different; their actions vary. The Father is God the Father Almighty, Maker of heaven and earth, and the Father of all who believe. The Son is the express image of the Father, His Revealer, and further-

---

[1] Henry L. Mencken, *Prejudices: A Selection*, ed., James T: Farrell (New York: Random House, n.d.).

more He is the Redeemer of the world. But the Spirit is the One by whom these things become actual, real, and operative within us. He guides us into "all truth" about God. If we would know what God is like, we must go to the Holy Spirit and He is, as Luther says, "the plainest teacher in heaven or earth."

Similarly, He guides us into all truth concerning man. It is through the Holy Spirit who inspired holy men to write the Scriptures that we learn what man essentially is — originally made in the image of God but fallen as a result of sin. The Spirit reveals to us the way by which we may be delivered from sin and its dreadful results. He brings us to Calvary, shows us our dying Savior, and points to the sacred blood of the Savior flowing from the cross. In the same way, He teaches us that "to be carnally minded is death, but to be spiritually minded is life and peace" (Rom. 8:6). He guides us into the truth concerning God's law and how our conscience may obey that law. He shows to us the path by which we may become true disciples of our Lord, following Him in all things and serving Him as best we can. He guides us into the wonder of the Church, the living Body of Christ. He shows to us the many ministries that can be fulfilled by us in the Church as we exercise the specific gift or gifts that the Holy Spirit has granted us. He opens to us the Scriptures and teaches us from them all that God requires of us. He tells us how the Scriptures came into being: "Holy men of God spoke as they were moved by the Holy Spirit" (2 Peter 1:21). In short, there is no branch of truth into which He will not guide us as we open our entire personality to His control. We are filled with the Spirit, and as we are filled, we are led and directed into all facets of truth and grace.

Love's greatest surprise — we may glorify Christ

"He shall glorify me" (John 16:14).

The sublime objective of the Holy Spirit is to exalt the Savior, the Son of God, the Man of Galilee, the One who was born "for us men and for our salvation." He shows Him as Lord of all redemption, Author of our salvation, the One whom God has appointed "heir of all things, by whom also he made the worlds" (Heb. 1:2).

And to this life that glorifies, we are called! We must exalt the Son, worship Him, praise and adore Him. We must follow Him, serve Him, obey and love Him. This is what a true disciple does. A disciple of Jesus Christ is primarily one who is glorifying the Son of God in his own personal life. He refuses to draw attention to himself. He is continually pointing away to Jesus. His life is a signpost to Bethlehem and Calvary. His mouth declares the greatness and the glory of his Lord and Master.

And this can be done only by the aid of the Holy Spirit. Without the constant prompting, supporting, upholding, and directing of the Holy Spirit, the disciple will come far short of his first responsibilities — to reverence and honor the Son. He must be altogether under the control of the Holy Spirit of God.

From this experience there emerges another of the surprises of the Holy Spirit. We become like the One we glorify. As Paul writes to the Corinthians: "We all, with open face beholding as in a glass the glory of the Lord, are changed into the same image from glory to glory" (2 Cor. 3:18); and this happens because of the indwelling presence of the Spirit of the Lord. Can there be greater surprise than this? Is there any wonder that C. S. Lewis named his autobiography *Surprised by Joy?* It is for this, therefore, that we pray unceasingly. We must glorify Christ. His mind must be our mind. His will must be our will. His commandment must be our delight. Words like those of Kate Wilkinson should be constantly on our lips and rising from our hearts —

> May the mind of Christ my Savior
> Live in me from day to day,
> By His love and power controlling
> All I do or say.
>
> May the word of God dwell richly
> In my heart from hour to hour,
> So that all may see I triumph
> Only through His power.
>
> May the peace of God my Father
> Rule my life in everything,
> That I may be calm to comfort
> Sick and sorrowing.
>
> May the love of Jesus fill me,
> As the waters fill the sea;
> Him exalting, self abasing,
> This is victory.

> May I run the race before me,
> Strong and brave to face the foe,
> Looking only unto Jesus,
> As I onward go. [2]

Like Moses, we shall not know our faces shine with the glory of God. But it will be part of the divine surprise that we "shall be like him" (1 John 3:2) and that there will be a day when we shall come "in the unity of the faith, and the knowledge of the Son of God, unto a perfect man, unto the measure of the stature of the fulness of Christ" (Eph. 4:13). The future holds for us many surprises of God. They will all be the Holy Spirit's and they will all be to the glory of the everlasting Son of the Father.

Surprising destinations

How the Holy Spirit surprised the disciples by the unusual ways He led them, and some of the very unexpected destinations to which He brought them!

Remember how Paul and Silas on the second great missionary journey of Paul crossed the mountainous plateaus of Asia Minor and wanted to go into the Roman province of Asia to preach the good news in the area of Ephesus and Smyrna, but they were not allowed to do so. Indeed, the verb is very strong: "They were forbidden by the Holy Spirit to preach the Word in Asia" (Acts 16:6). The same happened when they wanted to turn northward into the province of Bithynia. The door was closed. "The Spirit suffered them not" (Acts 16:7). Why not? They could not understand it. But a voice summoned them beyond these mountainous ranges and at last they came down to Troas, a seaport and, indeed, the end of the road for them in Asia. There came the vision. Paul saw a man of Macedonia, who begged him, saying, "Come over into Macedonia and help us" (Acts 16:9). When morning came, Paul shared the vision with the rest of the party and suddenly they possessed that amazing consensus which the Holy Spirit always gives to those who are walking in the light with Him and with each other. They knew that they had been brought to this place for one specific reason, namely, to travel by sea northwestward in the direction of Macedonia. This they did. Surprised? Of course they were. *They* had planned to evangelize some Roman provinces. But *God* had

---

[2] Kate B. Wilkinson (1859-1928).

planned that they should break through into a neighboring continent. So they set sail with merry hearts, certain that God had called them by His Spirit to preach the Gospel to the people of Macedonia.

Paul knew other surprises. He was determined to see Rome. He did see Rome. But he little expected to see it as a prisoner of Caesar. God often fulfills our wishes but not in the way we would choose. Not always are we "surprised by joy." Sometimes we are surprised by the silences of God, His mysterious ways, His strange commands. Yet He is always working wonders, and in the end we are surprised at His sovereignty and glorious power.

> His purposes will ripen fast,
> Unfolding every hour;
> The bud may have a bitter taste,
> But sweet will be the flower.

Every true disciple can fill in this wonderful story of the leading of the Holy Spirit. We have all known it. We should all be rejoicing in it.

One naturally shrinks from introducing personal testimonies to the guidance of the Spirit. But there are times when we fail our Lord if we are dumb. He can be glorified as we declare His mighty acts in our own lives. Let me be specific and personal just for a moment.

I have been in three pastorates — one in Ayrshire, Scotland, the second in Glasgow, Scotland, and the third in Toronto. The story of our commission to Glasgow is a saga in itself which must be passed over. But our coming to Canada was equally surprising. It was the last thing in our minds. Yet after eleven years in Glasgow, by the strange intuition of the Spirit we began to sense that the time might have come for us to be moving on. We committed everything to God and waited. One Sunday night I drove my assistant to his home and we sat and talked for a while when we reached his residence. I told him then of the incipient thoughts that were rising in our minds about possibly not being there much longer and I was surprised to hear him say: "That is exactly how I am feeling. As I have prayed for you I have felt that the time was drawing near for your departure." The next morning when I picked up my mail the first letter that caught my eye was one from Knox Church, Toronto. It contained an invitation to cross the Atlantic and preach with the possibility of being called. Surprised? Yes and no.

I preached in Toronto and was duly called. But there was no assurance that this was really God's perfect will. My wife and I decided that we must test God — and ourselves — still further. So we put out certain fleeces as Gideon did. We set a timetable, asking for a renewal of the invitation by September 30 — then several months away — as a sign from the Lord. We watched, and waited. And God, who only does wondrous things, met our request and humbled us in the dust before Him. There was only one thing we could do — worship and adore Him for the greatness of His glory. "He led them forth by the right way, that they might go to a city of habitation" (Ps. 107:7).

Leaving the third pastorate was even more difficult. Again, we were faced with many dilemmas. Almost in desperation one Thursday afternoon, my wife and I asked for special guidance, suggesting in prayer that if on the following Sunday morning a young minister would come and invite me to share his pulpit for a series of renewal meetings, we would accept that as being the definitive leading of the Holy Spirit. Thirty seconds after I left the pulpit that Sunday morning, a young minister of the Canadian Presbyterian Church knocked on my vestry door and asked me to go and help him. All I can say is that God in His great mercy accepted the longing of our heart to be in the place of His will. Since that day in 1971 we have travelled multiplied thousands of miles in a ministry of church renewal. I believe that God will stoop to our fearfulness if we are sincere and desperate enough to call upon Him with intense desire.

God's guidance is a continual surprise. It is always supplied on time — never too early, never too late. Divine guidance is the lot of every true disciple of Jesus Christ.

> In Thee is fire of love,
> And sacrifice;
> A lamp lit on the cross
> At costliest price.
>
> Give us Thy lamp of truth,
> Thy Spirit's fire,
> With courage, wisdom, faith,
> Our lives inspire.

> Then, in Thy growing light,
> We shall arise
> To shape the vision seen,
> By open eyes.
>
> (author unknown)

"I will guide thee with mine eye" (Ps. 32:8). There is a whole language in the silent communion of the eye. As we worship, we receive God's light. "They looked unto him and were lightened" (Ps. 34:5). Such guidance is always memorable and surprising.

Surprising visits of the Holy Spirit

Oswald Chambers has written a striking paragraph in which he describes the ways in which God surprisingly visits His people. Let me quote it fully!

> As workers of God we have to learn to make room for God — to give God "elbow-room." We calculate and estimate and say that this and that will happen, and we forget to make room for God to come in as He chooses. Would we be surprised if God came into our meeting or into our preaching in a way we had never looked for Him to come? Do not look for God in any particular way, but *look for Him.* That is the way to make room for Him. Expect Him to come, but do not expect Him to come only in a certain way. However much we may know God, the great lesson to learn is that at any minute He may break in. We are apt to overlook this element of surprise, yet God never works in any other way. All of a sudden God meets the life — "When it was the good pleasure of God. . . . " Therefore, keep your life so constant in its contact with God that His surprising power may break out on the right hand and on the left. Always be in a state of expectancy, and see that you leave room for God to come in as He likes.[3]

What a surprise it was for the two disciples on the way to Emmaus! "Did not our hearts burn within us?" (Luke 24:32). He came to them in a way and at a time when they least expected Him. And it is thus the Lord loves to come. Yet we are so slow to look for His visiting, so hesitant. How often do we leave our homes on a Sunday morning with an eager assurance that the Holy Spirit is going to break in on our worship today? The Mount of Trans-

---

[3] Oswald Chambers, *My Utmost for His Highest* (London: Simpkin Marshall, 1927), p. 25.

figuration must be climbed in urgent hope and thrilling expectation that the Lord will meet us there.

Surprises of revival visitation

In 1949 I shared a series of services with the late Duncan Campbell whom God so mightily used in bringing the fires of revival to the island of Lewis. One morning we were passing a field and he told me how the farmer of that particular farm had left home one day in a hot fit of temper against his son who had become a Christian the week before. He was determined to meet his son and lead him back to what he considered a more normal way of life. But, as he crossed a river that meandered through that field, suddenly the Holy Spirit convicted him of sin, of righteousness, and of judgment. All he could do was fall on the ground and cry, "God be merciful to me a sinner!" God was merciful. He rose from the green meadow a changed man. No one had spoken with him. Only the Spirit of God had dealt with him. He met God where and when he least expected Him.

Jonathan Goforth tells about a similar act of divine power:

My diary lay open on the table in front of me. I had just been writing a note in it. "Just read this," I said, handing the book to my wife. "This is the third day, with not the slightest sign of any spiritual awakening among the people. But, as surely as God is omnipotent and His Word like a hammer that breaks the rocks in pieces, so surely shall His people bend into the dust before Him." Mrs. Goforth handed the diary back to me. "I won't go home," she said. "I'll wait and see what God is going to do." Just then the Chinese pastor was ushered in. He was greatly worked up over there being no sign of revival, and he told us that the leaders felt so keenly about the matter that they had that morning started an extra prayer meeting.

From then on our difficulty was to get the meetings closed. Sometimes after a meeting had lasted three of four hours I would pronounce the benediction, and immediately dozens would come running up to the platform, pleading with me to give them a chance to confess. Each day the unconverted came in large numbers, and many were brought under conviction. One Christian said to me: "Before these meetings there was no special interest in the Gospel in my village. But today, when I went home for my noon-meal, about ninety of my fellow-villagers gathered around me and asked me to tell them about 'this Jesus and the way of salvation.' " Among the new converts were two noted witches. They had Pastor

Hsi go back with them to their villages and the pastor with the elders held a service. All in their families turned to the Lord.[4]

These days of revival continued. The results were permanent. The love that the people of that land came to have for Dr. and Mrs. Goforth is indicated by a plaque in the vestibule of my own church in Toronto — a plaque dedicated to the glory of God and in memory of Jonathan Goforth, donated by the Christians of Manchuria.

Expectancy and surprise

Our Lord taught that all the things we ask for in His Name we should believe we have received, and we shall have them.

Surely much of our modern Christian discipleship is breaking down here. We simply do not trust God to honor His Word. We pray, but there is so little of passion, so little of belief, so little of spiritual heat in our prayers that God is not entreated and revival tarries. We do not expect that God will honor His Word and give us souls when we truly witness to Jesus. We think of a God who is largely moribund, a God who stopped working years ago. Nothing could be more dishonoring to God. He wants to bless us. But we have fallen into the habit of busy-ness in work for the Lord and are not ready to meet with Him face to face. We must learn to face *Him.* He rarely comes when we expect Him. Seldom does He appear as we think He should. We must learn, however, to be ready at all times for our Lord's surprise visits. We must seek Him earnestly and only. To do so is to be ready for anything. To do so is to be His disciple indeed.

The great need of the hour in the Christian Church is revival after the biblical pattern. David knew this. "Wilt thou not revive us again: that thy people may rejoice in thee?" (Ps. 85:6). Every true disciple of Christ must commit himself to praying for and working towards this. Revival rests, of course, in the sovereignty of God. Yet, at the same time, there are conditions that we can meet which will help promote revival, which indeed will be in themselves revival. A true disciple of Christ is one who is constantly reproducing himself. Witnessing to Christ in the power of the Holy

---

[4] Jonathan Goforth, *By His Spirit* (Minneapolis: Bethany Fellowship, 1942), p. 68.

Spirit means that others are going to hear all that we have experienced and here and there we shall find some who want to become what we are.

Surprising? Yes, of course, it will surprise us. God loves to surprise His children. Let us move forward through days of victory to claim the crown and the honor for our Lord alone. And let us tell others confidently that all God has done for us He can, by the Holy Spirit, do for them. Let this be our confident hope.

> O could I tell, you surely would believe it!
> O could I only say what I have seen!
> How should I tell or how can you receive it,
> How, till He bringeth you where I have been? [5]

"He shall glorify me." That too is our task. What angels desire to do He has permitted us to do. Surprising? Yes, indeed, above all our highest, wildest dreams. May He make us willing in the day of His power.

---

[5] From "St. Paul" by F. W. H. Myers (1843-1901).

21

The Communion of the Holy Spirit

The grace of the Lord Jesus Christ, and the love of God, and the communion of the Holy Spirit, be with you all (2 Cor. 13:14).

THE QUESTION IS OFTEN ASKED: Should we pray to the Holy Spirit? The time has come for us to note what the Bible has to say on this.

First of all, there is no recorded prayer in the Bible to the Holy Spirit; but the communion of the Holy Spirit is spoken of, and it is natural to ask: Can there be communion without communication? No doubting it — as we have already seen, we are dependent on the Holy Spirit for everything. We therefore look to Him. And this implies prayer. Communion means partnership. The word goes through many shades of meaning in the New Testament but the idea of sharing runs through them all. James and John were partners with Simon (Luke 5:10). Paul speaks of Titus as his fellow-laborer and partner (2 Cor. 8:23). They were colleagues in the ministry of the Church. Onesimus and Philemon share an even more intimate sense of oneness and companionship: "a brother beloved . . . both in the flesh and in the Lord" (Philem. 16). When we therefore share "the communion of the Holy Spirit" we are co-laborers, colleagues, comrades with the Spirit of God: one in vocation, one in power and resources, one in fellowship. This is the heritage of every true disciple. It is to this high calling that we are summoned of God.

Communion and communication with the Spirit

There can be no communion if there is not first union. But we are united to Christ in the bonds of the Holy Spirit. "If any man have not the Spirit of Christ, he is none of his" (Rom. 8:9). Union is the basic or common ground on which we stand. The bond of union is, of course, Jesus Christ through whom we become a member of the family of God. This union extends into communion and surely true communion implies communication.

Ought we, then, to pray to the Holy Spirit?

If the Holy Spirit be God, equal in power and glory with the Father and the Son, surely we must be at liberty to address Him when we are so led. In writing of worship, Dr. Torrey says,

> The only prayer that is acceptable to God is prayer in the Spirit. The only thanks that are acceptable to God are thanks in the Spirit. And the only worship that is acceptable to God is worship in the Spirit. Would we worship aright, our hearts must look up and cry, "Teach me, Holy Spirit, to worship," and He will do it. [1]

Now that is definite. Communion with the Holy Spirit I therefore assume to be communication with the Holy Spirit. Even as we pray to the Father and to the Son, so we ought to pray to the Holy Spirit. He is our Teacher. Shall we not ask Him questions? He is our Advocate. Shall we not confer with Him on how to plead our cause? He is our Guide. Shall we not inform him of the problems we are meeting and share them with Him? We cannot be independent of one another. He indwells us; naturally, therefore, we talk with Him. Any power that we shall know in the work of the Gospel will come as a result of our communion with the Holy Spirit.

Our hymns are rich in great addresses to the Holy Spirit. True, they are often wrong in what they say! (So often the Holy Spirit is entreated to "come" — but the Comforter has come already.) Even so, some hymns to the Holy Spirit perfectly express the longing and hunger of the disciple of Christ. Think, for instance, of Bessie Porter Head's hymn:

> O Breath of life, come sweeping through us,
> Revive Thy Church with life and power;
> O Breath of life, come cleanse, renew us,
> And fit Thy Church to meet this hour.

---

[1] Reuben A. Torrey, *What the Bible Teaches,* 20th edition (Old Tappan, New Jersey: Fleming H. Revell Co., 1933), p. 476.

O Wind of God, come bend us, break us,
Till humbly we confess our need;
Then in Thy tenderness remake us,
Revive, restore; for this we plead.

O Breath of love, come breathe within us,
Renewing thought and will and heart:
Come, love of Christ, afresh to win us,
Revive Thy Church in every part.

Revive us, Lord! Is zeal abating
While harvest fields are vast and white?
Revive us, Lord, the world is waiting,
Equip Thy Church to spread the light. [2]

Another hymn of prayer to the Holy Spirit which is not sung often enough in our modern churches is "Come, Holy Spirit, Come" by Joseph Hart (1712-1768). It is reminiscent of Wesley's "He is the Advocate on High: Thou art the Advocate Within." Let me quote the final three stanzas of it:

Convince us of our sin;
    Then lead to Jesus' blood,
And to our wondering view reveal
    The secret love of God.

'Tis Thine to cleanse the heart,
    To sanctify the soul,
To pour fresh life in every part,
    And new create the whole.

Dwell, therefore, in our hearts;
    Our minds from bondage free;
Then we shall know and praise and love
    The Father, Son and Thee.

There is a hymn that I have usually found in children's sections of hymnbooks — and there is good reason for it to be there — but it is good for adults as well. It is one of the purest expressions of desire ever communicated to the Holy Spirit.

Holy Spirit, prompt us,
    When we kneel to pray;
Nearer come and teach us
    What we ought to say.

---

[2] Copyright © 1968 by Singspiration, Inc. Used by permission.

Holy Spirit, give us
Each a lowly mind;
Make us more like Jesus,
Gentle, pure and kind.

Holy Spirit, help us
Daily by Thy might,
What is wrong to conquer,
And to choose the right. [3]

The fact is that the Church in her hymnody has found it impossible not to address the Holy Spirit. And if this be so of our communal worship, shall it not be equally true of our personal day-to-day praying?

The Spirit who gave the Word gives the words

An interesting word that has come into use in recent times expresses this very beautifully. It is a compound word — "communification"! It expresses that a church which knows the communion of the Holy Spirit also knows how to share this with others. The church that has power "to bind and to loose" by the power of the Holy Spirit is a church that has learned to pray to Him in the name of Jesus Christ.

But we can hinder Him, grieve Him, quench Him. Dr. Chadwick, writing of this, says:

> The Spirit seeks partnership with us. His resources are inexhaustible, and His power invincible, but! but! but! There are reserves, conditions, interests; barriers that hinder, grieve and quench the Spirit. He is held up by the barriers of unbelief, and prayerless living, worldly ambition, stupid vanity, and inflated pride. He longs for our fellowship. For the sake of Christ and the Kingdom of Grace, He longs to be admitted to the life of the soul. He comes to co-operate, and co-operation waits for confidence and consent. Where there is "agreement" there is power. Service becomes mighty in this fellowship. All the conditions of power are met in "the Supply of the Spirit." Personality is quickened and sanctified. Sympathy is deepened and enlightened, and in sympathy are the discernment that understands and the appeal that woos and wins. Weakness becomes strength when the Spirit of might is upon

---

[3] From the hymn "Holy Spirit, Hear Us" by William Henry Parker (1845-1929).

us fully. Ordinary men become wonderful when clothed with the Spirit of Power. [4]

A word that has gained some usage and recognition in this connection is the word "interiority." "Interiority" implies the communication of life with life, heart with heart, mind with mind. And, by implication, all along the line this process suggests the use of words. Communication is a two-way street in which one spells out to another the real thoughts and intents of the heart; and when the other is the Holy Spirit Himself, then there can be no doubt that He who waits to hear us pray will speak and answer.

So words come to us — words hot and burning with tears at times when we have to confess to the Holy Spirit that we have failed Him and tarnished the glory of the One He delights to honor; words that express our heart's longing to be pure as God is pure; words that cannot be refused passage through the womb of our hearts to Him who searches and cleanses and renews us in the image of God.

Inspiration and communication

The Holy Spirit is the Agent of the Godhead. When God chose to use the book method in guarding and making available His saving truth for every generation, it was the Holy Spirit who became the divine inspirer of men so that they wrote what was the mind of the Holy Spirit, which meant they wrote what was the true desire of God the Father Almighty, and God, the Son, the Redeemer of men. Peter speaks of this in a wonderful passage in the first chapter of his second letter where he describes the real nature of inspiration. We have already noted his words, but they should be stressed again and again. Let us read and inwardly digest them.

> We were not following a cleverly written-up story when we told you about the power and coming of the Lord Jesus Christ — we actually saw His majesty with our own eyes. He received honor and glory from God the Father Himself when that voice said to Him, out of the sublime glory of Heaven, "This is my beloved Son, in whom I am well pleased." We actually heard that voice speaking from Heaven while we were with Him on the sacred mountain. The word of prophecy was fulfilled in our hearing! You

[4] Samuel Chadwick, *The Pathway to Pentecost* (London: Hodder and Stoughton, 1934), p. 55.

should give that word your closest attention, for it shines like a lamp amidst all the dirt and darkness of the world, until the day dawns, and the morning star rises in your hearts.

But you must understand this at the outset, that no prophecy of scripture arose from an individual's interpretation of the truth. No prophecy came because a man wanted it to: men of God spoke because they were inspired by the Holy Spirit (2 Peter 1:16-21 *Phillips*).

Here is the emphatic word of the apostle. Scripture did not arise because of the ingenuity of any man, because of the fertility of his mind or the depth of his understanding of the mysteries of life. No! Scripture came because "holy men of God" were carried, lifted up — the word is the same as that used in Attic Greek of surf-riders being lifted up and gliding along the topmost wave — carried, borne, upheld by the Holy Spirit. The Spirit communicated the truth. Yet, when He did so, He did not detract by one iota from the fullness of their own personality. They spoke, but under the sovereign control of the Holy Spirit. They were not automata. They were not simply God's amanuenses (though could one be summoned to a greater honor?). No! They were men; and their characteristics are all visible through the pages they write. Yet, it is the word of the Holy Spirit, the *verbum Dei*.

And Peter says that this is the word to which all believers should give heed. He has been testifying to the wonder of his own experience — how on the Mount of Transfiguration they actually heard the voice of God. Yet, he says, there is something even more wonderful than that. The Scriptures of truth are far more glorious. They abide forever. God's Word lives and abides forever. When the Holy Spirit communicated that Word, He intended it to be heeded and responded to, even as men heed and respond to a light that shines in a dark place. The communion of the Holy Spirit is the communication of the very words of God.

Rejection of this communion

Among the most awesome facts of which Christ spoke is the possibility of rejecting the communion of the Holy Spirit. There are different ways in which this is described in the Bible but none is more terrifying than what our Lord teaches about blasphemy against the Holy Spirit.

The words are found at Matthew 12:31, 32:

> Wherefore I say unto you, All manner of sin and blasphemy shall be forgiven unto men; but the blasphemy against the Holy Spirit shall not be forgiven unto men. And whosoever speaketh a word against the Son of man, it shall be forgiven him; but whosoever speaketh against the Holy Spirit, it shall not be forgiven him, neither in this world, neither in the world to come.

Now, this is admittedly a very difficult passage. But we cannot avoid it simply because of its difficulty. We have been thinking about the communion of the Holy Spirit and indicating that this means address and prayer to the Holy Spirit. We have seen also that through this communion the thoughts of God were so communicated to holy men that they wrote as they were moved by the Holy Spirit. But these verses of Matthew speak of the very reverse of what we have been considering. Instead of addressing the Holy Spirit, here is address against the Holy Spirit. Instead of communion with the Holy Spirit, here is condemnation of the Holy Spirit. Sin of that kind, says Jesus, will never know forgiveness. This is the unpardonable sin.

Under the Old Testament regimen, blasphemy against the name of God was punishable by death (Lev. 24:15, 16). So, under the New Testament economy, blasphemy of the Holy Spirit is *the* sin on which eternal judgment rests.

But what is this blasphemy? Is it ascribing the holy actions of Christ the Son of God to evil spirits? Is it the simpler view that all who ultimately refuse to acknowledge the Son of God and so remain finally unrepentant are guilty of this sin? These are part of this sin; but there is even more to be said.

To blaspheme means to slander, revile, rail at, or speak falsely of things that are sacred or Persons that are divine. But how can blaspheming the Holy Spirit be a greater sin than blaspheming the Son of man? Well, our Lord obviously uses the phrase "Son of man" deliberately. He is speaking of Himself in His humiliation; but the Holy Spirit is never known in humiliation. He is the Spirit of the ascended Christ. He is the Spirit of the Lord of glory. To blaspheme therefore against the Holy Spirit is to blaspheme against the very essence of the Spirit of God; it is to communicate to others that Christ is anti-Christ or that the anti-Christ is Christ.

This sin is unpardonable because it places the man who commits it in the very place where God cannot come. Man sets himself beyond even the reach of God when he states that the holy is unholy, the pure unpure, the truth is untruth. It is unpardonable because to reach a place where you slander the Spirit of God and call Him a Spirit of darkness is not an unpremeditated act but a persistent and deliberate preference of darkness to light. As Bishop Ryle says, it is the union of light in the head and hatred in the heart. It is the full and final rejection of all the moral demands which the Holy Spirit makes upon the conscience.

The rejection of the communion of the Holy Spirit is therefore in a very real sense the unpardonable sin. It is the ultimate denial of the Word that God has spoken. It is never a sin of ignorance but a sin against knowledge and understanding. It is a habitual attitude. It is a sin of character, not of an isolated moment of crisis. It is sin committed against the constant strivings of the Holy Spirit who, having convicted us of sin, righteousness, and judgment, continues to plead with us to repent and believe the Gospel. It is a sin therefore of the heart, not merely of the tongue or mind — and out of the heart are the issues of life.

J. Oswald Sanders has written a pointed paragraph on this awesome subject.

> Why is there no forgiveness for this sin? Because there is not sufficient virtue in the blood of Christ? Because God is capricious? Surely not! There must be always two parties to forgiveness — the forgiver and the one who is to be forgiven. If the one who has sinned obstinately refuses to be forgiven, what more can God do? For His Spirit to continue to strive would only increase the sinner's responsibility to no purpose. The sin is unforgivable, because it rejects forgiveness, and for such sin there can be no provision in the nature of the case. Let all who as yet have not yielded to the wooings of the Spirit, cease to gamble upon the grace of God, and yield at once, lest they cross the fatal line. [5]

These are fearful words. We have been told that "in the beginning was the Word, and the Word was with God, and the Word was God. The same was in the beginning with God. All things were made by him; and without him was not anything made that was made. In him was life; and the life was the light of men. . . .

---

[5] J. Oswald Sanders, *The Holy Spirit of Promise* (Fort Washington, Pennsylvania: Christian Literature Crusade, Inc., 1940), p. 136.

And the Word was made flesh, and dwelt among us (and we beheld his glory, the glory as of the only begotten of the Father), full of grace and truth" (John 1:1-4, 14). When we by the power of the eternal Spirit are made to know what that Word is and is saying, and yet reply with words that are of a totally contrary nature, we show ourselves perverse, foolish, sinful, and depraved. Our only hope is to cry now for mercy to the One who delights in mercy. If there is still concern in your heart about this, it is a sign that you have not yet committed the unpardonable sin. Flee then from the wrath to come while yet there is time. God's Spirit will not always strive with man.

Fullness of communion

Earlier in this book we reviewed the particular emphases of the charismatic movement on the "baptism" or "indwelling" of the Holy Spirit. The Pentecostal view is that the full gift of the Spirit is not received when Christ is received; that is, the fullness of the Spirit is not just a privilege, received simply or almost unconsciously receiving Christ. Rather, on this view it is an obligation to be sought specifically and experientially along with, or as a result of, receiving Christ. It is said that we are commanded to seek this fullness and are not obeying God unless we do. On this view, the gift of the Spirit, and thereby the communion of the Holy Spirit, does not come simply as a result of (a) receiving (b) salvation in Christ (c) by faith. No! An obligation rests on all believers to (a) seek (b) the fullness of the Spirit (c) through conditions, including, of course, the condition of faith in Christ.

We do not accept this view. The Gospel proclaims that the Father sends His Son for the salvation of men but also that He sends His Spirit, downward in the Word of the Gospel, then upward in Christian prayer. "Through the Spirit, we receive the spirit of adoption whereby we cry, 'Father, dear Father'" (Rom. 8:15, translation mine). Frederick Dale Bruner declares,

> As God fulfils in Christ the *conditions* for the reception of His gift, and as He *communicates* this gift through the preaching of Christ, and baptism in His Name, so finally, and through the same gospel, He enables even the *response* of prayer Godward. From heaven through history into the heart and back to heaven again the whole circuit is God's (cf. Rom. 11:36: "from . . . through . . . and *to*

Him are all things"). And the Spirit who comes enabling Christian prayer is not an influence or principle alien to the Father and the Son but in Paul's understanding He is God's own Spirit, or in Paul's exact, even trinitarian expression, He is "the Spirit of His Son." The work of salvation is the work of the triune God, Father, Son and Holy Spirit. So that even in the *closing* of the circle of salvation — in the prayer "dear Father" — the Spirit of God's Son is the Giver and men are not burdened with themselves or with their works. [6]

To enjoy the communion of the Holy Spirit in fullness we do not need any new baptism of the Holy Spirit. All things are ours when we receive the Son. We are heirs of God and joint heirs with Jesus Christ. At the same time, it is indisputable that all Christians in answer to believing prayer may receive an inflow of the Spirit of God which may well appear as a fresh baptism of the Holy Spirit and of fire.

The communion of the Holy Spirit is given us so that Christ's joy may be fulfilled in us. This communion is all of grace, glorious in holiness, and a continual fountain of praise. The life of the Holy Spirit within us is a sharing of the life of God as manifested in Jesus Christ, God's Son. It is a life of love, joy, peace, longsuffering, gentleness, goodness, meekness, faith, self-control. The fruit of the Holy Spirit is always known when we share the communion of the Holy Spirit. His presence is light. His being is an ocean of irresistible mercy. His nearness is illumination. His power is all-sufficient for every need.

Nothing can mar this communion except sin and love of self. The way to this communion therefore, as to all things in the Christian life, is the way of the cross. To abide in fellowship with the Holy Spirit means that we abide beneath the shadow of that wondrous cross on which the Prince of glory died. It is the experience of this communion that will mark out to others that we are of another Kingdom than that of this world. The world around us is on fire. In many areas the Christian Church is simply disappearing and with it the entire culture that Christianity has granted us for many years. We live in a post-Christian world that is clearly under the judgment of God. What are we to do? There is only one thing I can say to those Christian disciples who can still be seen on the

---

[6] Frederick D. Bruner, *A Theology of the Holy Spirit* (Grand Rapids: Wm. B. Eerdmans Publishing Company, 1970), p. 269.

ramparts: Live in the communion of the Holy Spirit. Live and walk in the light with God — that is the communion of the Father, the Son, and the Holy Spirit. In the midst of the world, and particularly the western world that has known so much of the illumination of God but today is busy blocking out that light with demonic and devilish delight, it is our destiny to show that the communion of the Holy Spirit is not just a mere phrase coined by well-meaning but ignorant men. Walk in the light of God's Word. There is no chasm between any denominational disciple who bows before the living God and therefore before the verbal, propositional communication of God's Word, the Scriptures. This makes us brothers in Christ. The communion of the Holy Spirit is nothing less than the communion of a divine brotherhood. Let us walk fearlessly therein.

22

The Holy Spirit and Counseling

His name will be called "Wonderful Counselor . . ."
(Isaiah 9:6 RSV).

*I will pray the Father, and he will give you another [of
the same kind of] Counselor* (John 14:16 RSV).

TO THINK OF THE COMMUNION of the Holy Spirit leads us on naturally to consider how the Spirit helps us to counsel one another.

The communion of the Holy Spirit is never a monopoly of any single class. He is given to "all that believe." All that a minister who has been ordained to the ministry of the Word and sacraments is able to do, all other disciples may equally do. The Holy Spirit enters into partnership with all who believe in Jesus as Savior and Lord. He becomes Helper, Teacher, Witness, Guide, and Strength — for all who believe. All things become possible to them that believe in Him. He strengthens with might and leads with wisdom. His resources are inexhaustible. His power is invincible. His wisdom is unconquerable. In the train of Christ's triumph He leads us — and leads on. He makes us more than overcomers. He even makes us to be spoil-gatherers on the field of testing and temptation.

I stress this in order to move one step further and say that the Holy Spirit can give us the wisdom that we need to counsel others. We preach Christ, as Paul says, "teaching every man in all wisdom; that we may present every man perfect in Christ Jesus" (Col. 1:28). But if we are to "teach every man in all wisdom" we need the aid of the Holy Spirit. Effective counseling cannot be done without the aid of the Holy Spirit. Christian counseling must be done in and with the help of the Holy Spirit.

Now, counseling is greatly needed within the Christian Church as well as beyond its borders. We live in an age of the psychiatrist. Recently I heard a very famous lady say that she went regularly to her psychiatrist "in the same way as people used to go to the priest for help and absolution." It was a very telling description of our age. Our secular world needs someone in whom to confide as much as did the religious generations of centuries ago. Nothing that I say here will be directed against psychiatrists as such. They have acquired certain qualifications and under certain circumstances help the needy. But do the qualifications a psychiatrist obtains at a university equip him to help those who have lost their self-control if he himself has not found the true secret of self-control? Self-control is part of the fruit of the Holy Spirit. Can a man who does not know the Holy Spirit, however learned he may be, impart such grace and spell out the secret of a balanced life if he has not for himself found the peace that passes understanding?

The Holy Spirit and the means of grace

For the most part, the Holy Spirit effects changes of character in the lives of disciples by showing them how they should properly use the means of grace. The Word of God, the sacraments, the fellowship of the Church, prayer and fasting are the means He employs to create the life of God within the soul of man in ever-deepening evidence and authority. Likewise, the disciple, being taught by the Holy Spirit how to use these means of grace for himself, learns how to show others the mode of their employ. These means of grace are the basic tools all counselors should have before they attempt to counsel others. Holiness is wholeness. True wholeness (or holiness) consists of love, joy, peace, longsuffering, patience, kindness, goodness, faithfulness, gentleness, meekness, self-control and this is the "fruit" of the Holy Spirit. It is obviously useless to try to impart these virtues apart from Him. To so try is to deny the essential depravity of the human heart (which the Bible emphasizes on every page) and also to underestimate the work of Christ on the cross and man's need for forgiveness and justification before God.

Every Christian disciple can teach another what Christ has done for Him and how. Where any work of grace has occurred, the recipient of that blessing should be able to testify about it. In doing so, he becomes a counselor of others. And in a very real sense, because he starts with the first premises of the Gospel, he is probably able to do more for his brother in need than anyone without the Gospel though with all the psychiatric pharmacopeia of today. Medication is no substitute for a work of grace. Yet all too frequently, a minister will "refer" a needy person to the care of a psychiatrist who knows nothing of the grace of God, nothing of the fruit of the Holy Spirit, nothing of the biblical ways of helping a troubled soul.

When anyone comes to you in need of psychiatric counseling, your first responsibility is to look to the Holy Spirit and to pray that the Holy Spirit will begin His work of healing. Much of the problem may have been created by the Holy Spirit as He has convicted of sin and guilt. Why should He not therefore be the first One to whom we turn, pleading that the efficacy of the blood of Jesus be applied and that all the means of grace be pursued and possessed?

Counseling from the Word of God

The experience of Augustine is helpful here. He had lived a riotous life of lust and license, but in his heart there was a deep conviction of his need for cleansing. It was A.D. 372 and spring was in the air. Augustine, a young man of thirty-one, in great distress of mind, entered a garden near Milan. The sins of his youth, a youth spent in following after the sins of the flesh and impiety, weighed heavily on his soul. Lying under a fig tree, pouring out abundant tears, he heard from a neighboring house a young voice saying and repeating in rapid succession, *Tolle, lege! Tolle, lege!* (Take and read!) Receiving this as a word of counsel from God to read the holy Scriptures, he returned to the place where he had left his friend, Alypius, to procure the roll of the epistles of Paul, the apostle of the Lord, which he had a short time before left with him. "I seized the roll," he tells, in describing this occurrence; "I opened it and read in silence the chapter in which my eyes first lighted." It was the thirteenth chapter of the epistle to the Romans. "Let us walk honestly, as in the day; not in rioting and drunkenness, not in chambering and wantonness, not in strife and envying. But put ye on the Lord Jesus Christ, and make not provision for the flesh, to fulfil the lusts thereof" (Rom. 13:13, 14). All was decided by that word. "I did not read any more," says Augustine, "nor was there any need; every doubt was banished." The morning star had risen in his heart. Old things had suddenly passed away and all things had as suddenly become new. His saved soul entered a new world of grace and mercy and peace, and to God he gave the glory.

I have often wondered what would have been the result if Augustine, with an identical experience and the same sense of need, had lived in our time and been counseled about his burden of guilt and sin. No doubt he would have been sent to a psychiatrist — or at least there would have been some who would have urged that course. It may, however, have happened to him today as it occurred in his own day. A voice might have been heard urging him to turn to the Word of God. In his own time, it was the voice of a child who pointed to him the right way. It could happen again. In any case, the guidance to go to the Word of God from whatever source it came would be helpful and instructive. The Holy Spirit still counsels from the Word He inspired holy men of God to write. And the humblest of Christians who knows the Word of God, who has hidden that Word in his heart and is being taught daily from its holy mysteries, is able well and wisely to show the way by which true peace can be found, the way in which real deliverance from the fever of guilt can be secured.

Jay E. Adams has a comment on this which is worthy of most careful study:

> The Holy Spirit is the source of all genuine personality changes that involve the sanctification of the believer, just as truly as He alone is the One that brings life to the dead sinner. It is time that Christian ministers and other counsellors asked again, "Who has bewitched you. . . ? Having begun in the Spirit, are you now being perfected in the flesh?" Why are Christians without peace turning to men who themselves know nothing of the peace of God that passes all understanding? How is it that Christian ministers refer parishioners to a psychiatrist who has never been able to discover the secret of control in his own life? Outwardly he may appear calm and assured, mature, patient and even suave. Can this be his actual condition if he does not know Jesus Christ? Can he have the fruit of the Spirit apart from the Spirit?

---

[1] Jay E. Adams, *Competent to Counsel* (Nutley, New Jersey: Presbyterian and Reformed Publishing Company, 1970), p. 21.

Counseling is the work of the Holy Spirit. Effective counseling cannot be done apart from Him.

Counseling from sovereignty

Too often when men think of the Holy Spirit, they think of something impersonal, an influence, a force, but never a Person. Yet the personality of the Holy Spirit is affirmed on every page of holy Scripture. The Holy Spirit is shown as One who speaks (Rev. 2:7), prays (Rom. 8:26), calls out missionaries, oversees the Church, and gives commandment concerning the life and practice of the apostles and the entire Church (Acts 13:2; John 16:13). He may be grieved (Eph. 4:30), insulted (Heb. 10:29), blasphemed and sinned against (Matt. 12:31, 32), quenched (1 Thess. 5:19). He is God *with* us. As a Person of the Godhead He is sovereign; therefore all who would counsel others with the aid of the Holy Spirit must be prepared to allow Him to determine the times and seasons when and how He will intervene and work miraculously. This means that when counseling others from the Word of God, we must recognize that the Holy Spirit may work immediately but that also He may in His sovereignty take time to effect His work of grace. Even though He is sovereign, He nonetheless usually works through human agencies. But if human agents ever take to themselves the glory that is the prerogative of the Holy Spirit to give to Christ Jesus alone, power departs and the miracle does not happen.

I use the word miracle advisedly. All true counseling from the Word of God and by the aid of the Holy Spirit ought to issue in miracle. If, however, we rebelliously circumvent the ministry of the Holy Spirit, we divest ourselves of powers that are vital for the aid of any needy soul. Paul speaks of the Word of God being given by inspiration of the Spirit of God and being profitable to the end that the man of God might be perfect, thoroughly furnished for every good work. Now this is miracle. The creation of a man of God is a miracle. It is to this end that the Holy Spirit in sovereignty works through the disciple who depends entirely upon Him and upon the Word of Scripture. When this happens, miracle happens.

The conversion of Augustine to which we have referred is a classic example of the way in which the Spirit operates. A needy soul, convicted of sin and longing for release, is led by the Holy

Spirit to the Scriptures and hears in them the voice divine. All true counseling should point on to the same living Word.

The witness of the Holy Spirit

"The Spirit bears witness with our spirit that we are the children of God" (Rom. 8:16). Now all creation is shown to be the work of the Holy Spirit — witness Job crying aloud: "The Spirit of God has made me and the breath of the Almighty has given me life" (Job 33:4) and compare this with Psalm 33:6: "By the Word of the Lord were the heavens made; and all the host of them by the breath of his mouth." Even so is unregenerate man born anew into the family of God by the Spirit of God. "Marvel not that I said unto thee, you must be born again. The wind bloweth where it listeth, and thou hearest the sound thereof, but canst not tell whence it cometh, or whither it goeth; so is everyone that is born of the Spirit" (John 3:7, 8). The Holy Spirit brings the believer in Christ to life eternal. He indwells the believer. He gives assurance of salvation through this indwelling, an experience which is called being sealed "with that Holy Spirit of promise" (Eph. 1:13). He empowers the disciple for all forms of service. We are never promised sinless perfection in this life. Neither, however, are we engaged to lives of sinless imperfection. The entire eighth chapter of Romans should show us that we are called to a life of victory and that in Christ old things pass away and all things become new.

But a young Christian must be taught these things. He can and should be taught by the disciples who have come to know the power of the Holy Spirit, His wisdom in guiding, His amazing grace in directing into all truth. It is to this kind of counseling that every Christian is called. We must not fail our Lord. He has sent us forth into all the world to make disciples of all nations; but He has expressly stated that this can be done only in and through the power of the eternal Spirit. We must, accordingly, seek this gracious endowment of wisdom that will make us wise counselors of all who are in trouble and will especially make us soul winners — thrusting in the sickle at the time when the need is greatest and the opportunity is glorious.

Counseling is an art which most disciples can learn. The Christian must first of all become acquainted with the best of books; then he must inwardly digest all that the holy Scriptures teach.

Thus he is readied to supply the kind of help that others need. Indeed, he is far better prepared, as he depends entirely on the guidance of the Holy Spirit, to direct others into healing and health of mind and spirit than the most learned person can hope to be without the Spirit's aid. Of course, every area of life is open to our sovereign and illimitable God — and any worker may unknowingly be subjected to divine overruling in his practices and insights. Nonetheless, it remains true that human techniques can never supplant the sovereign work of grace of the Holy Spirit.

The Holy Spirit and the imago Dei

When sin entered, the image of God in which man was first created was ruined and destroyed. True counseling aims at the re-creation of that image. This means that in the work of sanctification, which is another name for the re-creating of the image of God in the soul of man, the ministry of the Holy Spirit is absolutely essential and any counselor who is truly following Christ will seek His leading and light and strength.

First, communication between God and man must be reestablished. Where there is no divine life, there is no true communication. That is what Paul stresses in 1 Corinthians 2:8: "None of the princes of this world knew [about this wisdom] for had they known it, they would not have crucified the Lord of glory." Further on in the same chapter he adds, "These things we speak, not in the words which man's wisdom teaches, but which the Holy Spirit teaches; we interpret what is spiritual in spiritual language" (vs. 13, translation mine). By means such as these, extraordinary personality changes can be effected. This is the goal of the Holy Spirit. It is also the goal of the true Christian counselor.

As we depend on the Holy Spirit and learn to use the sword of the Spirit which is the Word of God, we enable our brother in need to put off his old patterns of life and to become involved in the new disciplines which Christ enjoins. This is our task as Christian counselors. It is one the whole Church needs to learn. This responsibility of the disciple must be spelled out very clearly. When our Lord sent His disciples out into the world, He said, "You will be witnesses unto me" (Acts 1:8). This same responsibility rests on us today. Our responsibility is to establish new Christians in their faith. They must first, of course, be brought to faith in Christ.

Thereafter, they have to be confirmed in it. This was Paul's great burden. He wrote to the Colossians:

> So naturally, we proclaim Christ! We warn everyone we meet, and we teach everyone we can, all that we know about him, so that, if possible, we may bring every man up to his full maturity in Christ Jesus. This is what I am working at all the time with all the strength that God gives me. . . . How I long that you may be encouraged, and find out more and more how strong are the bonds of Christian love. How I long for you to grow more certain in your knowledge and more sure of your grasp of God himself. May your spiritual experience become richer as you see more and more fully God's great secret, Christ himself! For it is in him, and in him alone, that man will find all the treasures of wisdom and knowledge (Col. 1:28, 29; 2:2, 3 *Phillips*).

All that the Holy Spirit was to Christ He will be to you. All that the Holy Spirit accomplished through Christ He is willing to accomplish in you. And it is this tremendous message we bear as we witness "in the power of the Holy Spirit." Filled with Christ's Spirit, we warn every man concerning his responsibility to God and show him how wonderfully God has made provision for his every need. As our Lord taught His disciples, so we teach by the grace of the Holy Spirit. This is our glory. This is our task. "When the fulness of time was come, God sent forth his Son. . . . " (Gal. 4:4). Even so He sends us forth to make disciples and to speak a word to them that are gone out of the way. "As my Father hath sent me, even so send I you" (John 20:21). In His strength we go. In utter dependence on the Holy Spirit we move out toward them that sit in darkness and under the shadow of death. For we are the light of the world. We are the salt of the earth. We are under commission of the Lord God, the Father Almighty. Dare we falter or fail Him?

A glorious ending

Our Lord's life was mapped out for Him. He came forth to do the Father's will and day by day that will was unfolded and interpreted to Him by the Holy Spirit. He grew in wisdom and in favor with God and man. He was led by the Spirit, taught by the Spirit, strengthened by the Spirit. He made no mistakes. He never needed to say, "Perhaps." His sagacity never erred. His power never failed, for He was continually upheld by the Spirit of God. Upon Him the Spirit was poured without measure.

The coming of Christ is the mightiest act of God in history. All that happened in the life span of our Lord was under appointment of the Holy Spirit. And as He sought the lost and brought them back into His fold, so are we called of God to do. It is our joyous and happy privilege to tell others about Him who was the everlasting Word and of the words He taught all men everywhere to say. To point another to that Word and to open another ear to the entrance of those words He so truthfully spoke is the responsibility of every disciple. God grant that through the counsel we shall give in the illumination of the Spirit of God, some will one day "see His face" and in the terrible glory of that day know that God alone in Christ can be, through the eternal Spirit, unutterable love.

23

The Temple of the Holy Spirit

Know ye not that ye are the temple of God, and that the Spirit of God dwelleth in you? (1 Corinthians 3:16).

What, know ye not that your body is the temple of the Holy Spirit which is in you, which you have of God, and you are not your own? For you are bought with a price: therefore glorify God in your body, and in your spirit, which are God's (I Corinthians 6:19, 20).

HERE IS A REMARKABLE ANALOGY. The temple was dear to every Jew. It was built to divine specifications. Moses was commanded to build the tabernacle according to the pattern that he had seen on the holy mount. He did so. And when the tabernacle was raised, the glory of the Lord covered it. So also, when Solomon completed the temple, "the cloud filled the house of the Lord, so that the priests could not stand to minister because of the cloud: for the glory of the Lord had filled the house of the Lord" (1 Kings 8:10, 11).

Now, says Paul, the body of the Christian is the temple of the Holy Spirit. He expresses the same thought in Romans 8:9: "You are not in the flesh, but in the Spirit, if so be that the Spirit of God dwell in you." And again in verse 11 of the same chapter: "But if the Spirit of him that raised up Jesus from the dead dwell in you, he that raised up Christ from the dead shall also quicken your mortal bodies by his Spirit that dwelleth in you." The temple is in his mind. He thinks of the way in which the glory of God filled the temple. And now he says that, even as the glory filled the temple made with hands, so will the Holy Spirit dwell with the disciple and glorify the One who is the chief cornerstone of the temple, even Jesus Christ our Lord.

245

But what is meant by the phrase "He dwelleth in you"?

Andrew Murray in *The Spirit of Christ* compares the three parts of the temple — the outer court, the holy place, and the holy of holies into which the High Priest alone could enter, and that only one day each year — with a threefold division of man — the outer, visible life in the body; the soul with its power of mind and feeling and will; and then that place where God dwells "with him that is of a humble and contrite heart, the holy place of the Most High." When there is true regeneration, God dwells in that holy place and man can commune with his God in holiness and peace. This is ingenious, though not all would agree with the tripartite division of man that Dr. Murray suggests. And yet unmistakably, the Holy Spirit, as a living Person, literally indwells us. If this be not so, if the terms used in the New Testament do not involve personality, there is an end to intelligible speech. The indwelling of the temple of our bodies by the Spirit of God is a real indwelling of a real, personal, spiritual Presence.

The incarnation of the Holy Spirit

In the marginal reading of Judges 6:34 we read that "the Spirit clothed himself with Gideon." As we read this in the light of the New Testament, we see that even as "a body was prepared for the Son of God," so is a body furnished for the Spirit.

The miracle of the incarnation of the Son of God is that the eternal Son came to inhabit a living body, miraculously conceived within the womb of the virgin Mary. So is it with the Spirit. When Christ is believed in as Savior and Lord, the Holy Spirit incarnates Himself within the body of the believer. A body was prepared by the Holy Spirit for the Son. Even so, a body for the Holy Spirit is made possible by the Son. Gideon became a mighty man of valor by the aid of the Holy Spirit. The Spirit clothed Himself with Gideon as with a garment. The life of Gideon became the life of the Spirit. The man was empowered and the Spirit was incarnate. The Holy Spirit wrought through Gideon's hands, thought through Gideon's brain, felt through Gideon's heart, spoke through Gideon's voice. Yet all the time Gideon was still Gideon and the Holy Spirit was still the Holy Spirit.

In no other way can we think of the indwelling Holy Spirit. He is real. He is a living Person, a divine Presence, a fountain of fire indwelling the heart of the true disciple. When the Spirit of God dwells in us, we "are not in the flesh, but in the Spirit" (Rom. 8: 9). In Jesus Christ incarnate, two whole, perfect, and distinct natures — the Godhead and the manhood — were inseparably joined together in one Person, without conversion, composition, or confusion. This Person is very God of very God, yet one Christ, the only Mediator between God and man. Even so does the personality of the Holy Spirit indwell the life of the Christian disciple, becoming the life of his life, the soul of his soul. And this happens in such a way that the disciple has the Holy Spirit ruling in him, leading him, guiding him, sanctifying him, preparing him body and soul for glorification. He indwells the believer as the animating Soul of his soul, Spirit of his spirit, repeating in Himself the mystery of the union of two natures in one personality, again without conversion, composition, or confusion.

The perpetuation of the Incarnation

It is in this way and by this means that the incarnation of Jesus Christ is continued in the Church, which is the Body of Christ. Even as every disciple is indwelt by the Holy Spirit, so is the Church, the Body of Christ.

This is, of course, divine mystery. It could be nothing else. But we fail to scan God's works completely if we do not see this divine gift of grace. He gives His Spirit without measure to all who believe in Jesus Christ as Savior and Lord and are serving Him faithfully within the fellowship of the Church, His Body. As the life of my life and the soul of my soul, the Holy Spirit indwells me and glorifies Christ in me. This is the mystery of all the ages. Yet it can be understood by a little child. In Christ God invaded history to redeem and make propitiation for the sin of all the world. In like fashion the Holy Spirit invades the temple of my body, assumes residence therein, and begins the mystical, yet so real, re-creation of Christ to the glory of God the Father.

"At that day you shall know that I am in my Father, and you in me, and I in you" (John 14:20). Could anything be plainer or more emphatic? The truth transcends human achievement and the promise surpasses all human understanding. But this work of divine omnipotence and love is real. Through this divine indwelling of the

Holy Spirit, the continuation or perpetuation of the Incarnation is fulfilled. There is nothing more wonderful than this. Only to think that a mortal man can be filled with all the fullness of God should send us to our knees in rapturous adoration. This is the ultimate blessing of Pentecost — the world shall know the Son of God and it is the Spirit indwelling the believer and giving him the ability of witness to his Lord, that makes all this come most gloriously true.

> God moves in a mysterious way,
> His wonders to perform;
> He plants His footsteps in the sea
> And rides upon the storm.
>
> His purposes will ripen fast,
> Unfolding every hour;
> The bud may have a bitter taste,
> But sweet will be the flower.

If we have recognized that our body is the temple of the Holy Spirit, we must keep it undefiled for Him. We must remember constantly that our conscious life, though it be only a tiny part of our personality, is to be regarded by us as a shrine of the Holy Spirit. He will look after the unconscious part that we know nothing of. But we must see that we guard the conscious part for which we are responsible. We have to account to God for the way in which we rule our body under His domination. "I beseech you," says Paul, "that you present your bodies a living sacrifice" (Rom. 12:1). We cannot fail to do this if we realize that our bodies are temples of the Holy Spirit. All God's law for me and my body is summed up in this tremendous and amazing utterance: "Your body is the temple of the Holy Spirit." To recall this moment by moment is to walk with God in the light and to perpetuate the incarnation of Jesus Christ, Son of God, our Lord and Savior.

The Spirit's indwelling and the simplification of life

In Kelly's *Testament of Devotion* there is a passage that almost takes one's breath away with the potential of the life with the Holy Spirit. Kelly is thinking of the simplicity that lies beyond complexity, the naiveté that is on the yonder side of sophistication. He calls it "the beginning of spiritual maturity that comes after the awkward age of religious busyness for the Kingdom of God." Then he goes on:

The mark of this simplified life is radiant joy. It lives in the fellowship of the transfigured face. Knowing sorrow to the depths, it does not agonize and fret and strain, but in serene, unhurried calm it walks in time with the joy and assurance of Eternity. Knowing fully the complexity of men's problems, it cuts through to the love of God and ever cleaves to Him.

I have in mind something deeper than the simplification of our crowded programmes, our absurdly crowded calendars of appointments through which so many pantingly and frantically gasp. These do become simplified in holy obedience, and the poise and peace we have been missing can really be found. But there is a deeper, an internal simplification of the whole of one's personality, stilled, tranquil, in childlike trust listening ever to Eternity's whisper, walking with a smile into the dark.

This amazing simplification comes when we "centre down" and when life is lived with singleness of eye, from a holy centre where the breath and stillness of Eternity are heavy upon us and we are wholly yielded unto Him. . . . We are called beyond strain, to peace and power and thorough abandonment of self. We are called to put our hands trustingly in His hand and walk the holy way, in no anxiety, assuredly resting on Him. [1]

When we enter into full realization that the Holy Spirit is making our bodies His temple, it is to this quality of life that we hasten with unrelenting pace. Otherwise, we live in double-mindedness. We miss the certainties of His love. We lose the pearl of great price — and there is no need for losing it. May He whose Spirit is everlasting love and joy and peace keep us rejoicing in the indwelling Presence and "centred down" in the true simplifying grace of His Holy Spirit.

The quickening of our mortal bodies

In Romans 8:11 Paul utters one of his profoundest sayings. "If the Spirit or him that raised up Jesus from the dead dwell in you, he that raised up Christ from the dead shall also quicken your mortal bodies by his Spirit that dwelleth in you." Here again we meet with this phrase: "[He] dwelleth in you." But with it there is this other phrase — "shall quicken your mortal bodies," or, as Phillips translates, "He . . . will bring to your whole being new strength and vitality."

---

[1] Thomas R. Kelly, *A Testament of Devotion* (London: Hodder and Stoughton, 1943), p. 63.

To know our bodies as the temple of the Holy Spirit is to experience His bringing to our being "whole new strength and vitality." Is not that what we all need? New strength and vitality! Not new faculties necessarily, but the awakening of the faculties we possess to fresh and vigorous action. The Holy Spirit brings to us fullness of life. This is the very essence of His ministry. He gives us sanity and spiritual power; but He also gives us vitality and vigor for the work we have to do. He enables us to fulfill the commandment: "Whatsoever thy hand findeth to do, do it with thy might" (Eccles. 9:10). The Holy Spirit redeems the material through the spiritual. It is the joy of the Holy Spirit to clothe Himself with consecrated humanity. He loves to accomplish extraordinary things through very ordinary people who have learned the art of allowing Him to dwell within them in ungrieved sovereignty and to rule and reign supreme within the temples of their mortal bodies.

John Masefield has written of this beautifully in *The Everlasting Mercy:*

> I did not think, I did not strive,
> The deep peace burned my me alive;
> The bolted door had broken in,
> I knew that I had done with sin.
> I knew that Christ had given me birth
> To brother all the souls on earth,
> And every bird and every beast
> Should share the crumbs broke at His feast.
>
> O glory of the lighted mind.
> How dead I'd been, how dumb, how blind,
> The station brook, to my new eyes,
> Was babbling out of Paradise.
> The waters rushing from the rain
> Were singing Christ has risen again.
> I thought all earthly creatures knelt
> For rapture of the joy I felt.
>
> The narrow station-wall's brick ledge,
> The wild hop withering on the hedge,
> The lights in huntsman's upper storey
> Were parts of the eternal glory,
> Were God's eternal garden flowers.
> I stood in bliss at this for hours. [2]

---

[2] Published by Heinemann, London, 1923.

Through the everlasting mercy of God, the Holy Spirit indwells the disciple of Christ. By that same eternal Spirit we are renewed in strength and vitality through our entire body.

The Holy Spirit and faith healing

Can we go on without a passing reference to the question of miraculous healing? Surely not! Paul speaks of the "renewing of the Holy Spirit" when he writes to Titus (Titus 3:5). He is referring to the great work of regeneration by the Holy Spirit, but there is a further sense implied in the words. The Holy Spirit is the Spirit of all true physical and spiritual renewal. He who indwells the temple of our bodies is the Spirit of holiness — i.e., of health. We must therefore learn the art of discussing everything with the Holy Spirit. He loves to hear us as we share our hopes and fears with Him daily.

> To talk with God, no breath is lost,
>   Talk on!
> To walk with God, no strength is lost,
>   Walk on!
> To wait on God, no time is lost,
>   Wait on!
> Little is much when God is in it,
> Man's busiest day not worth God's minute;
> Much is little everywhere
> If God the labor does not share;
> So work with God then nothing's lost;
> Who works *with Him* does best and most.

(author unknown)

If sickness comes, don't hesitate to talk to the Holy Spirit about this. He is interested in your health and is concerned about your sickness. Tell Him all. Pray about every detail of your sickness.

But is it the will of God that His people should suffer sickness? Is it not possible that God plans that His servants should be able to escape from sickness? Does not He, who quickens our mortal bodies, mean that we in faith may claim complete deliverance from all the evil of suffering, sickness, and pain?

There are those who say so. Some months ago I was invited to attend a service being conducted by Miss Kathryn Kuhlman. For some time I had been asked my opinion of Miss Kuhlman's ministry and wished to see for myself how she conducted herself and her meetings. I had read her book *I Believe in Miracles* and I also knew that some well-known and widely respected ministers of evangelical persuasion had invited her to their pulpits and were strong in their support of her ministry. Let me in the simplest terms give my appraisal of what I saw and heard as well as the results of my thoughts during that meeting and since.

After giving a brief statement of the heart of the Christian Gospel, a statement with which I could not disagree one whit, Miss Kuhlman proceeded to invite those who wished to be healed to come to the platform. I observed that a careful screening of those who did come had actually taken place by officers of the organization before they were permitted to reach the platform. I noticed also that from time to time Miss Kuhlman would state that in a certain part of the audience some person was suffering from a certain condition and that healing was there and then being given. This person was invited to the platform and in course of time he or she came. Some who stated that they were deaf when they entered the hall now claimed they could hear. Some who had been lame were able to walk. One who came to the platform on crutches walked down the steps from the platform without his crutches. In every case, after declaring that healing had been given and received, Miss Kuhlman touched the shoulders of the healed persons and it was as though an electric shock struck them, for each time they fell backwards into the arms of some strong men delegated to catch them as they fell.

In Miss Kuhlman's second book, *God Can Do It Again,*[3] cases of healing are cited which are vouched for by medical specialists, whose names, qualifications, medical positions, and other data are duly cited. They say quite definitely that they have known people with organic diseases who have been fully cured as a result of their contact with Miss Kuhlman. In some cases medical men themselves were the subjects of such healing. Further cases could be cited. Dr. D. Martyn Lloyd-Jones in a lecture he gave in May, 1971, at Bournemouth, England, to the Annual Conference of the Christian Medical Fellowship, lists further instances of medically attested cures when all the evidence pointed in the direction of

---

[3] Kathryn Kuhlman, *God Can Do It Again* (London: Marshall, Morgan and Scott, 1969).

death. Concerning this, he writes of the changing attitudes of scientists in our times and says:

> Scientists are realizing more and more the limitations of the scientific observer, and that there is so much more in the cosmos than the scientist dogmatically assumed in the past and especially in the past century. There is a new kind of humility in truly scientific circles, and all the recent discoveries about the DNA and the RNA have greatly encouraged this new view of science — indeed made it inevitable. [4]

Furthermore, research teams in various parts of the world have been gathering lists of case histories in which there have been spontaneous cures and particularly regressions in the case of cancerous growths. The fundamental question that all this raises is this: Can we dismiss as impossible the fact of miraculous healing? And is the Holy Spirit today still dispensing in His sovereign will the "gifts of healing" to those He has chosen for this ministry?

Some biblical principles

Our guide in this as in all else must be the Word of God. We must not allow ourselves to be guided in our thinking on this kind of subject by experiences such as Kathryn Kuhlman is able to produce. It is the teaching of the Bible that must determine questions of this kind. And the Bible has a great deal to say about it. There are sick saints in the Bible. Job suffered greatly. Timothy had stomach trouble and was urged by Paul to take medication for it. Epaphroditus was "ill, near to death. But God had mercy on him" (Phil. 2:25-27 RSV). And Paul speaks frequently about his own physical weakness. A book could be written about Paul's sickness. He speaks of it as "a thorn in the flesh." He is very explicit. It was given to make sure that he did not become a victim of pride. Listen to his own version: "To keep me from being too elated by the abundance of revelations, a thorn was given me in the flesh, a messenger of Satan, to harass me, to keep me from being too elated" (2 Cor. 12:7 RSV). He prayed for deliverance. But God said no. "Three times I besought the Lord about this, that it should leave me; but he said to me, 'My grace is sufficient for you, for my power is made perfect in weakness.'" (2 Cor. 12:8, 9 RSV).

---

[4] D. Martyn Lloyd-Jones, "The Supernatural in Medicine" (London: C.M.F. Publications, 1971), p. 9.

Our Lord healed people who were troubled with many kinds of illnesses: leprosy, fevers, haemophilia, blindness, dumbness, lameness, plagues, lunacy, and demon-possession. He also gave authority to apostles and disciples to heal. He sent out the Twelve and said to them, "Heal the sick, raise the dead, cleanse the lepers, cast out demons" (Matt. 10:8 RSV). Our Lord used means in His healings; e.g., spittle (Mark 7:33); clay (John 9:6); and the hem of His garment (Matt. 9:20-22). The book of Acts has many instances of healings by the apostles and others; e.g., Peter and John healing the lame man at the Beautiful Gate of the temple (Acts 3:1-9); Peter casting out unclean spirits and raising the dead (Acts 5:15; 9:36-41); and Paul touching the cripple (Acts 14:8-10); casting out the spirit of divination (Acts 16:16-18); and shaking off the serpent from his hand with no harm to himself (Acts 28:3-6).

Nowhere in the New Testament is there any clear statement that such ministry of healing would end with the apostolic age. The arguments of those who claim that the closing of the New Testament canon ended the dispensation of such miracles of healing are unsure and suspect. But at the same time, nowhere in the New Testament do we read of announcements being made that there was going to be a great healing service. No! On the contrary, the healings we read about occur almost naturally on the road where Christ's servants are. They make no parade of any specific gifts of healing. They act as God appoints and directs.

The prayer of faith

Probably there is no passage more frequently quoted in connection with miraculous or divine healing than James 5:14, 15: "Is any among you sick? Let him call for the elders of the church, and let them pray over him, anointing him with oil in the name of the Lord; and the prayer of faith will save the sick man, and the Lord will raise him up; and if he has committed sins, he will be forgiven" (RSV). How often have we heard this verse quoted as though it were a panacea for all ills of the Christian. The emphasis here is on faith — "the prayer of faith will save the sick man." That this is obviously a special kind of faith — a given faith — is surely clear from the context. Our Lord taught us to pray and said, "Whatever you ask in prayer, believe that you receive it, and you will" (Mark 11:24 RSV). The "prayer of faith" is a particular kind of faith that the Holy Spirit alone can inspire. But when He gives it, and when we truly ask in the name of Jesus, God hears this prayer and answers. This is a kind of faith that cannot be worked up. It does not come through emotionalism or ecstasy. It is a gift of God. Even as the faith by which we are saved is God's gift, so is this gift of faith that enables us to pray "the prayer of faith." Spirit-taught prayer is the foundation of all such effectual prayer that God hears and answers.

Now we should bear this in mind as we think through this great question of divine or miraculous healing. God is sovereign. He can heal as and when He wills. But He can also send us sickness and suffering — as and when He wills. The true attitude of faith that comes through all the writings of the saints under the inspiration of the Holy Spirit is that we should be willing to trust God, whether He gives or takes away. "The Lord gave, and the Lord has taken away; blessed be the name of the Lord" — that is how Job reacted; and God was with him to the end.

We should therefore note most emphatically certain facts that the Bible constantly emphasizes:

1. All healing is of God. God is the Creator and He is the Re-creator. Hence, He is the only healer. Satan is a destroyer and not a healer. Any kind of healing, therefore, is divine healing, whether it is on behalf of godly or ungodly men, whether it is over a long or short space of time, whether means are employed or not. All healing is divine healing. Wherever healing takes place, it is the work of God.

2. In certain specific cases, to which we have already made reference, God refused to heal. The reference is, of course, to Paul as recorded in 2 Corinthians 12:7-10. His was a godly, a notable, and a most useful life. Health, we would naturally assume, would have made his effectiveness all the greater. Yet God refused to give healing. In this light, how can we ever state that it is a Christian principle that all sickness *can* be cured if we have only sufficient faith? An assertion of this kind is a declaration that what the Bible records is untrue.

3. God has allowed disease or infirmity to overtake the bodies of all mankind and finally brings all men to death, with two exceptions — Enoch and Elijah. Each of us, if the Lord does not

come before, will most certainly die, by accident, sickness, disease, or some other kind of fatal and terminal ailment. It is appointed for us to die. This is the concomitant of sin. There is no escape. If the claims of faith-healers who say that all sickness can be cured were valid, there would be no death for some. But it is not so. All men go down the valley to the river called death. From the moment of our birth, we begin to die.

4. In cases of healing in the Bible means are often employed: wine, as in 1 Timothy 5:23 and medicine, as in Isaiah 38:21 and Revelation 22:2. Obviously, God does not disregard or disapprove of the use of means in the granting of healing. He can take dust and clay and make them instruments of His glory in the healing of our mortal bodies.

5. In the ministry of our Lord, and this surely is a most important fact, He healed comparatively few. Evidently, He had three great purposes in mind when He healed: (1) the saving of an imperiled life, (2) the securing in a particular way the glory of God, and (3) the demonstration of the fact that He was indeed the Messiah. With two exceptions, He healed only Jews, though millions of Gentiles were in equal need of healing. The exceptions are found in Matthew 8:5-13 and 15:22-28. Likewise, when He sent out the Twelve to heal and to preach, He forbade their going to the Gentiles (Matt. 10:5-8).

6. Among the gifts of the Spirit there is one that is called "the gift of healing." But this, being a gift of the Holy Spirit, comes under the sovereignty of the Holy Spirit. It may well be that Kathryn Kuhlman possesses this gift. I do not know. But, if we are to be true to the revelation of the Scriptures, we must stress that God has by His Spirit given "to some" the "gift of healing." We must therefore not dogmatically exclude such things that appear to bear the marks of supernatural healing, nor should we be uncritically credulous of them. God is not limited to the measure of our understanding.

7. But having said what we have, let us also continue to thank God for all the amazing means that He has placed in skilled, medical hands today. Many diseases that once were plagues and fatal are today almost unknown. Medicine has moved into marvelous plateaus of service to humanity. This, too, is God's gift;

and every true physician should recognize that this is so. Whatever God does will be "through His eternal Spirit." Let us rest in Him and in Him alone for all that He knows we need, all that is necessary to make us people of God, "thoroughly furnished unto all good works" (2 Tim. 3:17). He gives us grace upon grace. Trust Him for everything.

The new dispensation of grace

Under the old dispensation of the Law, God had a temple for His people, but under the new dispensation of grace, He has His people for a temple. Much can be learned from the apostle's words: "You are the temple of God" (1 Cor. 3:16). Let us summarize briefly once more some of the all-important things that the Scriptures teach with such clarity, vividness, and power. Everything is in Jesus Christ.

"Christ *for* me" is only the preliminary truth to "Christ *in* me" and all who have been redeemed by His death are redeemed to the end that He may dwell in them by His Spirit, thereby making them and their lives the sphere of His operation and blessing. Because of this redemption it can fully and truly be said: "You are the temples of the Holy Spirit."

What are the inescapable truths that arise from this elemental truth?

1. The temple was the one place in all the land of Israel that was *given over entirely to God's use*. It was there for His service and it was completely separated from all secular purposes. It was essentially the house of God. So must it be with those who are now called to be His temples. Their whole lives without any reserve must be yielded up to Him. It is natural, therefore, that the thought of "separatedness" should be linked with the concept of the people of God as His temples. "Come out from among them, and be . . . separate . . . and touch not the unclean thing" (2 Cor. 6:17), "for the temple of God is holy which temple you are" (1 Cor. 3:17).

2. The temple thus dedicated was *handed over for His possession*. We see this very clearly in Solomon's prayer (1 Kings 8). God sealed the acceptance of this possession by fire coming from heaven and the glory of the Lord filling the temple (2 Chron. 7:1).

Nothing of self-effort, strength of resolution, or strenuous determination to live aright can be a substitute for the indwelling of God. "We will come unto him and make our abode with him" (John 14:23); that is the secret that alone transforms our total life. To be God-possessed and indwelt by Him, *this is* what it means to be His temple. It is a revelation we should believe and a promise we should claim: "The Lord, whom you seek, shall suddenly come to his temple" (Mal. 3:1). When we claim that promise and trust God to fulfill all that He has covenanted to do, then indeed we shall rejoice and will show forth His praise "in psalms and hymns and spiritual songs, singing and making melody in [our] heart to the Lord" (Eph. 5:19).

3. When God possessed the temple and indwelt it, He intended that this should result in blessing to His people. The temple became the sphere of His self-manifestation to man. There they learned His Law and received His blessing through ordinance and sacrifice. So it is still. We are temples of the Holy Spirit. We are "a light unto the nations." Holiness is therefore never an end in itself; it is only a means to an end, that end being the blessing of others through our lives and labors.

Five simple principles evolve:

1. What God claims, I yield.
2. What I yield, God accepts.
3. What He accepts, He cleanses.
4. What He cleanses, He fills.
5. What He fills, He uses.

This is the glory of the life of God within the soul of man. It is ours to possess today by faith. It will be ours throughout all eternity.

24

The Unity of the Spirit

Walk . . . with all lowliness and meekness, with long-suffering, forbearing one another in love; endeavouring to keep the unity of the Spirit in the bond of peace. There is one body, and one Spirit (Ephesians 4:1-4).

IN ONE OF THE GREATEST prayers of our Lord, the "high-priestly prayer," is the supplication "that they all may be one" (John 17: 21). The words occur and recur, emphasizing the one supreme objective Christ had for His Church. The phrase has, as we know, been taken by the World Council of Churches as its motto and, on another level, its goal; however, the unity there sought appears to be different in spirit and content from that which our Lord sought for His disciples.

Unity in the Body of Christ is clearly among the supreme objectives of the Spirit of God. No study of the great doctrine of the Holy Spirit would be complete without pondering "the unity of the Spirit."

In Ephesians, chapters 1 to 3, Paul, reflecting on the wonder of Christ as King and Head of the Church, shows how the Church is indwelt by the Holy Spirit, grows up into a habitation of God through the Spirit, and is thus destined to be filled with all the fullness of God. Then he brings the disciple down from that lofty eminence — dwelling "in the heavenlies," his life hid with Christ in God — and in the last three chapters of the letter shows how the disciple must walk worthy of his calling and in true fellowship, not only with Christ in heaven, but also with the Body of Christ on earth, with the whole company of Christ's disciples scattered all around the world.

259

> Elect from every nation,
>   Yet one o'er all the earth,
> Her charter of salvation,
>   One Lord, one faith, one birth;
> One holy Name she blesses,
>   Partakes one holy food;
> And to one hope she presses,
>   With every grace endued.

This is the relationship of Spirit-filled believers to each other. Anything short of this is certain to become an occasion of offense, division, and separation.

All one in Christ Jesus

Our Savior's prayer gives place in post-Pentecostal days to the great affirmations of our true unity in Christ and with one another. "By one Spirit we are all baptized into one body" (1 Cor. 12:13), and "You are all one in Christ Jesus" (Gal. 3:28). If there be division in the Church, it is occasioned by neglect of one sovereign truth — that our true position in Christ unites us as one. We are never intended to be isolated units, ships that pass in the night with scarcely a greeting, islands separate from one another by dividing seas. On the contrary: we are fellow-members of one body, fellow-citizens of one Kingdom, fellow-soldiers of one great army, and fellow-heirs of one divine inheritance.

Individualism has its place. God has given to some of His servants a number of talents that immediately place them in an unusual position. They stand head and shoulders above the rest. But there are also perils associated with this status. There is no doubt that the Church of Christ today as seen by the world is rent and weakened by divisions that are very largely the result of an exaggerated individualism and a neglect of our common magnetic focus around the living Lord.

One has only to ponder a little while to realize that both extreme Anglicanism and Romanism have in the past overstressed the visible unity of the Church to such a point that they deny the possibility of the life of Christ being known outside their communions. This is heresy. Now the wheel has turned almost full circle. In one area of Toronto the Presbyterians and the Roman Catholics have jointly contributed to a building in which Roman rites and Presbyterian preaching can both be heard, each in its proper time. Is this bringing us any nearer the mark of the truly Christian unity that expresses the unity of the Body of Christ? One hesitates to say so. Yet, on the other hand, many follow an exaggerated individualism, each man living for himself and in his own way contributing to the division and dissension that plague the Body of those who truly love and serve the Lord Jesus Christ.

We must get back to elementals. Some of them should be underlined very specifically.

1. "By one Spirit we are *all* baptized into one body" (1 Cor. 12:13, italics mine).

2. This one Body into which we are "baptized" is the "Body" of Jesus Christ and this is His Church.

3. "The body is not one member, but many" (1 Cor. 12:14).

4. Christ never calls us to independence but to interdependence. Paul states very clearly that we are "members one of another" (Rom. 12:5).

5. We become members of Christ's Body by faith. It is in "the unity of the faith" that we come "to mature manhood" (Eph. 4:13 RSV).

The unity of the Holy Spirit is seen and proved by the world when in the Church of Christ there is the true "fruit" of the Spirit — love, joy, peace, longsuffering, gentleness, goodness, meekness, faith, self-control. We can reduce this to a very simple rule. The unity of the Holy Spirit is apparent when Christ is the One who is glorified by all the members of His Body working together and sharing with each other the benefits of His death and risen life. To this we are called. In this we must learn to abide.

Unity in identity

All disciples share a common identity of life. Before Christ found us we were living in sin, turning away from the infinite gifts and graces of our Lord. But being born again by the Holy Spirit, we receive a transfusion of the heavenly life that will never pass away or end. The identity, therefore, that we share is first one of life. We are born of the same Spirit. We receive forgiveness for the same reason — all of us, without distinction or differentiation. We receive the Spirit of adoption in the same way; and we are led to call God our Father by the same Spirit of adoption. We are one in family name, family heritage, family likeness, family responsibilities, family privileges. We are all members of the redeemed family of God. We share a common identity of life. But that is not all. We share a common identity of ownership. "One is your Master, even Christ; and all ye are brethren" (Matt. 23:8). We belong to Christ. We are His and each of us can say, "He is mine." Too seldom, however, do we think through the implications of this great truth. If Christ is our Lord, Lord of us all, then we must recognize that we are one with each other. His sacred Person is the center of our unity; and this is so, for we yield to Him an uncompromising recognition that we all together acknowledge Him as Master and Lord. If He is Lord of us all, we should all do the things He says and commands. Not to do them is to deny that we have "one Master, even Jesus Christ."

A third element in our unity through the Holy Spirit is identity of service. Who can ever forget the occasion when the Holy Spirit spoke to the assembled elders and prophets of the Church at Antioch? "Set apart for me Barnabas and Saul for the work to which I have called them" (Acts 13:2 RSV). It seems as though for a little while they doubted the directive being given; for once again they fasted and prayed until the message came through loud and clear. "When they had fasted and prayed, and laid their hands on them, they sent them away" (Acts 13:3). This was the beginning of the first great missionary journey of Paul. It arose from a common obedience on the part of the leadership of the Church and of Paul and Barnabas themselves. From this unity of mission there is no escape even today. The task of world evangelization still confronts the disciple. The commandment of Christ has never altered. "Go therefore and make disciples of all nations" (Matt. 28:19 RSV). Yet, the tragedy of many church situations is that, faced with the awesome strength of the devil, people spend their strength either building up their own denomination or else contesting for positions that do not and can never glorify Christ. Has the time not come for Christian men and women at the heart of their own church fellowships to reconsider the words of the Psalmist: "How good and how pleasant it is for brethren to dwell together in unity . . . for there the Lord commanded the blessing" (Ps. 133:1, 3)? Service of our risen Lord should unite us in ministries that are glorifying to Him.

Broken fellowships

It would be unprofitable to write on the subject of unity and not deal with some of the grievous divisions that mar the Church of God.

This has been true of almost every century in the Christian era. But I believe that at the present time, the great accuser of the brethren is at work, stirring up strife, fomenting disagreements, breeding designs that should not even be mentioned within the house of God. Paul realized how difficult it was to maintain the unity of the Spirit in the bond of peace. Writing to the Romans, he said: "If it be possible, as much as lieth in you, live peaceably with all men" (Rom. 12:18). He recognized the subtlety of the enemy of souls. He knew the carnality of so many within the Christian Church. He realized that in a thousand cases there had been no true yielding to Christ, no acceptance of His law of unending love, no willingness to go all the way with Him who went to Calvary "for us men and for our salvation." Therefore, strife, contention, enmity, rivalry, dispute, discord, struggle, and violence erupted and in place of the unity of the Spirit there was left only the disunity of sinful minds and hearts.

Do I speak too strongly? I do not think so. I can point to many churches where the life of the minister is a veritable torture chamber, and those who are causing the greatest damage are the ones who should be standing by his side, upholding and sustaining him by prayer and brotherly love. But brotherly love does not continue. Instead, the very people who hold high office in the Church are often those who are found vilifying, slandering, and defaming the man whom, in calling, they have promised to support and obey. Anyone who knows anything about the Church at all in our times knows that what I say is true. Only recently, a brother minister told me of incident after incident in his own denomination where godly men were being persecuted by leaders within their own fellowship and in a number of cases being forced to resign. Is this the unity of the Holy Spirit? Did Christ die and rise again from the dead to no effect among us? Surely not! We are summoned to a fellowship that should be God-glorifying every moment of recorded time. But it is not so; and we only compound the sorrow of many if we refuse to recognize that it is not so.

I think especially of one great man of God. He ministered to me as few have ever done. I little knew the story that was behind his shining face. He had been maliciously pursued by a band of people who, because he would not do the things they did, resented him and ultimately got him thrown out of his ministerial office. What a travesty of the Gospel of Christ! How tragic the drama when within the very house of God these things are permitted to happen. This is not unity. This is demonism. This is Satan sowing tares among the wheat. This is the denial of everything for which the holy Bible stands. Yet it is happening on every side. Let us beware lest we become partakers in such wrongdoings. It is so fatally easy to be drawn into the misrepresentation and maligning of our brother Christian. It is equally easy for us to build up in our own minds defense mechanisms that lull us into thinking that we bear no responsibility for the state of things. May the Spirit deliver us from all such disunity and strife.

Cultivating unity

In quest of unity our minds must always be directed to the holy Scriptures. They remind us, they command us, to "keep the unity of the Spirit in the bond of peace" (Eph. 4:3). The mood is present-tense imperative. This is the new covenant of which Jeremiah wrote, where the Word of God will dwell in our hearts freely.

> After those days, saith the Lord, I will put my law in their inward parts, and write it in their hearts; and will be their God, and they shall be my people. And they shall teach no more every man his neighbour, and every man his brother, saying, Know the Lord: for they shall all know me, from the least of them unto the greatest of them, saith the Lord: for I will forgive their iniquity, and I will remember their sin no more (Jer. 31:33, 34).

This is the new commandment, that "we love one another." It was the commandment that our Lord expressed so forcibly: "A new commandment I give unto you, that you love one another; as I have loved you, that you also love one another" (John 13:34). He added, "By *this* shall all men know that you are my disciples, if you have love one to another" (John 13:35, italics mine).

If we would cultivate this Christian unity, we must live close to Christ. Living close to Him, we will live close to one another. There is much in all of us that would give bridgeheads to the enemy — the carnality of our natures, the selfishness of our spirits, the hypocrisy of our beings. If these things are indulged, then the work of the Holy Spirit is certainly going to be hindered and we will not grow into the unity which is Christ. More and more, therefore, we must walk in the spirit of 1 John 1:7. This is a verse every true disciple should repeat daily to himself, praying that its truth may be wrought out in him: "If we walk in the light, as he is in the light, we have fellowship one with another, and the blood of Jesus Christ his Son cleanseth us from all sin." There is no other way of cultivating unity. Walking in the light with Christ and experiencing the blessed cleansing of His precious blood will guard us from all assaults of the adversary of our souls and bind us in one unbroken fellowship of love, joy, and peace.

We forget too often that God has only one desire for us. It is that we should become holy people, people of God, with the character of God stamped upon us. Holiness is not some idle state of spirit in which we glide along the way of life with no call for resourcefulness and determination. Holiness is health; it is the true life of God of which we have so frequently spoken. To such a life of unbroken fellowship with God and with our brother disciples we are called. To fail to follow where God leads is to give place to the devil and to his disunity.

Helps to unity in Christ

Undoubtedly, one of the greatest means of furthering unity in Christ is the formation of little prayer cells where in intimacy of heart and mind we can be honest with one another and with God and totally transparent in His sight. It is good even to meet with one other Christian, to pledge to pray together at fixed times, to covenant to come before God at appointed times. From this togetherness there comes a bond of unity that is truly divine. But we must work at this. We must be steadfast in our covenant. It must be our common determination never to miss this appointed hour and place of prayer. We must be faithful to one another and to God.

In such a fellowship, the Word of God will, of course, be acknowledged and obeyed. God's mind will be sought. It will become a most natural thing for us to talk about ourselves, our weaknesses, our hopes, our dreams, our longings after the will of God, our sense of failure and sin when we come short of His glory.

Only when the Scriptures rule in any assembly is there truly a meeting of the Church. Our Lord said, "Where two or three are gathered together in my name, there am I in the midst of them" (Matt. 18: 20). In the verse immediately preceding He makes an even more daring statement: "If two of you shall agree on earth as touching any thing that they shall ask, it shall be done for them of my Father which is in heaven."

Matthew Henry has a beautiful comment on verse 20:

> Though but two or three are met together, Christ is among them; this is an encouragement to the meeting of a few when it is either, *first,* of choice. Besides the secret worship performed by various persons, and the public services of the whole congregation, there may be occasion sometimes for two or three to come together, either for mutual assistance in conference, or joint assistance in prayer, not in contempt of public worship, but in concurrence with it; there Christ will be present. Or, *secondly,* by constraint; when there are not more than two or three to come together, or, if there be, they dare not, *for fear of the Jews,* yet Christ will be in the midst of them, for it is not the multitude, but the faith and the sincere devotion, of the worshippers, that invites the presence of Christ; and though there be but two or three, the smallest number that can be, yet, if Christ make one among them, who is the principal one, their meeting is as honorable and comfortable as if there were two or three thousand.

A spirit of mutual forgiveness is also essential if unity is to be known. Almost immediately after Christ spoke these words that have just been quoted, Peter came to Jesus and asked: "Lord, how oft shall my brother sin against me, and I forgive him? till seven times?" (Matt. 18:21). How singularly apt is the work of the Holy Spirit in placing Scripture next to Scripture. Here is another sure way in which we shall together promote the spirit of unity. We must forgive one another, not just seven times, but until seventy times seven, as our Lord said. Forgiveness must be a continual outgoing spirit from our inmost heart. As we forgive, we demonstrate that we love. As we love, we are one.

If we would promote unity, we must constantly look for the best in our brethren. Now, let it be immediately granted that this is not easy nor is it natural to us. We are far more prone to look for offensive things in our fellow Christians. We harbor resentments against them; we are rebellious against their counsel; we refuse to see in them qualities that are God-given; we are unwilling to give to them the higher place that God has in all probability ordained for them. If we are to promote unity, we must see our brother as he is in Christ and not only as he is in himself. When you see him in Christ, you will in a miraculous way recognize also that the same life is in him that is in you. You share the same royal bloodstream. You are heirs together of the same promises. And although you need not be ignorant of his faults or failings, you will be enabled by the Holy Spirit to give him his rightful place in your mind and life. You will see to it that you outdo others in showing honor (Rom. 12:10).

The prayer of our Lord

We have already noted that our Lord, on His last night on earth, had one great prayer for His disciples: "Holy Father, keep . . . those whom thou hast given me, that they may be one" (John 17: 11). His one desire was to see us as a united flock, all gathered and kept and united in one great fold under one great Shepherd. As He is on the throne, we may be sure that this is the same prayer that He is pleading today. He intercedes for us on the throne on high. Through the eternal Spirit, He pleads the same prayer within our hearts. He prays that we may be one; that we may be perfect in one; that the world may know that the Father loves us, as He loves His Son, and has sent us as He sent His Son.

We must be very much aware of the stirrings within the Church as she reaches out after fellow-Christians. Life is always marked by a capacity to respond to the environment; and where there is the true life of Jesus Christ within the soul, you can be sure that there will always be a straining after contact with others of like spirit, a reaching out or response to those who have the same precious hope within them. Every token therefore of an awakening within the Church to desire the unity of God's people should be a theme for praise. There can be spurious and false endeavors after such unity. Of that we are very much aware. But there is a real desire that is born of God. And every true disciple knows this and recognizes this within his own heart when he is brought into contact with others who have received the same baptism he has received. In lowliness and love we must keep the unity of the Holy Spirit with those whom we contact. We must pray also that all who lead and guide the Church be attuned to the whisper of the Holy

Spirit, and, being enlightened from above, become true guides to those who follow their leading. The unity of the Spirit must be more than human bonds in creed and church order. Unification is not necessarily unity. Yet true unity, true oneness in Christ Jesus, must ever be our single desire.

This is something that we must determine to learn. Our natural carnality can so easily lead us away from one another. Matthew Arnold was thinking of this, I believe, when he wrote these lines from "The Scholar Gypsy":

> For early thou didst leave the world, with powers
> Fresh, undiverted to the world without,
> Firm to their mark, not spent on other things . . .
> O life unlike to ours;
> Who fluctuate idly without term or scope,
> Of whom each strives, nor knows for what he strives,
> And each half lives a hundred different lives.

When our Lord prayed for the unity of His disciples, He asked that "they may become perfectly one" (John 17:23 RSV). Christians approach perfection as they approach unity. True perfection is impossible in a state of alienation from our brother. Indeed, we might almost say that I can appropriate fullness of life only as I receive that part of life which has been given for me to my brother in Christ.

The unity of all believers is the goal of the Incarnation. It is only in the unity of the Body that the Holy Spirit can fully display His power, either in the Church or to the world. Note the times and occasions when God spoke in power to His people: He spoke in greater fullness to great companies than to single individuals or solitary watchers at His feet. The voice that spoke on the day of Pentecost came to a company of disciples who had reached such a place of unity that of them it could be said "they were all with one accord in one place." Then God spoke in a fuller tone, an intenser fervor, and in a Pentecostal revelation that was never surpassed.

As we look around the world today, we might well ask, Where is this unity to be found? The Church is fragmented and therefore weak. She is separated and therefore impotent. All the more reason for us to seek the unity of the Holy Spirit in active exercise and to strive, to seek, and not to yield until we see love's banner riding high above all the living Church of God throughout all the world.

25

The Pentecostal Life

Walk in the Spirit and you won't fulfil the desires of the flesh (Galatians 5:16, translation mine).

SINCE THE DAY OF PENTECOST, the Holy Spirit has assumed a new office. It is vital that we recognize the meaning of living in the Pentecostal age.

Our Lord used the word "baptism" when He promised His disciples that they would experience the coming of the Holy Spirit in power. "John truly baptized with water; but you shall be baptized with the Holy Spirit not many days hence" (Acts 1:5). You will have noticed that uniformly throughout this volume I have spoken of the "infilling" of the Holy Spirit — not of the "baptism" of the Holy Spirit. I have done so for very specific reasons. It is my belief that the "baptism" of the Holy Spirit which the disciples received on the day of Pentecost was a climactic, once-for-all experience. Our Lord confers great honor on John the Baptist when He refers to that day and John's saying: "I indeed baptize you with water . . . but he that comes after me . . . shall baptize you with the Holy Spirit" (Matt. 3:11). We have noted that when the word "baptism" is used of the operation of the Holy Spirit it is (in our view) the "baptism of a believer into Christ" by which means he becomes a member of His body. "By one Spirit are we all baptized into one body . . . and have been all made to drink into one Spirit" (1 Cor. 12:13). At no other point is the word "baptism" used in the sense of a special endowment of power from the Holy Spirit for our service in the Church of God. In referring to John the Baptist, our Lord confirms the word of his messengers. He reaffirms what John the Baptist had foretold: "He . . . shall baptize you with the

Holy Spirit." This certainly happened on the day of Pentecost. Even there, however, the distinctive word used to describe this is "filled" — "they were all filled with the Holy Spirit." On the day of Pentecost the Spirit assumed a new role. The entire administration of the affairs of the Church became His responsibility. Hitherto, the Spirit had come and gone, never abiding forever in any one of God's servants. Now, He had come to indwell them *forever*. J. Elder Cumming, a senior statesman of the true faith of more than a century ago, once said, "That Day was the installation of the Holy Spirit as the Administrator of the Church in all things." This is the age of the Holy Spirit. Beyond this age we look for the second coming of the Lord. Till then, we live in the Pentecostal age and under the rule of the Holy Spirit.

The manifestation of the power of God

The chief characteristic of the disciples of our Lord before Pentecost was *powerlessness*. Occasionally, as when the seventy were sent forth, they were able to perform some mighty deeds. But these were very few. Though devoted to their Lord, they were continually defeated by Satan. All of their lives stand out as a startling disappointment. But Pentecost changed everything. Viewed from the standpoint of heaven, it might be said that the Church on that day came of age. She entered into the fullness of the inheritance that God had planned for His own from the first of time. She became filled with all the fullness of God.

From that day the disciples moved out to meet the needs of their times. They did so "in power and demonstration of the Holy Spirit." They attacked the foundations of the secular world and triumphed. They encompassed the decline and fall of the Roman Empire. Filled with the Spirit, guided by the Spirit, taught by the Spirit, empowered by the Spirit, illuminated from day to day by the Spirit, they stormed the citadels of hell and won. This could never have happened without the Holy Spirit. The power that their Lord had promised them when the Holy Spirit came upon them made them valiant, daring, dauntless, and undismayed in every situation. Persecution arose. Driven by persecution, they crossed land and sea proclaiming everywhere that "Jesus Christ is Lord." After the death of the first Christian martyr, many of them were forced to flee and came to Antioch where they preached to both the Jews and

Greeks with the result that a great number of them believed and turned to the Lord. Antioch became the center of great missionary action. From that city, the Christians sent forth Barnabas and Saul as missionaries. In the name of Jesus, signs and wonders happened as they, Barnabas and Saul, pioneered the ministry of the Gospel into Asia Minor. Churches were founded. Many were converted. Returning to Antioch, they "gathered the Church together [and] rehearsed all that God had done with them, and how he had opened the door of faith unto the Gentiles" (Acts 14:27).

Is this not the kind of power we need today? Is it not true that in so many churches there is no evidence of this kind of power? Yet a powerless Christian is at once both needless and sinful. I have heard "responsibility" defined as "our response to God's ability." Surely this is so. And surely there is no need for us to spend one more day without the power of God. "You will receive power after that the Holy Spirit is come upon you" (Acts 1:8). This is God's promise to us all. To live without such power is to deny the promise of God. On our response to God's all-comprehensive promise of power depends the fulfillment of our large responsibility to the world.

A great sense of forgiveness

For many years after becoming a Christian and even after she had received acclaim as a hymn-writer, Francis Ridley Havergal was burdened with a great sense of sin. This passed from her only after much diligent research into the Scriptures on the nature of God's forgiveness. Mrs. Jonathan Goforth tells of a similar experience and how, even after going to China as a missionary, she would find herself oppressed and burdened with a sense of sin. One evening, when all was quiet, she settled at her desk with Bible and concordance before her, determined to discover God's attitude towards the failures, the faults, and the sins of His children. Here is the result as she recorded it in her diary:

What God does with my sins:

1. He lays them on His Son — Jesus Christ (Isa. 53:6).
2. Christ takes them away (John 1:29).
3. They are removed an immeasurable distance — as far as east is from the west (Ps. 103:12).
4. When sought for, they are not found (Jer. 50:20).

5. The Lord forgives them (1 John 1:9; Eph. 1:7; Ps. 103:3).
6. He cleanses them ALL away by the blood of His Son (Rev. 1:5).
7. He cleanses them as white as snow or wool (Isa. 1:18; Ps. 51:7).
8. He abundantly pardons them (Isa. 55:7).
9. He tramples them under His foot (Mic. 7:19 R.V.).
10. He remembers them no more (Heb. 10:17; Ezek. 33:16).
11. He casts them behind His back (Isa. 38:17).
12. He casts them into the depths of the sea (Mic. 7:19).
13. He will not impute us with sins (Rom. 4:8).
14. He covers them (Rom. 4:7).
15. He blots them out (Isa. 43:25).
16. He blots them out as a thick cloud (Isa. 44:22).
17. He blots out even the proof against us, NAILING IT TO HIS SON'S CROSS (Col. 2:14).[1]

This is the life of Pentecost. The Holy Spirit "witnesses with our spirit" (Rom. 8:16). As Christ is our Advocate on high, so is the Holy Spirit the Advocate within us, assuring us of the infinite benefits of Christ's blood and helping us to trust entirely in Him and His completed work. With this kind of forgiveness, there comes a unique enabling of the Holy Spirit to witness to others about the possibility of their sins being forgiven. Pentecostal power is the power of a soul that knows itself ransomed, healed, restored, forgiven.

A great ability to forgive

The story of the New Testament disciples reveals the way they learned to forgive one another. Pentecostal power will never be known until we have learned to forgive. "If you forgive men their trespasses, your heavenly Father will also forgive you; but if you forgive not men their trespasses, neither will your Father forgive your trespasses" (Matt. 6:14, 15).

I could multiply instances. But having already referred to Mrs. Goforth and her experience of the forgiveness of God, it seems good to go on and relate how she was led into the miracle of being able to forgive others.

---

[1] Rosalind Goforth, *Climbing* (Toronto: Evangelical Publishers, 1940), pp. 90, 91.

Much was wrong on the mission station where they lived. Something had happened which had hurt her husband and she found it impossible to forgive the one who had been responsible for it. Dr. Goforth had quietly laid it all before God and left it there and pled with his wife that she should do the same. She found she could not. Or rather, would not. A long time passed and she found herself with her husband and other missionaries on the way to the religious fair at Hsunhsien, where annually an intensive campaign of evangelism was carried on. She was in charge of the women's work.

But she had no peace. She felt she could not speak with authority. Then the Holy Spirit came near and said, "Write and ask forgiveness from the one you hate!" She tells in her diary: "My whole soul cried out, 'Never, never can I forgive him!'" But as she prayed again, the inner voice of the Holy Spirit spoke clearly as before. Again she cried out, "Never, never! I will never forgive him!" Three times this was done, and after the third time she rose from her knees, saying, "I'll give it all up, for I'll never, never forgive!"

Her journal continues:

I joined the others and laughed and talked to hide my agitation. Then followed the saddest part of my life. For several months I preached and prayed to keep up appearances but all the while my heart was becoming harder, colder, and more hopeless.

Then one day that passage in the Pilgrim's Progress came to me (I think I was reading to the children), where Christian, when going through the House of the Interpreter, came to the man in the cage who said, "I have grieved God's Spirit, and He is gone: I have provoked God to anger, and He has left me." As I read this passage, a terrible conviction came upon me that the words I have quoted were true of me. During the two days and nights that followed, I was in the depths of despair, believing God's Holy Spirit had left me. My husband was away from home, and there seemed no one to whom I should turn. Then God in His mercy sent someone to me.

A young missionary whose wife had died under peculiarly sad circumstances, when passing through our station, came over to see me. It was evening, and the children were in bed. We sat on the front steps together while he sobbingly told me of his wife's death. Suddenly, the very flood gates loosed within me, and I gave way to uncontrollable weeping. When able, I told all the story as I have related it, and its sad, early details, then ended with, "I have grieved the Holy Spirit of God, and He has left me."

"But Mrs. Goforth," he said, "are you willing to write that letter?"

I replied: "I now know what it would be to be without God and without hope; and if I could only have another chance, there is nothing I would not do."

Again he asked, "Are you willing to write that letter?"

"Yes," I replied.

"Then go at once and write it."

With a glorious ray of hope dawning in me, I ran into the house, and in a few minutes returned with the letter. It was just a few lines of humble apology for *my actions,* without any reference to the other part. Oh, the joy that came, and thankfulness that it was indeed not *too late.*

From that time, I have never DARED *not to forgive.* There have been times when for hours, or even days, the battle was on again, but always the remembrance of this experience has enabled me to conquer and forgive.

She closes the chapter in which this story is related with words of Longfellow: "If we could only read the secret history of our enemies, we would find in each man's life sorrow and suffering enough to disarm all hostility." Then come the following lines:

> O God! that men would see a little clearer,
> Or judge less harshly when we cannot see!
> O God! that men would draw a little nearer
> To one another. They'd be nearer Thee
> And UNDERSTOOD.

The apostle Paul gives his own special footnote: "Let all bitterness, and wrath, and anger, and clamour, and evil speaking, be put away from you, with all malice: and be kind one to another, tenderhearted, forgiving one another, even as God for Christ's sake has forgiven you (Eph. 4:31, 32).

The joy of the Lord

We have, of course, referred to the joy of the Lord, which is part of the fruit of the Holy Spirit. We must note it again as we think of the Pentecostal life in all its fullness.

All true joy is touched with pain. The ecstasy of Christian joy is never far removed from the agony of sacrifice. It was under the shadow of the cross that our Lord spoke of His joy (John 15:11; 17:13). And the writer of the epistle to the Hebrews says of Him: "Who for the joy was set before him, endured the cross, de-

---

2 Ibid., p. 101. Used by permission of Evangelical Publishers, Toronto.

spising the shame, and is set down at the right hand of the throne of God" (Heb. 12:2). Job tells us that in the day of creation "the morning stars sang together, and all the sons of God shouted for joy" (Job 38:7). Song greets the creation of God. Joy fills the universe as God unfolds it. And joy is among the truest indicators that the Holy Spirit is present within the heart of the believer and fulfilling the perfect will of God. Dean Inge once said that he detected in the records of the New Testament church "a vein of sacred joy running through them all." Indeed, Augustine confesses that the first thing that drew him near to Christ was the joy he saw in the lives of the disciples of Christ.

Do we know this joy? We should if we are abiding in Christ. Our Lord has said, "These things have I spoken unto you that my joy might remain in you, and that your joy might be full" (John 15:11). Our Lord's joy was the total self-surrender and self-sacrifice of Himself to the Father. "I delight to do Thy will" — that was His joy. His joy was in God. There we too find the joy of Christ. In God. Not in service. Our Lord cautioned against this when He said, "Notwithstanding in this rejoice not . . . but rather rejoice because your names are written in heaven" (Luke 10:20). Christ in effect is saying that we should not rejoice in successful service but only in the fact that we are rightly related to God. We tend to emphasize service. It is not what we do for God that really counts. There is a sense in which that scarcely matters at all. But we must be ready to allow God to work in us what He pleases by being rightly related to Him, by living a life hidden with Christ in God. When we are in that position, then out of us flow the rivers of living water and the joy of the Lord is our daily strength.

Be rightly related to God. Keep the lines of communication Godward open continually. Whatever the circumstances may be in which you find yourself, let God pour through you His blessing for others. He will do this and in His mercy He will not let you know that it is happening. "Moses did not know that the skin of his face shone" (Exod. 34:29 RSV). If in the days of creation the morning stars sang, what should be our song in the days of the new creation? Joy in inseparable from the handiwork of God. Where God is, joy is always known.

This is one of the reasons why praise is at the heart of the Christian faith. You cannot think rightly of the life of discipleship without associating it with songs of joy. If praise is removed from our walk with God and from our worship together in the fellowship of God's presence, we are far separated from the spirit of true discipleship.

> Songs of praise the angels sang,
> Heaven with hallelujahs rang,
> When Jehovah's work begun,
> When He spake, and it was done.
>
> Songs of praise awoke the morn
> When the Prince of Peace was born;
> Songs of praise arose when He
> Captive led captivity.

So James Montgomery sang as he surveyed the glories of the work of God. And in similar vein he asked,

> And can man alone be dumb,
> Till that glorious kingdom come?
> No! The Church delights to raise
> Psalms and hymns and songs of praise.

Praise is the only answer to the grace of God. Joy is the truest manifestation of the work of the Holy Spirit within the heart of man. Joy is strength. And the promise from of old is with us: "The joy of the Lord is your strength" (Neh. 8:10). It is a truly Christian prayer that says:

> Make us joyful with gladness unforced,
> Contagious, abounding,
> That all whom we meet may be kindled from us,
> With Thy fire of joy.
> (author unknown)

Yes, it is truly Christian, for when love is directed towards the eternal and infinite, the mind is fed with pure joy. Even here on earth we taste the pure and unsullied joy of heaven. This is the life of Pentecost.

Knowledge and glory

The Pentecostal life is lived out in the inner recesses of our life where the indwelling presence of the Holy Spirit permeates, energizes, and controls all the faculties of our nature. It is another Incarnation — this time with the Holy Spirit indwelling the body of the consecrated believer. In the upper room the Holy Spirit clothed Himself with the waiting disciples and He still is prepared to do this with every consecrated believer. In us who believe and want to be the Lord's disciples He will find a body and through Him we shall be given spiritual expression, the power of living, divine words, the action that spells new life for multitudes. Even as it is true of the union of the Father, the Son, and the Holy Spirit, so is it true of us: the Spirit indwells us without confusion, without any loss of individual consciousness and in perfect unity of operation.

When this happens, the Pentecostal life is experienced to the full. We see this in the disciples on the day of Pentecost and the same is still being seen in our midst today. Our Lord promised that with the coming of the Spirit the disciples would be led into fullness of knowledge. "At that day you shall know" (John 14:20). "I have yet many things to say unto you; but you cannot bear them now. Howbeit, when he, the Spirit of truth, is come, he will guide you into all truth" (John 16:12, 13). By the aid of the Holy Spirit they would have an ability to grasp heavenly things which for the present they could not. Thus it happened. The Scriptures were opened to them. Prophecy shone with new meaning. The death of Christ was seen in the light of the sovereign purposes and predestinating will of God. The resurrection was the beginning of a new day. History took on a new meaning. In the light of the Holy Spirit the Word of God became luminous and glorious.

So they were changed from contentious, proud, and boastful men to daring, yet gentle, disciples. From fear to faith, from wrangling to righteousness, from weakness to walking in the light — it all happened as the Lord had promised. And it is still happening. This is the life in the Holy Spirit. It is the life predestined for you if you truly believe in the Son of God. Christ did not die and rise again merely to introduce us to a dull, joyless, and sick life. No! He came that we might know the exceeding greatness of His power toward us who believe. This life you may know *NOW*. It is His promise. He cannot deny Himself.

26

Preaching in the Power of the Holy Spirit

My speech and my preaching were not with enticing words of man's wisdom, but in demonstration of the Spirit and of power (1 Corinthians 2:4).

PREACHING IS A CHRISTIAN exercise. "Now after John was put in prison, Jesus came into Galilee, preaching the gospel of the kingdom of God, and saying, The time is fulfilled and the kingdom of God is at hand: repent, and believe the gospel" (Mark 1:14, 15). Jesus came *preaching*. Here is the authority for every preacher of the Gospel. He follows his Lord in the greatest of all ministries — preaching. When our Lord came to Nazareth, He entered the synagogue and was asked to expound the Scriptures. He found the place, opening the book at Isaiah 61:1, 2. This occurred immediately after His baptism in the river Jordan when the Spirit descended on Him like a dove. The wilderness temptation had also occurred, but from that time of testing by Satan we read that "Jesus returned in the power of the Spirit into Galilee: and there went out a fame of him through all the region round about" (Luke 4:14). Then came Nazareth and His preaching in the synagogue. He said, "He hath anounted me to preach the gospel to the poor. . . . " Thus He emphasized that He was anointed by the Holy Spirit to preach the Gospel of salvation, "to preach the acceptable year of the Lord" (Luke 4:18, 19).

Our Lord came preaching. He did so in the royal line of the prophets who, being filled with the Holy Spirit, turned the hearts of many to the Lord by the power of their proclamation of the truth of God. "Holy men of God spoke as they were moved by the Holy Spirit" (2 Peter 1:21). And Jesus specifically stated in the synagogue at Nazareth that He was able to preach the acceptable year of the Lord to the poor only because, as He said, "The Spirit of the Lord is upon me" (Luke 4:18). He stated very emphatically that even He could not have exercised this unique ministry on earth were it not for the fact that He had received this special, unusual "endowment" or "anointing" of the Holy Spirit to fulfill His task. Even He could not preach without the unction of the Holy Spirit. But when that happened, He came *preaching*.

After His resurrection, He appeared to the disciples in the upper room and told them:

> Thus it is written, and thus it behoved Christ to suffer, and to rise from the dead the third day: and that repentance and remission of sins should be *preached* in his name among all nations, beginning at Jerusalem. And you are witnesses of these things. And, behold, I send the promise of my Father upon you; but tarry in the city of Jerusalem, until you are endued with power from on high (Luke 24:46-49).

This leads on to Acts 1:8, and by a straight course to the fulfillment of this promise in Acts 2.

The difference fullness makes

On the day of Pentecost the disciples were "baptized with the Holy Spirit and with fire" (Acts 1:5; 2:1-4). The symbols of wind and fire manifest the nature of the endowment, but the real truth is that the disciples were "filled with the Holy Spirit." Joy, power, courage, fire — they all had their source in the fullness of the indwelling Spirit. They overflowed for the simple reason that they were filled to overflowing. Salvation was already theirs. In the upper room, their Lord had breathed on them and said, "Receive the Holy Spirit" (John 20:22). But Pentecost was the second gift, verifying and completing the first in an overflowing power through an infilling Presence. Fullness makes all the difference.

Not many in our day know William Arthur's once-famous book *The Tongue of Fire*. In a memorable passage he illustrates the difference that the fullness of the Holy Spirit makes:

> A piece of iron is dark and cold; imbued with a certain degree of heat it becomes almost burning, without any change in appearance;

inbued with a still greater degree, its very appearance changes to that of solid fire, and it sets fire to whatever it touches. A piece of water without heat is solid and brittle; gently warmed, it flows; further heated, it mounts to the sky. An organ filled with the ordinary degree of air is dumb; the touch of the player can elicit but a plucking of the keys. Throw in but an unsteady current of the same air, and sweet, but imperfect and uncertain notes immediately respond to the player's touch; increase the current to full supply, and every pipe swells with music. Such is the soul without the Holy Spirit; and such are the changes which pass upon it when it receives the Holy Spirit, and when it is filled to the uttermost with Him. [1]

This is the fullness that the Church of today needs. We need what happened in those sun-drenched days of Pentecost. "With great power gave the apostles witness of the resurrection of the Lord Jesus: and great grace was upon them all" (Acts 4:33). This is the difference that "fullness" makes. We should be content with nothing else.

The real significance of the records of Pentecost is that here are men whom we might have expected to be in a perfect position for fulfilling the ministry of preaching. They had been with their Lord for three years; they had heard Him preach (what a thrill that must have been!); they had watched Him perform miracles; they had had personal tuition from Him day after day; theirs had been the benefit of being with Him and watching His methods with men and women. Some of them had been with Him on the Mount of Transfiguration. All had witnessed His crucifixion, even though from afar. Every one of them was an eyewitness of His resurrection as Paul tells us in the fifteenth chapter of first Corinthians. Was that not a seminary course of sufficient length and depth? Surely, if ever men were trained for the ministry of preaching, these disciples should have been. But they were not. They possessed knowledge, but that was not enough. They needed the fullness of the Holy Spirit; and this had to happen on God's calendar at a specific time. Not until the Holy Spirit had filled them to the uttermost, had baptized them with all the fullness of God, were they fitted to erupt onto the streets of Jerusalem and confront a hostile crowd and

---

[1] William Arthur, *The Tongue of Fire*, first published in 1901 (Winona Lake, Indiana: Light and Life Press, n.d.), p. 60.

make it become a congregation waiting for the Word of God. This is preaching. Without the Spirit, there is no preaching.

The inauguration of the Church

The day of Pentecost may well be spoken of as the day of the inauguration of the Church. This is not in the sense in which in the counsel of God it first began. From the first of time, God had called unto Himself His own and all of them of former ages form part of the Body of Christ. Our Lord said of the heathen, "Many shall come from the east and west, and shall sit down with Abraham, and Isaac, and Jacob in the kingdom of heaven" (Matt. 8:11). The Church is as old as Adam and Eve. To them God first preached the Gospel. But until the fullness of time was come when God sent forth His Son who died and rose again and ascended on high to pour forth His Spirit, God kept a mystery from His people. It was the mystery that the Gentiles would be heirs with the children of Israel; and when the fiftieth day after the resurrection of our Lord was fully come, the hour on God's calendar struck and the Church emerged, a glorious Church; her tongue was loosened and she was transfigured, her fashion like a mighty army. The Church began to speak. "They were all filled with the Holy Spirit, and began to speak with other tongues, as the Spirit gave them utterance" (Acts 2:4).

Now appear the differences that God has planned from the beginning. The altar of the old economy becomes the pulpit in the new. The priest becomes a preacher. The sacrifices become the two blessed sacraments ordained by Christ Himself — baptism and the Lord's table. The Sabbath becomes the Lord's day — naturally, the first day, the day on which He arose triumphant from the dead. Instead of a priestly elect from the tribe of Levi, all of the disciples are filled with the Holy Spirit. Each believer is made a witness, a preacher. All are instantly prepared for spiritual service by the infilling of the Holy Spirit. All are led to become active witnesses for Christ and for His cross.

Preeminent in all the amazing miracles of the day of Pentecost is the gift of preaching, a gift which was immediately shown to be the most influential instrument for the recovery of mankind. Out of the company of the disciples Peter stands forth. He has not been trained in the art of public speaking. He is not a product of learned schools. He does not speak, it appears, in a foreign language but in his native dialect. Many a time he has spoken before; but today there is in his speech a qualitative difference that is the gift of the Holy Spirit. He speaks, but there is a different element in what he says. He not only speaks, he prophesies. That is, he delivers a message from God, under the impulse of the Spirit of God, and by His aid. He proves the presence of the "other Comforter." He demonstrates immediately that "greater is he that prophesieth than he that speaks with tongues" (1 Cor. 14:5). Peter faces the world and presents a new faith, one without a history, without a priesthood, without a college, and without a patron. But he is filled with the Spirit. He is anointed with the Holy Spirit. Therefore he speaks as none has ever spoken before. The day of preaching has come.

Preaching in the modern world

The twentieth century has seen great changes in attitudes to preaching. We live in days when not only preaching but the very life of the Church is being brought under serious question. There is talk about "religionless Christianity," whatever that may mean. Perhaps it means that the institutionalized Church has become for many one of the greatest barriers to true devotion; and, on their protestations, the only hope for any revival of true religion is for the Church to disappear and some form of free and unrestrained worship to arise. Coupled with this is a great disparagement of preaching. The pulpit that someone has described as a place "six feet above contradiction" is viewed as one of the supreme architects of the malaise affecting Christianity. For one man to stand and declaim his views of religion for a period of time in a church service is among the greatest reasons why people will not listen and think they ought not to listen. Give us dialogue, they say. Let us discuss. In the interplay of our many minds we shall surely reach the truth faster than if we listen on and on to a preacher from behind a sacred desk. Oratory is not in vogue today.

There are good and valid reasons for this. For too long the preaching we have heard in the Church is of the kind adorned with literary prettinesses and pious exhortation — this, together with a veritable deluge of words. Professor Tait of Edinburgh once caustically described popular preaching as "the exercise of a man who understands a subject imperfectly addressed to people who wish to talk about it without understanding it at all." Still more fiercely Hermas, a writer from the second century, castigates preachers he has known: "Empty himself, he gives empty answers to empty people."[2] What a contrast to the preaching we see in the New Testament! Luke gives us in specific places some notes of apostolic sermons (e.g., Acts 17:3, 18; 18:5; 26:22, 23). At other points, as in the case of Peter, he gives us a fairly full summary of the message (Acts 2:14-40; Acts 4:8-20). The same is true of Paul's message (Acts 13:16-42). The content here is full of Christion truth. That the Messiah was bound to suffer is shown as the "Christian Credo." The New Testament preacher is first a teacher. He is a bearer of good news. He is a herald of divine grace. He indulges in great indicatives. This, however, is always done with a noble simplicity which is surely the crown and consummation of knowledge. The truth is uttered always with a personal signature. Nothing else can supply life to preaching. Preaching in its truest, Christian sense is always "truth through personality in the power of the Holy Spirit."

But this is not what we commonly find today. There are, unfortunately, attitudes within the Church that have brought to pass this discounting of preaching. First and foremost, there has been a fatal loss of belief in the truth of the Bible. The authority of the Scriptures has been undermined — or defied. Therefore, if a man stands to speak from the Scriptures to a congregation with no supreme conviction that the Bible is the Word of God, what else can you expect but that the man in the pew will become fidgety and soon lose any interest in what is being said? One of the great Roman orators forced his pupils to memorize the rule *Rem tene, verba sequentur* — "Get your theme and the words will naturally follow." This is universally true. All great speaking is ennobled by the theme discussed. Likewise, great preaching rests upon and is dependent upon great themes. And what themes the Christian preacher has before him! If you are not persuaded that the truths you are speaking about are the greatest themes on which man can meditate, you will never preach greatly. There was a time in Scotland when practically everyone knew the Shorter Catechism, and

---

[2] From *The Shepherd of Hermas*.

thus had at his command a scheme of teaching about God and life, superbly concise in its phrasing, profound and spacious in its conception. The same was true of the Methodists in England. John Wesley's sermons were so definite in doctrine that they could be made the standard of faith for the church he founded, and the greater Nonconformists never failed to teach. When Robert William Dale came as a young minister to Carr's Lane in Birmingham, he was told the members would reject doctrinal preaching. "They will have to take it," he replied. Regrettably, there has been great deterioration in this aspect of church life. No longer do the Scriptures speak as once they did. Men have speculated, conjectured, made suppositions, surmised, and made inferences about the Bible, and the result is a loss of confidence in the Bible. This is our situation now. It could scarcely be worse.

Another facet of this distressing situation should be noted. From about the second half of the nineteenth century, there was a certain amount of idolatry in the minds of church people about preachers. It was a time when there seemed to be an unusual number of men with oratorical gifts in different pulpits across the world, speaking to vast congregations of people who often had queued up long before the church doors opened. These preachers might well be called pulpiteers. They ruled the pulpit and they ruled the people. There was a great deal of exhibitionism in their work. They were deft in their handling of crowds. They were skilled in playing on emotions. How vividly I recall some sermons preached in a great Edinburgh pulpit which were enthralling, engrossing, engaging. To this day there are sections of these sermons that I could repeat with ease. But of Gospel content there was not a trace. They were bookish and semi-scholarly in their own way; but I would not dignify them by the term "preaching."

Inevitably, there came reaction. The hungry sheep looked up and were not fed. Permissiveness followed — in education, ethics, politics, and life in general. Apathy and resistance set in against such effusions. A cry for debate, discussion, dialogue, and often disputation was heard throughout the Church. Youth seminars and young people's groups set themselves to be the guides and directors of this new movement; and since in so many churches the eleventh commandmnt is "Thou shalt not restrain the youth of the church," there was every facility granted to steer the pulpit away from its greatest ministries. Where this has happened, there has usually been an increase in the formal part of the service. The sermon has become an address and almost a tag-on to the rest of the service. The service has become increasingly ritualistic. Ceremonial, processionals, form, and style have increased as the place of the sermon has been taken over or as a new concept of what the sermon should be has grown. The result? The norms of preaching as we see them in the Scriptures and as we also see them in periods of great revivals when the Church has returned to the Word of God and sought and found God's message of redemption and salvation in Christ — these norms are almost unknown. You are considered old-fashioned or "Victorian" if you hold to principles such as those presented in the New Testament. To court the favor of the people and, tragically, often of the leaders of the people in the Church, you have to indulge in a style that is a veritable mockery of what preaching ought to be.

Entertainment?

In his book *Preaching and Preachers,* Dr. D. Martyn Lloyd-Jones has a fascinating half page which should be underscored on every line. He says:

Still worse has been the increase in the element of entertainment in public worship — the use of films and the introduction of more and more singing; the reading of the Word and prayer shortened drastically, but more and more time given to singing. You have a "song-leader" as a new kind of official in the church, and he conducts the singing and is supposed to produce the atmosphere. But he often takes so much time in producing atmosphere that there is no time for preaching in the atmosphere! This is a part of this whole depreciation of the message.

Then on top of this, there is the giving of testimonies. It has been interesting to observe that as preaching as such has been on the decline, preachers have more and more used people to give their testimonies; and particularly if they are important people in any realm. This is said to attract people to the Gospel and to persuade them to listen to it. If you can find an admiral or a general or anyone who has some special title, or a baseball player, or an actress or actor or film-star, or pop-singer, or somebody well-known to the public, get them to give their testimony. This is deemed to be of much greater value than the preaching and the exposition of the Gospel. Have you noticed that I have put all this under the term "entertainment"? That is where I believe it truly belongs. But this is what the Church has been turning to as she has turned her back upon preaching. [3]

The great god "entertainment" has certainly invaded our sanctuaries and assumed a role that you do not see in the Scriptures anywhere. The New Testament preaches Christ. The New Testament preachers refused to get themselves involved in politics nor did they deal with social conditions as such. The Spirit that was in them signified that there was sufficient dynamite in the message they were proclaiming that social conditions would be arraigned, convicted, and condemned as and when God determined. They refused to pander to the tastes of their listeners. Facing the problem Christians of Corinth, Paul dealt with them and their special needs in the most direct and categorical way. He had no time to waste on lesser things. He went straight to what was distinctively Christian even though to his hearers this may have seemed offensive. For from attempting to entertain them, he admonished, warned, rebuked, and reproved them. This is "preaching in the power and demonstration of the Holy Spirit." If this has departed from us, it is time for us to repent and to seek God's forgiveness. The time has come for judgment to begin at the house of God. It is high time for us to awake from our sleep of folly and return to the old paths. When we do, there may be hope that God will be entreated again and will "restore to us the years that the locust has eaten" (Joel 2:25).

The Spirit's baptism that created great preachers

The book of Acts os our principal textbook for this great theme of preaching. Upon the disciples there came an effusion of power that was a divine endowment for service. From being men and women terrified at the very thought of Caiaphas and Pilate, hiding behind closed doors for fear of the Jews, we see them out on the streets of Jerusalem, dauntless and undismayed. With great confidence, in divine assurance and boldness, Peter declares the whole counsel of God and there is no trace of fear in him.

---

[3] D. Martyn Lloyd-Jones, *Preaching and Preachers* (Grand Rapids: Zondervan Publishing House, 1972), p. 17.

What has happened? Why are things so different? There is only one answer that meets the case. He has been "baptized" by the Holy Spirit. This has meant an outpouring of power upon him that no man had ever known before. As a man, he is not so great as John the Baptist; our Lord said that John the Baptist was the greatest man ever born of woman. But Peter is now greater than the Baptist, for he has received this new anointing which all true disciples may receive if they seek it. Peter is Spirit-filled. This is what the "baptism" of the Spirit has meant for him — and for all of those in the upper room. The "baptism" of the Holy Spirit at this time did not mean for Peter conversion or regeneration. He was already born of the Holy Spirit. He had received the Spirit when the Lord said, "Receive the Holy Spirit." But the baptism that he has received is to make him a witness, a telling, triumphant witness to the glory of his exalted Lord. So we see him, standing forth among the people, calling them to himself, and saying, "Men of Israel, hear these words."

Now this happened on the fiftieth day after their Lord's resurrection, on one of the high and holy days of the old dispensation. Peter was given power to witness, power to preach. We see the same thing in the third chapter of Acts. Peter and John are going to the temple at the hour of prayer and suddenly they encounter the impotent man who was laid daily at the beautiful gate of the temple. Immediately after the lame man is healed, they witness and they preach also in the temple. Brought before the Sanhedrin, the same things are seen. The record is in Acts 4:7, 8:

> When they had set them in the midst, they asked, By what power, or by what name, have you done this? Then Peter, filled with the Holy Spirit, said unto them, Ye rulers of the people. . . .

Why is the phrase "being filled with the Holy Spirit" repeated? Surely for one reason: to demonstrate that from henceforth they are to preach and to proclaim the good news only as the Holy Spirit enables them to do so. They are in difficulties. They need help. Then comes the Spirit and fills them anew. A new endowment of power was needed for this critical moment before the Sanhedrin. The Holy Spirit gave just this. He gave a fresh filling for this unique duty.

Following through the book of Acts, we note this happening

again and again. It happened when the Church was at prayer, fearful for very good reasons, and wondering what was going to happen next. Well, what did happen? This: "When they had prayed, the place was shaken where they were assembled together; and they were all filled with the Holy Spirit" (Acts 4:31). The experience is not new. They had been filled with the Holy Spirit previously. But now, in the face of awesome threatenings, they are once again "filled" and prepared to do what God has called them to do. Clearly, this infilling of the Holy Spirit can happen repeatedly. There is evidently truth in the old saying "One baptism; many fillings."

Deacons are appointed, according to Acts chapter 6. Here is the record:

"It is not right that we should have to neglect preaching the Word of God in order to look after the accounts. You, our brothers, must look round and pick out from your number seven men of good reputation who are both practical and spiritually-minded and we will put them in charge of this matter. Then we shall devote ourselves wholeheartedly to prayer and the ministry of the Word." This brief speech met with unanimous approval and they chose Stephen, a man full of faith and the Holy Spirit, Philip, Prochorus, Nicanor, Timon, Parmenas, and Nicolas of Antioch who had previously been a convert to the Jewish faith (Acts 6:2-5 *Phillips*).

Here is a new ministry within the Church. As the apostles found themselves overwhelmed with routine work, the Church determined that others should be appointed to relieve them of their load of administrative duties. But this is not done without ensuring that men "filled with the Holy Spirit" are called. Indeed, it is clear that a new endowment of power is given to them as they assume the ministry. What else can be intended by Luke when he adds that "they chose Stephen, a man full of faith and of the Holy Spirit" (Acts 6:5)?

When Stephen was martyred for his faithfulness to the Gospel, Luke again stresses this. He notes that "he, being full of the Holy Spirit, looked up steadfastly into heaven, and saw the glory of God, and Jesus standing on the right hand of God" (Acts 7:55). Here is another new experience. The fullness of the Holy Spirit is given to Stephen to enable him to die aright.

The greatest passage has not yet been reached. We come to it when Paul is writing to the church in Corinth. He recalls how he had come to them from Athens in weakness and fear. Whether or not Athens was for Paul a disheartening experience, unquestionably Paul came on to Corinth without any dependence on his own strength or capabilities. He wrote,

> I was with you in weakness, and in fear, and in much trembling. And my speech and my preaching was not with enticing words of man's wisdom, but in demonstration of the Spirit and of power: that your faith should not stand in the wisdom of men, but in the power of God (1 Cor. 2:3-5).

This central, emphatic statement makes it crystal clear that only the anointing of the Spirit can make preaching great. Paul was, as we know, a man of exceptional gifts. But with cool and calm determination he resolved never to let these enormous natural gifts of his be the foundation on which his preaching would be built. Otherwise, there would always be the possibility that men might be swayed through the use of these unusual gifts and not really be touched by the power of the Holy Spirit. Therefore he determined "not to know any thing among [them], save Jesus Christ and him crucified" (1 Cor. 2:2). In his preaching there must be nothing of the attractiveness of the clever mind. Faith must never rest on man's cleverness but only on the power of God mediated through the Holy Spirit. He repeats this further on in the letter when he reacts to the carping criticism of some of his enemies. "The kingdom of God is not a matter of the spate of words but of the power of Christian living" (1 Cor. 4:20 *Phillips*).

When Paul writes to the Thessalonians, the same emphasis is apparent. He says,

> Our gospel came not unto you in word only, but also in power, and in the Holy Spirit, and in much assurance (1 Thess. 1:5).

Even more precisely he speaks to the Colossians of Christ,

> Whom we preach, warning every man, and teaching every man in all wisdom; that we may present every man perfect in Christ Jesus. Whereunto I also labour, striving according to his working, which worketh in me mightily" (Col. 1:28, 29).

The apostle's stress is that the Gospel by which they had been saved had come to them not only in the words of man but in the fullness of the power of the Holy Spirit. The Gospel had come to them not "in word only" but also "in power" — and therein lies the secret of the apostolic understanding of the basis of their preaching. Had they gone on their recognizances, they would have been total failures. They might have gathered around themselves a coterie, a company of interested scholars wanting to share in the brilliance of the rhetoric. But this, at every point, all the apostles are eager to forego. Preaching is preaching only when it is in "demonstration of the Spirit and of power."

The record of history

Some might argue that this was all right for the apostles but that since their time we have moved into a new era. Thank God that we have the record of history and that the record we see there authenticates the New Testament pattern and program. In every great period of revival and reformation, preaching has been at the center. The great Protestant Reformation was basically a discovery of the Bible, a discovery of the heart of the Gospel, and a discovery of the way in which the Gospel had to be proclaimed. Luther and Calvin were both mighty preachers. John Knox was a preacher without peer, and the evidence of the impact of his messages is visible to this day. Hugh Latimer preached at St. Paul's Cross in London and he preached with the unction of the Holy Spirit. Then think of Robert Bruce of Scotland. I turn my eyes as I write and see his great volume of communion sermons on my bookshelves. Nothing nobler has ever been produced. "The Cross is the meridian splendour of God's love" — that was his great theme elaborated and illustrated with telling effect on multitudes of listeners. John Bradford? One of England's earliest and most outstanding preachers: one too of England's martyrs for the faith once delivered to the saints. Preaching was their highest calling. And who can forget the Reverend John Livingstone of Ancrum? Dr. Alexander Smellie in *Men of the Covenant* has left us what is probably the greatest account of this remarkable man's preaching. I quote:

> One of the greatest revivals in the annals of the Church is linked with the name of a young probationer whom the bishops pursued with hate. He was John Livingstone. His words had the flame of the Holy Ghost glowing in them and they conquered and captivated the souls of men. Monday, 21st of June, 1630, found him as preacher designate at the post-communion services in Kirk of Shotts. With some friends he had spent the night before in laying fast hold on the promise and grace of heaven. When the mid-

summer morning broke, the preacher wanted to escape from the responsibilities before him. Alone in the fields, between eight and nine, he felt such misgivings, such a sense of unworthiness, such dread of the multitude and the expectation of the people, that he was consulting with himself to have stolen away; but he "durst not so far distrust God, and so went to sermon, and got good assistance." Good assistance indeed; for after he had spoken for an hour and a half on the text "Then will I sprinkle clean water upon you and ye shall be clean," and was thinking that he must close, he was constrained by His Lord Himself to continue. "I was led on about an hour's time in a strain of exhortation and warning, with such liberty and melting of heart as I had never had the like in public all my life." No fewer than five hundred men and women, some of them ladies of high estate, and others poor wastrels and beggars, traced the dawn of the undying life to John Livingstone's words that day. [4]

That is preaching "in demonstration of the Holy Spirit and of power." Such preaching could never be were it not for the continuous infilling of the Spirit of God. Here lies the reason why men refuse to listen when we speak, why our words fall like dead leaves on frozen ground; we have not been "filled by the Holy Spirit" for this major exercise of the Christian ministry. Only when we are, will the hearts of multitudes be touched and miracles of grace be seen.

History is replete with illustrations of this kind. The lives of George Whitefield and the Wesleys, the ministries of Edwards and Brainerd, D. L. Moody, and W. P. Nicholson — all of them tell the same wonderful story. The Holy Spirit filled them and made them to be men afire for God, aflame with love for the souls of men, and irresistible in speech as they preached the everlasting Gospel. "It pleased God by the foolishness of preaching to save them that believe" (1 Cor. 1:21). God has not changed His methods. Preaching is still the greatest instrument the Church possesses. How tragic that she is so unaware of the power that lies so near to her!

Anointed to preach

We have referred already to our Lord's visit to the synagogue at Nazareth. There he stated, "The Spirit of the Lord is upon me, because he hath anointed me to preach the gospel to the poor"

---

[4] Alexander Smellie, *Men of the Covenant* (the Andrew Melrose edition of 1905), p. 99.

(Luke 4:18). He was very specific about this. Anointing is essential for preaching. In the old days, it was customary for elders to ask of each other concerning some preacher: "Does he have the anointing?" They knew full well that unless there was an endowment of power from the Holy Spirit, no minister could bring the Word of the Lord with authority and in power. Therefore they asked that all-important question. The question should still be asked. Every preacher should ask it of himself. "Am I anointed by the Holy Spirit?" It is high time that we decided with the firmest of resolve to abandon all gimmickry in the pulpit and to return to the God-appointed paths. "Then will I sprinkle clean water upon you, and you shall be clean" (Ezek. 36:25). This is our greatest need, the sprinkling of the power of God upon us, the infilling at the deepest levels of our lives of all His fullness.

Then we shall preach the Word with boldness. There will be no "ifs" and "buts" in our declarations. We shall point away from ourselves to Him whose glory exceeds the glory of the heavens. We shall never need to draw attention to ourselves. Indeed, that is the last thing we shall wish to do. John the Baptist will become our ideal — "I am a voice." Our chief objective will be to become a voice for God. Preaching is the greatest of such voices. May God restore this gift again to His Church.

It is possible that one of the major reasons preaching is discredited in our times is that God is judging us for our idolatry of popular preaching in the past. God will not share His glory with another. He has raised up the pulpit to be the principal instrument of reaching a lost world and if this divine method has been misused or wrongly idolized, we can expect nothing but judgment. In our preaching we should see to it that we are absolutely lost in our message. There must be nothing mechanical, contrived, or artificial about our speech. I have heard of a preacher who "practiced" his sermon three times every Saturday before a mirror, ensuring, he thought, that every gesture would be right and nothing outré or uncongenial permitted. How foolish! True preaching is the presentation of truth through personality, through a personality that has been burned over with heavenly flame. We must never offer to the Lord anything that costs us nothing. We must give our all for this all-demanding task. We must wait His will for the Word to be declared and then await His power to declare it.

The assurance the Holy Spirit gives

How do we know we are "filled with the Spirit?" Paul tells the Thessalonians, "Our gospel came not unto you in word only, but also in power, and in the Holy Spirit, and in much assurance" (1 Thess. 1:5). Much assurance! Is this boastful? Not at all! He knew within his own heart the assurance that the Holy Spirit gives to those who obey Him. The assurance was not that of self-conceit, self-dependence, self-esteem. No! The assurance was born of the Holy Spirit, communicated to him through a deep sense of peace, and attended by an unusual authority. All this the Spirit gives.

When this assurance is known, the disciple possesses a new power for service. Pentecost brought to the followers of Christ awakening, conviction, conversions, and the baptism of fire. Nothing else will counteract the dearth of conversions that we know so well. The Spirit's gift is the gift of power and a deep assurance that God is over all, in all, and through all. Abundant fullness overflows in abundant assurance. You know that the Holy Spirit is upon you and is anointing you to preach the good news. He comes to glorify Christ in and through you and rejoices to do this especially in the calling out of a people for God.

Yes! The supreme need of the Church today is for Pentecostal fullness issuing in authoritative witnessing and preaching. Such Pentecostal floodtide could fertilize and water every desert. No work of the Holy Spirit can ever be perfected without our knowing the fullness of the Spirit, and God still waits to hear us ask for this greatest of all gifts. "How much more shall your heavenly Father give the Holy Spirit to them that ask him?" (Luke 11:13). It is the will of God that every child of His should be filled with the Holy Spirit, be renewed continually in the mind and power of the Spirit, and prevail through the Spirit. This blessing is for anyone, for all, and now. God's conditions have never altered. They never will. He wants to fill ordinary people with extraordinary power. He longs to transform our frustrated faith into an all-conquering life of triumph. This He will do. He will do it for you. He will do it now.

To this give all the prophets and apostles witness. The apostles before Pentecost were workers, believers, stewards, healers, followers — but there was no Pentecostal power. Then came the promised Spirit upon them. Immediately, everything changed. Immediately, also, they set out to claim, to grasp and never yield all the Spirit had covenanted they should know. The Spirit came. They were all filled with the Holy Spirit. They began to speak. They are speaking still.

Bibliography

Adams, J. E. *Competent to Counsel.* Philadelphia: The Presbyterian and Reformed Publishing Co., 1972.

Augustine. *Confessions.* Harmondsworth, England: Penguin Books Ltd., 1971.

Barth, K. *The Word of God and the Word of Man.* Edinburgh: T. & T. Clark, 1957.

Bergsma, S. *Speaking With Tongues.* Grand Rapids, Michigan: Baker Book House, 1965.

Berkhof, H. *The Doctrine of the Holy Spirit.* Richmond, Virginia: John Knox Press, 1964.

Brengle, S. L. *When the Holy Spirit Is Come.* London: Salvationist Publication Supplies, 1896.

Bruner, F. D. *A Theology of the Holy Spirit.* Grand Rapids, Michigan: Wm. B. Eerdmans Publishing Co., 1970.

Buchanan, J. *The Office and Work of the Holy Spirit.* London: Hamilton, Adams and Co., 1857.

Bunyan, J. *Grace Abounding to the Chief of Sinners.* London: SCM Press, 1955.

————. *The Pilgrim's Progress.* Harmondsworth, England: Penguin Books Ltd., 1968.

Burdick, D. W. *Tongues — to Speak or Not to Speak.* Chicago, Illinois: Moody Press, 1971.

Candlish, J. S. *The Work of the Holy Spirit.* Edinburgh: T. & T. Clark, 1900.

Chadwick, S. *The Way to Pentecost.* London: Hodder and Stoughton, 1933.

Chantry, W. *Signs of the Apostles.* Edinburgh: The Banner of Truth Trust, 1973.

Conn, C. W. *Like a Mighty Army.* Cleveland, Tennessee: Church of God Publishing House, 1955.

————. *Pillars of Pentecost.* Cleveland, Tennessee: Pathway Press, 1956.

Cumming, J. Elder. *Through the Eternal Spirit.* London: S. W. Partridge and Co., 1894.

Cutten, G. B. *Speaking With Tongues Historically and Psychologically Considered.* New Haven: Yale University Press, 1927.

De Haan, M. R. *Holy Spirit Baptism.* Grand Rapids, Michigan: Radio Bible Class, 1964.

Drummond, A. L. *Edward Irving and his Circle, Including Some Considerations of the "Tongues" Movement in the Light of Modern Psychology.* London: J. Clark, 1937.

Dunn, J. D. G. *Baptism in the Holy Spirit.* London: SCM Press Ltd., 1970.

Ervin, H. M. *These Are Not Drunken, as Ye Suppose.* Plainfield, New Jersey: Logos International, 1968.

Frodsham, S. H. *With Signs Following: The Story of the Pentecostal Revival in the Twentieth Century.* Springfield, Missouri: Gospel Pub., 1941.

Goforth, J. *By My Spirit.* Minneapolis, Minnesota: Bethany Fellowship, 1942.

Goforth, R. *Goforth of China.* Grand Rapids, Michigan: Zondervan Publishing House, 1937.

Gordon, A. J. *The Ministry of the Spirit.* Fleming H. Revell Co., 1895.

Griffith-Thomas, W. H. *The Holy Spirit of God.* London: Longmans, Green and Co., 1913.

Gromackie, R. G. *The Modern Tongues Movement.* Philadelphia, Pennsylvania: The Presbyterian and Reformed Publishing Co., 1967.

Hayes, D. A. *The Gift of Tongues.* Cincinnati: Jennings and Graham, 1913.

Hoekema, A. A. *What About Tongue-Speaking?* Grand Rapids, Michigan: Wm. B. Eerdmans Publishing Co., 1966.

————. *Holy Spirit Baptism.* Grand Rapids, Michigan: Wm. B. Eerdmans Publishing Co., 1972.

Keiper, R. L. *Tongues and the Holy Spirit.* Chicago: Moody Press, 1963.

Kelly, T. R. *A Testament of Devotion.* New York: Harper and Brothers Publishers, 1941.

Kelly, W. *Lectures on the New Testament Doctrine of the Holy Spirit.* London: W. H. Broom, 1877.

Kelsey, M. T. *Tongue Speaking: An Experiment in Spiritual Experience.* Garden City, New York: Doubleday, 1964.

Kuyper, A. *The Work of the Holy Spirit.* New York: Funk and Wagnalls Co., 1900.

Lewis, C. S. *Surprised by Joy.* London and Glasgow: Collins, 1960.

Mackie, A. *The Gift of Tongues, A Study of Pathologic Aspects of Christianity.* New York: Doran, 1921.

Martin, I. J. *Glossolalia in the Apostolic Church.* Berea, Kentucky: Berea College, 1960.

Morgan, G. C. *The Spirit of God.* London: Hodder and Stoughton, 1900.

Murray, A. *The Spirit of Christ*. London: James Nisbet and Co., 1888.

Nuttall, G. F. *The Holy Spirit in Puritan Faith and Experience*. Oxford: Basil Blackwell, 1947.

Ockenga, H. J. *Power Through Pentecost*. Grand Rapids, Michigan: Wm. B. Eerdmans Publishing Co., 1959.

Owen, J. *On the Holy Spirit,* 2 vols. Philadelphia, Pa.: Protestant Episcopal Book Society, 1962.

Pache, R. *Person and Work of the Holy Spirit*. London: Marshall, Morgan and Scott, 1956.

Palmer, Dr. E. H. *The Holy Spirit*. Grand Rapids, Michigan: Baker Book House, 1958.

Rees, T. *The Holy Spirit in Thought and Experience*. London: Duckworth and Co., 1915.

Samarin, W. J. *Tongues of Men and Angels*. New York: Macmillan, 1972.

Sanders, J. Oswald. *The Holy Spirit of Promise*. Fort Washington, Pa.: Christian Literature Crusade, 1962.

_____. *The Holy Spirit and His Gifts*. Grand Rapids, Michigan: Zondervan Publishing House, 1971.

Sherrill, J. L. *They Speak With Other Tongues*. New York: Pyramid Books, 1970.

Smeaton, G. *The Doctrine of the Holy Spirit*. Edinburgh: T.&T. Clark, 1889.

Smellie, A. *Men of the Covenant*. London: Banner of Truth Trust, 1960.

Stott, J. R. W. *The Baptism and Fullness of the Holy Spirit*. Chicago, Illinois: Inter-Varsity Press, 1964.

Torrey, R. A. *The Baptism With the Holy Spirit*. New York: Fleming H. Revell Co., 1897.

Tozer, A. W. *The Divine Conquest*. Harrisburg, Pa.: Christian Publications, Inc., 1950.

Unger, Merrill F. *The Baptizing Work of the Holy Spirit*. Findlay, Ohio: The Putnam Publishing Co., 1962.

Walker, D. *The Gift of Tongues*. Edinburgh: T.&.T. Clark, 1906.

Walvoord, J. F. *The Holy Spirit*. Wheaton, Illinois: Van Kampen Press, 1954.

Warfield, B. B. *Counterfeit Miracles*. New York: Charles Scribner's Sons, 1918.

Winslow, Octavius. *The Work of the Holy Spirit*. London: The Banner of Truth Trust, 1972.

Wood, W. W. *Culture and Personality Aspects of the Pentecostal Holiness Religion*. The Hague: Mouton, 1965.

Wright, G. Ernest. *The Rule of God*. New York: Doubleday and Co., 1960.

General Index

Scripture Index